To D-Day and Back

The author and friends in the 507th PIR enjoy R&R in the Black Hills, 1943.
Top left: Wilson "Duck" Keith and Bob Bearden.
Bottom left: Private Burns, Howard White, and Chet Gunka.

To D-Day and Back

ADVENTURES WITH THE 507th PARACHUTE INFANTRY REGIMENT AND LIFE AS A WORLD WAR II POW

BOB BEARDEN

ZENITH PRESS

First published in 2007 by Zenith Press, an imprint of MBI Publishing Company LLC, Galtier Plaza, Suite 200, 380 Jackson Street, St. Paul, MN 55101 USA

© Bob Bearden, 2007

Zenith Press titles are also available at discounts in bulk quantity for industrial or sales-promotional use. For details write to Special Sales Manager at MBI Publishing Company, Galtier Plaza, Suite 200, 380 Jackson Street, St. Paul, MN 55101 USA.

To find out more about our books, join us online at www.zenithpress.com.

Designer: Tom Heffron

Library of Congress Cataloging-in-Publication Data
Bearden, Bob, 1922-
    To D-Day and back : adventures with the 507th Parachute Infantry Regiment and life as a World War II POW : a memoir / by Bob Bearden.
        p. cm.
    ISBN-13: 978-0-7603-3258-0 (hardbound w/ jacket)
    1. Bearden, Bob, 1922- 2. United States. Army. Parachute Infantry Regiment, 507th. 3. World War, 1939-1945—Personal narratives, American. 4. World War, 1939-1945—Campaigns—France—Normandy. 5. World War, 1939-1945—Aerial operations, American. 6. United States. Army—Parachute troops—Biography. 7. World War, 1939-1945—Prisoners and prisons, German. 8. Normandy (France)—History, Military—20th century. 9. Prisoners of war—Germany—Biography. 10. Prisoners of war—United States—Biography. I. Title.
    D769.348507th .B43 2007
    940.54'1273092—dc22
    [B]
                                                    2007015671
Printed in the United States of America

CONTENTS

PART III
TOURING EUROPE 10TH CLASS: MY LIFE AS A POW

Part IV
THE RUSSIAN EXPERIENCE: OR, HEADING EAST TO GO WEST

Acknowledgments

This book is the product of a fine education received through three years at John Reagan Grammar School, Dallas; four years at Adamson High School, Dallas; and five years at the University of Texas, Austin. To the teachers and staffs of all of these institutions, I am grateful.

I am who I am due to the influence of my Adamson High School brothers, later to be known as the Excelsior Club, and still later as the September Club: Bert Smith, David Ivy, Bob Hughes, Ed Kelly, Buck Haynes, Billy Maxwell, Nev Williams, Herbert Stice, and Ben Skelton. My great Adamson High School track coach and mentor, Pop Noah, may well have kept me out of serious trouble by providing his steady guidance.

I would have never been a paratrooper except for my love for a great young lady, Doris Cook, who with her mother Ruth Cook and sister Embelyne encouraged me throughout my high school days. I also thank Chuck Carrell, whose high school friendship was renewed aboard a ship bringing us home from World War II in Europe. Later as my roommate at the

University of Texas, he kept me in successful pursuit of my BBA degree.

This book is intended to introduce the world to the men of the 3rd Squad, 60mm mortar, 3rd Platoon, H Company, 507th Parachute Infantry, 82nd Airborne Division with whom I soldiered and whom I pushed out the door of a C-47 plane, tail number 42-92842, over Normandy at approximately 2:30 a.m., on June 6, 1944. These guys drove me nuts over about three years, and I loved them all like brothers.

I essentially owe the contents of the book to my mortar squad: Wilson (Duck) Keith, a New Hampshire dairy farmer; our gunner, Fred Kelly; our assistant gunner, Hubert McClain, the only squad member we lost, who was killed in action in Normandy; and our ammunition bearer, James (Bones) Lewis. This is also their story. Truly great and heroic young men from New England, Alabama, Texas, Ohio, and Indiana, they were drawn together and prepared to fight to the death for America. They inspired me.

I equally recognize and thank Howard White, who talked me into joining the Texas National Guard in July 1940, and whom I talked into joining the paratroops. I suppose we were even. He nearly lost an arm in the Normandy jump. He was a continuing support during my entire military career, save the POW stretch, which I did without him.

This book is also the result of having had the opportunity to speak about my war experience to many audiences over the years. There was never an audience in which someone did not say, "That must be put into a book." To all those encouraging listeners, I owe the spark that set the fire to try to put the stories on paper. To Raider Nelson, John Condich, Clarence Hughart, Bob Kelley, Lieutenant Bart Hale, First Sergeant Marco, and others at reunions who encouraged me to write this book, I am grateful. Clarence Hughart is, also, responsible for furnishing several of the photographs provided in these pages and for that I'm appreciative.

My five children, Perk, Brenda, David, Tim, and Terry, by being (for the most part) obedient kids, gave me the time to tell these stories over and over, and even encouraged me. An additional debt is owed my children's mother Doris Bearden, who led me out of a serious case of agoraphobia after the war by introducing me to a deeper walk with the Lord.

Debbie, my wife and dance partner of seventeen years, provided a steady support system during some dark periods. She is twenty-seven years my junior and provides another son, Greg, and grandson, Derek. I have struggled through some serious health problems over the years and most were corrected or treated thanks to a great Veterans' Administration Hospital and Clinic in Temple, Texas. Because of my number one doctor, Dr. Allan Price, and his staff, I am here to write this book.

Finally, I thank my editor and agent Dr. Gayle Wurst, of Princeton International Agency for the Arts. Without her, there would be no book. She not only nudged me along, she corrected much error in my effort.

These days, I never pass up an opportunity, whether it be service clubs, groups of history buffs, schools, or military associations, to speak about the crazy, unique, ordinary guys I knew who did extraordinary service in World War II. I think of this memoir as a continuation of those many talks. It was born, in part, as a response to the encouragement I received from my generous audiences, and in part as a tribute to my wacky, loveable friends, including Billy, Chet, Duck, Mac, and Pettus, who deserved so very much more than they received from this life. I hope that readers will think my book is entertaining and educational, but above all I pray that it will shout the truth that "freedom isn't free."

PART I

DOING MY BIT

Chapter One

Texas National Guard, 144th Infantry

My first night in the Texas National Guard, I was issued a full field pack and a .30-caliber Enfield rifle, then fell out to march to the downtown Dallas railroad station to board a train for Louisiana Maneuvers. It was August 1940, and I was seventeen. We marched to a bagpipe band, changing steps a hundred times per block, trying to keep in step with the band. As we marched past the Majestic Theater, the marquee lights announced the current movie—*All This and Heaven Too.*

My buddy Howard White was the one who talked me into the Guard. About a month earlier, he and I had been walking home from a Thursday evening Big Band dance at Kid Springs, where I got to dance with beautiful petite Betty Jane Mimms, who would one day beat Babe Zaharias for the Texas Women's Open Golf Event. If you enjoyed dancing, as all of my friends and I did, you could dance for four hours to the music of Glenn Miller, Tommy Dorsey, Artie Shaw, and others for three dollars a couple as the Big Bands came through Dallas. This often entailed "borrowing" my sister's jewelry to be hocked along with my Adamson High School letter sweater at Uncle

Sam's Hock Shop in downtown Dallas on "Deep Elum" Street.

Howard and another friend, Pinky Wade, were already in the Guard. As we walked home from the dance, he told me how the Guard would put weight on me, and I could play for the Leopards, the Adamson High football team, like he did. This was a point of great interest. I loved all sports, but my size of five feet six inches and about ninety pounds kept me out of everything but soccer, track, and boxing. Although I could not run fast, I could run forever it appeared, so I became a miler. In time, I would run a mile in 4:40 flat and take second place behind Jerry Thompson, an old Fort Worth track teammate. Even now, they still run the "Jerry Thompson mile" at the Texas Relays every year.

Then there was the fact that I was always trying to prove myself. My brief amateur boxing career was a source of pride among my buddies, but I had never received support from home for any personal or team activity. I vividly recall leaving to ride the streetcar downtown to box in the Golden Gloves for the first time. I was almost shaking as I walked out the front door of our apartment. Lou, my stepmom, said, "I'll bet they knock your head off." I gulped and thought, *You're probably right.* Several fights later, I read a little headline in the *Dallas Morning News*: BEARDEN FIGHTS IN FINALS. I walked around the house with a chest full of pride, one step closer to becoming a man.

Most of all, though, the money in the Guard sounded good. Howard had been promoted to sergeant squad leader and was earning a considerable income. He assured me I would make about a dollar a day if I could get in on the Louisiana Maneuvers, which were coming up the following month.

This proposition meant I could double my current earnings from the A&P grocery store. I'd been working weekends for twelve and a half cents an hour, serving in every department but the butcher's. My lunch at the corner drugstore consisted of a steak sandwich for a dime and a chocolate frozen malt for a nickel. Frequently, at noon, I would shoot dice and lose my pay for the day. It was a hard lesson in learning to handle defeat.

Another source of income was spending the hours from midnight to 4 a.m. setting pins at Bodecker's Bowling Alley for five cents per line. Most bowlers at that time of the morning were drinking heavily, and it was not uncommon to see bowler and ball come crashing down the alley. Of course, we were setting the pins by hand. Getting hit by flying pins was just a hazard of the trade.

I was also seldom without a newspaper route in those days, preferably the *Dallas Morning News*, which we threw every day about 3 a.m. One good thing about it was that most of us paperboys helped ourselves to the early morning delivery of delicious fresh-baked doughnuts at the local grocery store. I had been known to offer a warm doughnut to a Dallas police officer in his squad car when he came by checking on us.

In short, the National Guard was a tempting proposition. Soon after my conversation with Howard, eight of us got together and bought a Model T Ford for twelve dollars—or maybe twelve of us bought a Model T Ford for eight dollars. The details are hazy. All I know was that a dollar a night for every drill meant I could afford my share.

There was just one problem: I was underage, and my father objected. Eventually, I got the signature and so became a member of Company F, 144th Infantry Regiment, 36th Division. My family was proud of me, and I did not have to lie about my age, unlike Manuel Allen Deton, who at fifteen was my youngest squad member. "Pappy" Sanderson, at fifty-seven, was the oldest.

My first job in Company F was "runner" and "dog robber." A runner literally ran messages from officer to officer in the field. A dog robber took care of an officer—pitched his personal tent, cleaned his weapon, made his bed in the field, and did his bidding. The name came from an old army expression, saying any man who would serve an officer like that would "rob a dog of his bone!"

I was almost ashamed to admit that I loved the military discipline and work—and this in spite of my "baptism" in the 1940 Louisiana Maneuvers. What a way to experience the old army! All our equipment, from rifles to uniforms, was of World War I variety. We wore World War I campaign hats that looked better on Smokey the Bear.

We frequently went on thirty-mile marches, tromping day and night across the state. We marched through swamps observing alligators and other swamp creatures. We were said to have walked cavalry horses to death and tanks out of gas. Powdered purple eggs and potatoes were a common meal.

And to top it all off, I was taken prisoner through no good fault of my own. After we'd had a mock war for a couple weeks, we took a break and I got a pass to visit my sweetheart in Dallas. I was on my way back to camp, when the referees restarted the maneuvers prematurely. As soon as they heard the first official gunshot, some eager beavers started capturing "enemies" wherever they could find them. This particular enemy they carried off the bus starry-eyed with love for Doris Cook. I had given Doris her very first kiss on my sixteenth birthday, when she was sweet fourteen. She had short, dark hair and was about ninety pounds and five feet tall; she remains near that size today, in Dallas.

When the Texas National Guard was called up at the end of November 1940, I had to quit high school. I had never been much of a scholar, partly because I had a learning disability later identified as dyslexia. As a child, I could say the alphabet perfectly until I came to the letter J, at which time I stalled. I'd been whipped with a belt in my father's effort to get me to say that letter. No way! My dyslexia took a long time to identify because I never stayed put in any one school. We changed addresses so often that the Beardens were known as the family that moved every time the rent came due. I could remember another kind of life, when we had enjoyed the best that money could buy. My father had been an outstanding life insurance salesman in the early years of the industry, but we experienced all that sudden financial failure can hand a family in the great collapse of 1927 to 1929. Leading up to that crash, his investments became worthless when it cost more money to pump oil than the oil was worth on the market.

We loaded up our big, expensive Morman automobile and headed out for Irving, Texas, where my mother's aunt owned the only cafe-hotel in town. A series of crises and further moves ensued, including the loss of my mother, who died in childbirth, when I was seven. Soon after, my sister, who was eight, and I were shipped unaccompanied across the country in Pullman cars to live with a rich old German aunt in Washington State. I was still drinking from the "fingerbowls" when we pulled into Spokane. Looked like lemonade to me!

At age fifty-five, my father remarried—a nineteen-year-old girl who had been raised in a Texas orphanage, the Corsicana State Home. We called her Lou, for her name was Lula, and she had never seen a living adult relative. Raising me and my sister, Mary, would prove to be a real challenge. She was a beautiful person with a hopeless task and zero preparation.

By the time dad remarried, Mary and I had lived in three different states. Back in Texas again, we moved many times again as Dad tried every morning to come up with a dollar bill for my new mother to run the house. I attended five grammar schools in Fort Worth before we went back to Dallas, where I would attend another half dozen schools. It was in Dallas that a teacher finally came to suspect that I might have a "learning problem."

I nevertheless managed to get almost through high school. The rent must have been very modest in the Oak Cliff section of Dallas, because we moved there and stayed for seven years. We continued to change addresses, but always within the same school district.

When the Guard called me up, I had only about two months to go before my mid-term graduation from Adamson High. I missed the prom and all of that. I had no choice—I was in the U.S. Army. Even now, I keep waiting for the University of Texas to come after the BBA they awarded me in 1952. I entered that university in August 1945 without a high school diploma!

The Guard met daily for training at the Akard Street Armory in Dallas until we moved to Camp Bowie, Texas, on December 14, 1940. Marching with the Guard to the train station in downtown Dallas was really a blast, although it was not popular ever to admit you were enjoying army life. I was always a good soldier. I learned every weapon I was ever equipped with, and usually qualified as expert, although my discharge does not record such.

My first and only special weapon in the Guard was the 60mm mortar. Prior to Pearl Harbor, I taught the mortar for a year before I had even seen one, using make-believe mortars made of iron pipes to simulate the real thing. Obviously, nothing I said was correct, because I was teaching out of a 1918 Field Manual.

I had been assigned to a mortar squad because there was no one else in the slot, so making squad leader was no big deal. First of all, no one wanted to carry that little forty-eight-pound package everywhere the platoon went. I stayed with this weapon throughout my time in the army and came to love it. As a leader I had to be able to set up the mortar faster than anyone else, and this I did. We could and did get nine rounds of 60mm mortar ammunition in the air before the first one landed. Quite an unmatched accomplishment.

Our division took part in the VIII Corps Brownwood, Texas, maneuvers during the first two weeks of June. We'd not been long back at Camp Bowie before we headed off for the August and September 1941 Louisiana Maneuvers in Mansfield. Once again, I experienced the coldest and hottest days and nights of my life. We slept with snakes and mosquitoes. We were forced to drink polluted water into which the medics had poured iodine; it made the water safe, but almost undrinkable.

And once again, when we took a break to get everyone back in his right unit and place, I got a pass and hitch-hiked back to Dallas. Doris and I were still going strong, although you must keep in mind that a romance at that time rarely, if ever, included a sexual relationship. I was on my way back to Mansfield when the maneuvers started up early again. True to form, I was captured from another bus by gung-ho "enemy" units with the help of a cooperative referee. Later, I would realize that these early captures were something of an omen of my fate in real combat.

We returned to Camp Bowie from Louisiana on October 2, 1941. Changes were taking place in the division, which was reorganizing from the old "square division" with four infantry regiments to a "triangle division," with only three. On February 1, 1942, the division was redesignated the 36th Infantry Division and transferred to Camp Blanding, Florida, about two and a half weeks later.

Meanwhile, my regiment, the 144th Infantry, had been removed from the 36th when the division pared down to three regiments. On December 7, 1941, Pearl Harbor Day, we loaded up at Camp Bowie. We had about thirty-six hours to get packed and on a train bound for Fort Lewis, Washington. After a brief stay at Fort Lewis, we started to work our way south down the coast, laying barbed wire on likely invasion sites. The nation was anticipating a west coast invasion any day, and coastal residents lived fearful lives. We just knew for sure that the Japs were coming, and soon!

TO D-DAY AND BACK

By April 1942, the 144th Infantry had worked its way down to California, having created hundreds of defensive positions all along the coast. I guarded railroad bridges, radar stations, air bases—anything that might apply to the war effort. We fired our light and heavy machine guns, as well as Browning automatic rifles and 60mm and 81mm mortars. If the Japanese started coming ashore in an invasion, we were ready. We could simply drop our weapons in place and start firing pre-arranged fire patterns.

I'll always remember when Howard and I first talked about joining the paratroops. The 144th had worked its way a good stretch down the coast, and we were living in pup tents in the Petaluma, California, city park. We had initially heard about these supermen on Louisiana Maneuvers in 1941. By now, we had had it with pulling guard duty, waiting for the Japanese to attack.

Personally, I had several other reasons for wanting to be a paratrooper. First, it was an image thing with me. Because I had always been small for my age and class, almost everything I did was aimed at proving myself as a man. During my Adamson High days, I'd become known as "Boss Bearden," a title jokingly laid on me because I could think up so much of the unacceptable behavior my friends and I exhibited. I was always in trouble with school officials and had taken a number of trips to the Dallas city jail for vandalism. Most of the acts that brought me such pride and my friends' recognition were the source of great fear on my part—fear that I could never allow to surface if I was to continue to be "bad"!

I knew, and Howard knew, and everybody else in the army knew, that the airborne troops were the baddest of the bad. Anytime a paratrooper showed up on a military post in a recruiting effort, everyone wanted to see what he looked like. Were paratroopers really supermen? That image I envied.

We had also heard that troopers made an extra fifty dollars

a month just for jumping. Well, as a buck sergeant in 144th Infantry, I was making about eighty dollars a month. Just imagine how loaded I'd be if they added another fifty dollars jump pay to that!

Then, we had seen those paratrooper wings and how crazy the girls were for that hero image. More than one man had been talked into joining the airborne action by some guy who had just received his wings, gone home on jump school furlough, and had all the girls chasing him. Last, but certainly not least, I discovered on inquiry that I'd get a five-day layover in Dallas on my way to Fort Benning and jump school. Five days with Doris Cook, my love.

Sometime later, when Howard was on pass to San Francisco, I signed us both up for the paratroopers. When he returned, he was both surprised and delighted by my act. He quickly made his application official. Billy Blansett, another of our Company F buddies, joined up too.

Just before we left for jump school, an incident occurred that exemplifies much of our duty in the 144th Infantry. I was in charge of a half dozen men living at a radar station on top of Bald Hill, just outside of Fort Bragg on the northern California coast. Everything was made to look like a farm with an artificial windmill, barns, and other outbuildings. We overlooked a location that was considered to be an excellent site for an invasion. We had fired our machine guns and mortars at all the likely landing sites on the beaches and made many a run down Bald Hill in our jeeps in preparation for the Japs.

It was not uncommon for local citizens to phone us up on the mountain, exclaiming that the invasion was on and ships were coming ashore. Initially, we were very attentive to these calls, but in time, with so many false alarms, we pretty much ignored the spooked civilian community and their cries of "wolf"!

This time, however, a call got our attention. "Come quick, the Japs are here!" the caller exclaimed. I took my field glasses out to the west overlook position on our little post. Sure enough, out in the turf was a good-sized naval vessel, putting out a number of smaller crafts full of troops. They sure did look like landing craft to me.

I sounded our alarm, the six of us jumped in our jeeps, and we barreled down the hill for a war with the Japs. Imagine our relief when we arrived at the shore and discovered that the Coast Guard was tending their safety buoys! The landing craft were small rubber boats from which the crew had been operating. I took my men back up Bald Mountain, very thankful we were not in the war just yet.

So it was in the summer of 1942 that Howard, Billy, and I found ourselves on a train heading for Benning and the big bucks. A priceless layover in Dallas was included en route. We showed up in Columbus, Georgia, having no idea what was coming. In this, we were typical of airborne volunteers: none of us had ever been on an airplane, and if we had ever seen a parachute, it was at an air show put on by daredevils.

I was soon enlightened as to what might lay in store. The very day I arrived in Columbus, I saw a major from the Canadian Airborne School get hit in the air by a trailing photo plane and die crashing into the runway at Lawson Field. Several other new arrivals to jump school also saw this fatal jump. Some of them immediately went to school headquarters and withdrew from the course before they even saw an instructor or a parachute.

Chapter Two

PARACHUTE SCHOOL, FORT BENNING, GEORGIA

The parachute school in Fort Benning operated twelve months a year. Howard, Billy, and I began classes in August 1942. Four stages: A, B, C, D—each one week long, comprised the month-long course. The first three stages covered physical hardening, judo, jumping techniques, and parachute packing and maintenance. On the first day of D Stage, we began our "final exam"—to make five jumps from a C-47 transport plane, in flight, over Lawson Field. This was accomplished on five consecutive days. On each occasion, we jumped chutes we had packed ourselves.

The key to getting ordinary American young men to jump out of a perfectly good airplane was to have outstanding physical specimens as instructors. They would have to be just a bit crazy, we thought, not born as ordinary men. These exceptional beings, all endowed with the highest paratrooper qualifications, would party all night in Columbus or Phenix City bars, then show up at 6 a.m. to lead us on a five-mile run, barking commands all the way.

During the stage called physical hardening, the instructors successfully separated the men from the boys—and all of us felt like boys from time to time. Sometimes the exercises were painful; students frequently passed out from exhaustion.

As part of this killer training, our supermen instructors, or "Black Hats" as we called them, told us, in no uncertain terms that we were useless. There was no way any of us would ever make paratroopers. "You gutless wonder! Your mother must be ashamed of you," they'd yell. "Your old man won't let you come home 'cause you're not a man." Well, after three weeks of this sort of challenge on a minute-by-minute basis, most of us would have jumped out of a plane even *without* a chute just to prove to those sorry bastards that we were men, indeed.

It was during B Stage, I believe, that an incident happened to Howard that I'll always remember. The exercise took place on a six-by-six-foot platform about four feet off the floor in a gym. We were to raise our arms over our heads as if we were holding onto parachute risers. Then the instructor barked a command, and we jumped off the platform down onto a mat.

The instructors had us so jumpy that we hardly knew which way was up. "Jab!" they screamed. We banged our fists into our chests so hard that sometimes we knocked ourselves down. "Brace!" We hit an exaggerated position of attention until we could hardly breathe. These shouted commands came so often and so loud that all of us stayed freaked out.

I can still see Howard up on that platform, the instructor screaming at him. At the command "Go!" my friend leaped—straight off on his back. The fall totally knocked the breath out of him. I went crazy with laughter, bent over double at my buddy forgetting to land on his feet. I paid dearly for that moment of hilarity. The instructor sent me running around the area for what seemed like hours, hands raised overhead and shouting, "I will not laugh at my buddy."

The troops lived in two-story frame buildings during jump school. It was always a painful experience when one of us washed out of the program, either voluntarily or through dismissal. Many of us would probably have quit except for the fact that we could not stand the thought of going back to the barracks and packing our bags in the presence of other students. As impossible as it was to continue sometimes, the alternative was even more impossible. To the man, we developed a new level of determination to see this thing through. Yet at every stage of training, many still fell out.

Sometimes a trooper who had graduated only a week or two before would come by our barracks and tell us how impossible it was to complete the school. We just were not going to make it, he would say. All the while that special badge of courage, his paratrooper wings, was proudly displayed on his chest. If only he could have heard the comments when he left! They invariably went something like, "Where the hell did he get his wings?" Or, "If *he* made it, *I* sure as hell can!" These visits invariably added a considerable boost to our determination to complete the unbearable course.

During our early training, we must have jumped out of a hundred "mock" airplane doors, landing two to three feet below. Later, we went out of a forty-foot tower in a harness attached to a cable that allowed us to slide rapidly to the ground. At a certain point, the instructor released us so we could practice our landing technique.

This drill and many others taught us to trust the entire rig, tower, harness, cable, and so forth. Still, it was difficult to register that a flimsy piece of silk would be the means by which we would reach the ground, jumping from 800 to 1,200 feet in altitude.

Learning about the operation of the parachute, thus, was crucial to our education. We were required to pack our own chutes for the first five jumps in D Stage. In fact, we wound up packing the sixth and seventh chutes we jumped as well.

Many of us were the careless sort, not accustomed to paying much attention to instructions of any kind. Our high school records would bear witness to this fact. Yet here we were receiving instructions on how to fold a parachute. We had to remember each tiny detail and step in the packing process. One mistake, and the parachute we jumped with might not properly open. Good-bye life, hello Mother Earth.

We were assigned to pack our chutes in pairs. Because both of our names started with B, Billy Blansett and I were packing partners. Neither of us was known to be too studious, but there now came over us a brand new attitude about paying attention to detail, every detail.

I must say, no teacher ever had my attention like my instructors did now. There was no—that is, *zero*—horsing around in the packing sheds as we were taught how to pack our chutes. When you know what a squirrel you are, and how absent-minded you have always been, believe me, you think about trusting yourself to such a task. Time after time, I thought, *They are trusting me with this life-determining procedure?* I knew, even then, that I had some sort of learning disability, although my dyslexia was not identified as such for many years.

On the last day of C Stage, Billy and I packed the chute that I would use for the first jump, and it took about two hours. At one stage of the process, we were to leave a gap of say, half an inch between two halves of the folded parachute. Billy wanted to move on with his estimate of that half inch, and I was determined that it was a thirty-second-of-an-inch off. We redid that chute perhaps twenty times before turning it in, to be stored until our first jump the following Monday morning.

Sweat was pouring off both of us in that un-air-conditioned packing shed down by Lawson Field. We had already missed evening chow by the time we were starting to pack Billy's parachute. He was just a tad more careful with his chute than mine, so we spent at least another two hours packing it. The process would have made a great cartoon, with two scared clowns going through the tedious act of packing parachutes and fighting each other every inch of the way.

When we finally finished, we did not even trust the staff to properly store our chutes. We would have preferred to take them back to our barracks and sleep with them. Now we faced the interminable weekend wait to discover if we had done the job correctly. A sign over the packing shed door read, "Through these portals pass America's finest troops. Pack well, and pass again."

Finally, the big day came, Monday, the first day of D Stage, when we would make that first real jump that truly separated men from boys. Billy and I drew the chutes we'd sweated over and strapped them so tightly to our bodies that we could hardly breathe. We pulled up extra hard on the leg straps to our harness to ensure that no "special," personal body parts would be caught in the webbing during the opening shock, which, we had been told, would be significant. The single strap across our chest did nothing but keep us from falling out of our harness—that's all!

There was no laughter, for sure, as we boarded our jump plane. The two Bs, Blansett and Bearden, jumped next to each other, thus sharing one of life's wildest experiences. We talked as we came down over Lawson Field and tried out the parachute and body turns they'd taught us. This was the first and last time I ever tried a parachute turn. It required climbing up the risers and suspension lines until you had hold of the bottom hem of the parachute canopy. With all the air dumped out of one side of the chute, the whole canopy began flapping like crazy—but it did turn, just as we were told it would. I let loose of that canopy skirt and never thought about parachute turns again.

On the next day, Tuesday, Billy and I went to jump the second chute we had packed together. Everything was the same, except this time we all knew what was coming, and some, like me, were more apprehensive. I sat in my bucket seat next to Billy. No "ho, ho, ho," this day. When the jumpmaster cried out, "Stand up and hook up!" I froze. I did not move and could not move I was so overcome with fear.

Billy was already standing. He reached down, grabbed me by my harness front, and yanked me into the line. He hooked me up, checking both me and the trooper in front of me, ensuring every strap and every snap fastener was in place. When the jumpmaster shouted, "Sound off for equipment check!" Billy called out in his turn, "Number eight okay," for me and then okayed the number for himself.

At the command, "Close it up and stand in the door!" Billy pushed me forward toward the opening. On "Go!" he literally shoved me out the door. When the chute opened, I screamed out, "Blansett, the son-of-a-bitch opened!" I never expected it to open that day. That was the last time I had such an acute experience of ultimate fear that I was about to die in a jump. Oddly enough, the next day, jump number three, I performed the same procedure for a super-frightened Billy Blansett.

Billy, Howard, and I all made it through the first four jumps. On Friday, the morning of our last and qualifying jump, a bunch of us pinned a pair of jump wings on the inside of the upper left pocket of our coveralls, the standard student uniform, in an effort to put one over on our instructors. The wings were hidden, but sure enough, in a fit of hostility toward the staff, some crazy student had to reveal his wings to an instructor.

All hell broke loose. I've never been so belittled in my life as I was at that moment. The very idea that I, a gutless, spineless wonder, thought I'd ever make a paratrooper. I don't know where the wings landed when the instructor tore them off my coveralls, but I do know a thousand wild horses could not have stopped me from going out that fifth and qualifying C-47 door.

The Parachute School
Airborne Command
United States Army

This is to Certify That:

Private ROBERT L. BEARDEN — 20811340

has satisfactorily completed the prescribed course in Parachute Packing, Ground Training, and Jumping from a plane in flight. He is, therefore, entitled to be rated from this date, October 10, 1942 , as a qualified Parachutist.

G.J. Howell

Colonel Infantry
Commandant

Bob Bearden's Paratrooper Certification.

When the jumpmaster yelled "Go!" I must have leaped thirty feet out the door, screaming "Geronimo!" Thus, I experienced what Dr. Phil would call a "defining moment" of my life.

Billy, Howard, and I were no different from any of the other new jump school graduates. Having completed four weeks of the most intense, physically demanding training that any human body could take, we proudly displayed our original wings on a chest full of pride. We had gone through hell and now were qualified paratroopers, headed home for a ten-day furlough.

It is impossible to describe how proud we felt as young, brand new paratroopers walking down our hometown streets, chest out, airborne patch on our caps, the caps themselves positioned in such a way as to state: "Don't mess with me, I'm a U.S. Army paratrooper." At the time we graduated, there were only about two thousand of us scattered throughout America. No World War I soldier had seen a paratrooper during that war; in fact, few Americans at all had ever seen one of this new breed of combat soldier. We were *different*.

Walking down the Dallas street on jump school furlough in September 1942, I would sometimes see a little boy clutching his mother's hand, pointing at the proud new paratrooper and whispering, "Look, mama, a paratrooper!" Needless to say, I would swell up like a toad frog, push my airborne cap forward on my head, and pretty much float down the street. It was this national infatuation and adoration along with the fifty dollars a month jump pay that kept me and the rest of this new breed of soldier jumping.

Chapter Three

507TH
CAST OF CHARACTERS

B y September 1942, when Billy, Howard, and I returned
from furlough, the 507th was pretty well established on
the Alabama side of Fort Benning. Howard and I were both in
the 3rd Platoon of Company H, while Billy had been assigned to
Company I. We occupied barracks recently vacated by the 504th
PIR, which had moved to Fort Bragg where the 82nd Airborne
Division was being formed. The 504th had also furnished many of
the initial officers and men for the 507th.

Our new homes were one-story frame barracks with
tar-paper siding. Inside, metal bunk beds lined each side of a
single long room, which housed about thirty men. Coal- and
wood-burning stoves were at each end of the building, with a
door at each end as well. At the end of our Company H street
was a latrine, or bathing and toilet facility, also covered with
tar-paper siding. Behind the latrine was a swamp.

The official activation of the 507th had occurred about
two months previously, on July 20, 1942, at the hands of the
Secretary of War in Washington, D.C. If you could have

known us as individuals or units, you would have immediately been impressed with the fact that details such as this could not have meant less to us. When's payday? When do we get our next furlough or weekend pass? And what's for chow? Now that was important stuff.

Our fellow troopers hailed from everywhere imaginable. They came from a New Hampshire dairy farm to a Rio Grande Valley orange grove, from the position of accountant at a prestigious Midwest firm to the nonposition of a real-live hobo riding the country's rails. In some cases, they spoke with very distinct foreign accents; in others, rebel voices or a New England twang identified that section of their beloved America from which they had been born and bred.

At times one wondered, would they ever learn to communicate? Yours truly, a Dallas, Texas, high school drop-out, had to learn to give understandable orders to "Duck," aka Wilson Keith, his New England gunner. Duck was built so low to the ground he waddled, especially when shouldering the weight of a mortar. His assistant was his perfect counterpart—Pfc. Fred Kelly, from Wetumptka, Alabama, the tallest man in the squad, who spoke with such a Deep South drawl that he needed an interpreter to talk to Duck. Our monthly fifty-dollar jump pay was probably more money than Fred had ever handled in one lump sum, as was the case for most of us.

Then there was Bones Lewis, a private from Ohio and our first ammunitions bearer, the smallest member of the squad. I had to whip Bones just about every payday when he'd have a couple of beers and think he could beat his boss. And how could I forget Pvt. Hubert McClain, ammo bearer and Company H barber, whose particularity was falling asleep in unlikely places? Later, when we were stationed in Alliance, Nebraska, Mac regularly climbed into the rafters of the mess hall to get his "beauty rest," as he called it. Latrine orderly, another of his frequent duties, also provided rafters for his beauty rest. He even became fond of sleeping under the old, unreliable boiler, which threatened to burst at any time.

Presiding over the 3rd Platoon of Company H was Sgt. 1st Class Chet Gunka. Perfect for the task and quite a man, Chet became a good friend. At twenty-six or twenty-seven, he was older than most of us, a peacetime sailor from Ohio who had spent nine years in the U.S. Navy. Because he got sick every time they took up anchor, he had transferred to the paratroops, looking for a better life on land. The girls all thought he looked like a Greek god.

Most, but not all, of our officers were directly out of jump school. An exception was First Sergeant Marco. A little older than most of us, Marco was a tall, thin family man who must have had considerable rank in his previous military outfit. He came to Fort Benning slick-sleeved like the rest of us, and very soon became our first sergeant. I always liked Marco, though he once won seven hundred dollars off me in about ten straight hands of blackjack, sitting on his bunk in Alliance, Nebraska.

Another of our officers who came to the company with prior experience was 2nd Lt. Bart Hale, who had been an NCO in China or somewhere else in the Far East. Hale was Old Army and knew his stuff. I believe he was sent to Officers' Candidate School because someone had recognized that as a pre–World War II first sergeant, he demonstrated all the qualities needed in an officer. He was our contact with the officer ranks, and he even shared some of the prize officers' club booze with his men. All of us loved him and respected his judgment, and he loved and respected us.

Many of us, who had formerly been NCOs in our old outfits, soon made our rank back in the 507th and, as cadre, became squad leaders and platoon sergeants. Billy, who had been a cook in the 144th Infantry, led a rifle squad in Company I and became an outstanding soldier who later received a field commission to second lieutenant. Howard, a buck sergeant in the 144th like me, led a rifle squad in the 3rd Platoon of Company H, and I led the mortar squad in the same platoon.

Just like any team sport, a combat military unit has to get that "oneness" established. You need to know your twelve squad members like brothers. How will each react in a given situation? Which weapons can he fire and how well? Is he mechanically inclined—can he fix things, or does he break everything he gets his hands on? And, oh yeah, who always has coffee ready before the rest of the squad wakes up out in the field?

Teamwork in infantry combat is more essential than in any team sport I ever played. The stakes are obviously higher. Yes, we frequently fought with one another like brothers, but if you were not "family," you had better stay clear and not mess with any member of the squad.

Despite our diversity, this was the spirit in most of our companies. We worked on many "problems" that placed our units in simulated combat situations and then required us to maneuver out of them. Such exercises required long, forced marches, sometimes more than thirty miles. We marched in one-hundred-degree weather, we marched with the rain freezing on our uniforms, and we always marched with little rest, frequently at a very fast pace, and usually with full field packs while carrying all our weapons. It was not uncommon for us actually to run part of the way.

These forced marches unified us, building us up as teams that depended on trust and cooperation. Take the system I had with my gunner, Duck. Each of us could balance our forty-pound 60mm mortar on a shoulder and walk all night with it sitting there, hands free. We would tie a jump rope between us so the first could lead the other down a road at night with the second man carrying the mortar on his shoulder, fast asleep.

That's teamwork. I knew Duck like a book, and he knew me. When it came to firing on enemy soldiers in Fresville, Normandy, on D-Day morning, we worked together just as we had on many other occasions preparing for that day. I knew what to expect of Duck in Fresville, and what to expect of Fred Kelly, too, who was part of our mortar squad in that attack.

Chapter Four

Payday Parties

If there was one characteristic that identified most paratroopers, it was that we loved to party. Company H was no exception when it came to having to get 20 percent of the unit out of jail the day after almost every payday. We were usually paid in the morning after an inspection of our bunks, weapons, uniforms, and barracks. Then we lined up and went through the pay line filing through the front door of the orderly room and out through the supply room exit.

Most of the married troops sent the bulk of their pay home to the wife and kids. We single types had nothing to lose and monthly ideas of hitting it big. If we lost our paycheck, we could always bum cigarettes and wait for next month's payday.

You would think our modest pay, always in cash, was burning holes in our pockets. First of all, it was not all that much, regardless of the troopers' famous "extra pay." By the time we went into combat in Normandy, I suppose a private was making about forty-eight dollars a month, plus his fifty-dollar jump pay.

Payday weekends always meant four things in Company H. One was lots of alcohol, in whatever form it was to be had. Thus, our standard expression: "He only drinks when he is alone or with someone." It might come from a farmer's cornfield as an unlabeled bottle of twenty-five-cent firewater; it might come from a bootlegger as a pint of "crazy water" for whatever the traffic would bring—there was nothing we would not drink to get drunk.

The second item in every payday scene was girls. They, too, seemed to find their way into our barracks. We were never surprised at what might show up the morning after a payday. In England, the morning after our "baptism of fire" party, some units supposedly reported in 100 percent overstrength. It was bedlam, really crazy! But the same problem on a lesser scale was not uncommon in the States before we went overseas. Some of the married men also took part in these drunken parties, both in the barracks and nearby towns.

These drunken weekends often provided the atmosphere and conditions for a "let's get married" fiasco. Then the trooper would report back to his unit with a whole new set of problems. Sometimes, however, the soldier "found out" about his marriage weeks later, when the girl and her parents showed up in the company commander's office, seeking the girl's husband and the father of her baby-to-be!

The third, and also guaranteed issue at every Company H payday, was the fighting that took place either in the local bars and nightclubs or back in the barracks. It mattered not where—these men were going to fight someone. Frequently, the fights would be between two best friends, but troopers preferably fought with outsiders such as local civilians or Army Air Corps troops.

Item number four guaranteed to accompany every payday was gambling. Although a paratrooper would bet on daylight coming up tomorrow, for the most part we either shot craps or dice or played poker. My gambling skills had already developed in my first military unit, the old Texas National Guard division, so, fortunately, I had pretty good poker skills. Identifying cards by simply making a slight fingernail mark was the first trick the big boys taught me. I could also identify "honey cured" dice— dice so weighted that, nurtured by skillful hands, they could be made to turn over just so many times, thus winding up on the thrower's point and making him a winner.

There was a system of gambling throughout the 507th , as well as throughout the army and perhaps the entire U.S. military organization worldwide. In every barracks on every payday, there would be a couple card games, usually a couple kinds of poker and maybe blackjack. There would be at least one crap or dice game going, while troops talked to the dice and cussed one another in a variety of accents. One expression was, "Eighta from Decatur, the county seat of Wise," referring to Wise County, Texas, spoken when the thrower had eight for a point. Another crap shooter would observe, "The dice shooters in hell saw the point," meaning that he tried to throw an eight but threw a six, the point that's up when eight faces down. Shooting dice was somewhat of a math class, and we quickly learned percentages we never mastered in school.

By the end of each payday, a couple or three troops had won most of the available gambling money in each barracks. These winners moved on to the "company game," which involved the winners from each barracks. Within three days, there were a few really heavy winners and a lot more poverty-stricken losers. This was a monthly ritual in just about every outfit. The winners seldom pulled KP, the most hated duty of any soldier, for they bought their way out of the task by paying someone—often a loser—to take their place.

My good friend Chet Gunka was one of the big-time players. He had had to leave his former rank back with his naval outfit, but I doubt he lost much sleep over the change in pay grade. If that was his attitude, he was proven correct in short order. Unfortunately for troopers such as myself, Chet's lessons on how to win at army poker were not all that cheap—though they were good. His army pay was just one increment in his overall income.

Of course, part of Chet's gross monthly income also included his "banking business," or money-lending opportunities. Chet was only one of many money lenders, and given the system in place, he was a very fair financier. His finance charges were actually reasonable compared to the going rate of at least 400 percent. You see, in the G.I. barracks loan business, when you borrowed ten dollars on April 29, 1943, and got paid on April 30, you paid back twenty dollars for the ten-dollar loan. Figure what that means as an annual rate. And we stood in line to take advantage of these financial opportunities.

Chapter Five

Training Jumps
in a Peanut Patch

As members of the 507th, we jumped on the Alabama side of the Chattahoochie River, on a drop zone near the company area. The object of these training jumps, then as it is now, was to learn how to assemble in units after a drop and to get to our equipment on the ground.

Every C-47 we jumped from carried a maximum of six equipment bundles beneath its belly, weighing, on average, two hundred pounds, which were attached to its own secure canister. It was a real hassle loading or attaching the bundles to the canisters. Their weight was determined by the items they contained. For example, the medics' bundle would be rather light because it carried first aid supplies. Our mortar squad bundles were always very heavy because they were loaded primarily with HE (high explosive) 60mm shells, as many as we could crowd into the heavy canvas case.

The canvas measured about seven feet square. First, we laid the bundles out on the ground, then spread the loaded items toward the center of the canvas. After arranging the items from one end to the other, we folded the side flaps toward the center, thus covering the gear. Then we rolled the whole thing up like a rug, slipped a heavy round canvas cover over each end, and bound the end caps together with heavy canvas straps. Each bundle thus secured had its own cargo parachute, which was to open automatically, just as our personal chutes opened.

The bundles were released from inside the plane by a system of six switches near the jump door, each of which controlled one bundle. The timing of this was vital. The object was to release the bundles in the middle of the stick. Then everyone slipped his parachute toward the bundles, and we all landed together, next to our equipment. Right? Wrong! Great strategy but, as the old saying goes, "The best laid plans of mice and men. . . ."

My practice was to tape the line of all six switches together between two tongue depressors. Thus, when the middle man in the stick got to the door, he could hit all the switches with one swipe, simultaneously releasing all the bundles, which then would land in the middle of the stick. Or so we hoped.

Frequently, if the pilot and crew of the jump plane were not alert, we would "daisy chain" the bundles in an effort to keep them together. That way, no matter how dispersed the stick, at least our equipment would all be in one place. We took our jump ropes and tied the bundles together in every fashion imaginable. And, it never worked.

One day, we loaded all thirty-three of our platoon's personal backpacks into one bundle on a jump into some peanut patches around Fort Benning. When the chute opened, all the equipment came raining down in every direction. Each pack had an entrenching tool attached to it, either a shovel or a pick. The shovels made a deadly sounding swishing noise as they traveled toward earth. Troopers abandoned the assembly plan and headed for safety in every direction. Fortunately, no one was injured by the rain of trenching tools.

The Army Air Corps threw a fit about daisy chaining. It seems that on one occasion, someone hit the release system heading out the door, and all the bundles released but one. Because they were chained together, five of the bundles were dragging beneath the plane, while the one still in the rack kept them all attached. The crew chief failed to manually release the last bundle, and the load dragged the plane into the ground.

Fortunately, by this time, the pilot had returned to Lawson Field and made a landing with all the equipment bundles still dragging. No one was hurt, but the accident put a stop to daisy chains. We usually tried to get the chaining job done after the inspection, when we were loaded up and ready for takeoff. Crew chiefs thereafter always tried to be the last person entering the plane, so they could nab any trooper who had daisy chained the bundles and was making a hasty exit.

Our squad also came up with a system of identifying our bundles in the air in an effort to improve our assembly on night jumps. We attached a tin can to each bundle, indicating H-3-3—Company H, 3rd Platoon, 3rd Squad—on the sides and the end of the can. A small light in every can turned on when the bundle was released from the carrying pods under the plane. At one time we even had different colored lights in each can to identify the platoon or company. There was really no end to our ingenuity when it came to retrieving our equipment.

Of course, there were many personal near disasters as we practiced our maneuvers. On one jump, Bill Stoler, the regiment's best rifle shot and a known clown, came in really fast and overshot the drop zone. This put Bill into our company area. His chute blew over the top of the latrine and the canopy spread across the roof. With a crack-the-whip movement, his body whipped right into the end of the latrine. His feet went through the one-inch boards, and there he stuck, about four feet off the ground.

And when I say stuck, I mean good and stuck. He was on his back, held in place by sharp, shattered boards pressing hard against his torso. It was laughable because he wasn't seriously hurt, but carpenters had to come and gingerly remove the boards in order to free him. We had a great time with that one in our barracks.

More seriously, the drop zone on the Alabama side of Fort Benning was also bedeviled by high-tension electric lines. Our instructors warned us that if we touched any two of these lines at the same time we were certain to be "fried." On the same jump that Billy got stuck in the can, a trooper from another company got hung up on the high-tension lines. There he was, swinging back and forth, pushed by a strong wind, his body touching one wire, then almost touching another. He sucked in his belly going one way bent his back out of shape going the other, in an effort to avoid instant death.

Each time he swung away from a wire, he would try to get another snap loose on his harness. First, he got his chest strap, then a leg strap, and then the other leg strap loose. Whichever was the final strap that freed him, I don't recall, but he came loose and fell the sixty feet to the ground like a spinning top. Fortunately, he hit in sandy soil, arranged in neat rows for planting peanuts. It was as soft a landing site as you would ever see, more so, even, than a water landing.

On another jump on the Alabama side, our great regimental executive officer, Lieutenant Colonel Maloney, saved a trooper from serious injury. The fellow had gotten his feet tangled in his suspension lines so that his harness held his shoulders in place while the lines held his feet up. This meant that his back would be the first thing to hit the ground.

As the trooper descended, Colonel Maloney ran around the drop zone on his motor scooter trying to get to the spot where he thought the soldier would land. When the lad was about to hit, Maloney dropped his scooter, ran to the jumper, and caught him in his arms. They both were knocked to the ground very hard, but neither was seriously injured. There came loud cheers for Colonel Maloney and the trooper.

I think it was on that same day that a medical corpsman jumped with my platoon. I pushed the stick, so I was the last man out. The medic was just in front of me. When his parachute opened, I saw nothing but suspension lines all around me. It took a few seconds to realize what was happening. I was inside someone's suspension lines, and they certainly were not mine!

This was another "first" for me, and a "first" for the medic as well. It was funny to hear him shout, "Get out of my suspension lines!" as if I had worked hard to get right in the middle of this guy's lines. I don't know how it happened, but I darn sure didn't make a habit of trying to get tangled up with some other jumper. We had all the hassles we needed getting safely from plane to assembly on the ground.

When I discovered that my lines were obviously running through two of his, I found the point of intrusion, gathered up my lines in one hand, and separated his with the other. I pulled down hard on my lines, and my chute dipped sharply away from his. I had a little thrill as I dropped some distance before my chute gathered enough air to slow my descent. As I contemplated this near-serious encounter, I discovered that I was about to land in the swampy area behind Company H. Moreover, I was going in backward. I had lost quite a bit of preparation time dealing with the suspension lines. As I neared the ground, I heard someone shouting instructions, telling me what to do. I was busy, had just had the hell scared out of me, and now I had someone advising me on how to land backward in a swamp!

"Who the hell is riding this parachute?" I shouted. Crash! I was down, wet and dirty in the swamp water, but safe. Then an officer came plowing up, waist deep in water. He said, "Colonel Millett wants to see you." I gathered up my chute and stumbled out of the swamp a couple hundred feet to where the colonel was standing.

I then discovered I had smarted off to Colonel Millett. He called me on the carpet, and I suggested that what I had said was accurate—"Who was riding that rig to the ground?" Besides, I added, I didn't know who he was. He laughed and agreed that it was my business. As it turned out, he had also seen the deal with the medic. He said I had done a pretty good job through the whole affair and dismissed me with a kind word.

Chapter Six

Louisiana Maneuvers, 1943

In early March 1943, the regiment loaded up on passenger trains for a trip to Shreveport, Louisiana, and Barksdale Army Air Base, where we would spend twelve days on Third Army maneuvers. Poor Shreveport! This was the only large town in which we were ever stationed, and we really turned it loose. We stayed at Barksdale for quite some time, waiting out a jump to participate in maneuvers. This little hiatus provided the 507th with an excellent opportunity for many a night on the town.

Shreveport had never been exposed to a regiment of wild, frequently drunken paratroopers. Before we departed, we really loaded up the municipal jail. As an example of how a paratrooper went to jail in those days, I can tell you that my first trip to town found me behind bars for the behavior of another drunken paratrooper whom I scarcely knew. He told the attendant at a closed drugstore that if he didn't open up and sell us some cigarettes, he'd kick in the glass door. The door was not opened, and true to his paratrooper oath, he kicked in the glass. Hello, jailhouse! And, as I said, I scarcely knew the nut!

After laying around Barksdale Field for about ten days, we loaded up the regiment in C-47s, formed an air train in the sky, and flew down the Sabine River about one hundred miles, where we jumped into the heart of the maneuvering troops. I can't recall what our mission was to be, and probably wasn't the least bit interested then. All I knew was that I was back for another—my third—miserable Louisiana maneuver. I had spent some of the worst days and nights of my existence chasing all around the boondocks of that state. Would this new experience be a re-enactment of my previous trips? I prayed not.

The jump was attended with the usual extraordinary mishaps. I am not sure exactly what happened, but First Sergeant Marco did not make the jump. I am assuming he refused, because he was busted back to private. Because he was such a valuable soldier, they did not ship him off to the infantry in the Pacific, but kept him in the regiment on non-jump status.

Another friend of mine, Sgt. George Forte, a rifle squad leader in our 3rd Platoon, confirmed his talent for special landings. He had once come down at a Denver air base with one foot on each side of the very top of a tall telephone pole. He perched there long enough for his picture to be taken, standing on top of that pole, before falling fifty feet to the ground. As I recall, the photo was published in the *Denver Post* the following day.

In Louisiana, George was not so graceful. He came right down through an old, ramshackle farmhouse, shattering the roof and scattering the farmer's furniture as his big body crashed into the living room. He was not injured, as I recall, but the affair was the source of much laughter. I suppose the army gave the old couple a new roof.

Then there was the senior general, whose parachute got hung up over the top of a sixty-foot pine tree, leaving him too far from the tree trunk or branches to climb down. In that shape a trooper usually passes out as his harness tightens up on his body and cuts off circulation. We all carried a jump rope for just such occasions, but to use it safely, you couldn't be more than forty feet or so from the ground.

Having a general "up a tree" played right into the hands of the typical paratrooper. Many of the men who had safely made the jump walked under him, shouting up not-so-encouraging comments like, "What the hell are you doing up there, General?" In time, I reckon, his unconscious body was lowered to the ground by some tree monkey riggers.

I myself had a great landing in a typical sandy pasture full of pine tree stumps. As soon as my feet hit the ground, maneuver officials declared me a prisoner because I landed right in the middle of enemy forces. Three Louisiana maneuvers, three times a prisoner. It was becoming a habit.

The officials took me over to some tall pine trees under which they'd erected a barbed wire fence to make a prison camp. There were canvas cots inside the prison compound and a lister bag hanging there full of ice water. This was a rubber-lined fifty-gallon canvas bag suspended from a three-pole frame, with a handy spigot on the bottom. A chow truck with its own kitchen was backed up to the barbed wire enclosure. There were magazines to read and a life of leisure to be enjoyed as a prisoner of our enemy.

I had just settled down for a nap when a young, new lieutenant, the prison commander, came over to me, the only prisoner in his compound. "Take off those jump boots, Sergeant," he ordered. Our Corcoran jump boots were our pride and joy, unique to our branch of service. "Why," I asked. "You're not going to escape from my prison!" he exclaimed.

"Listen, Lieutenant," I said, "please sit down here and let me tell you about my experience in these Louisiana pine forests on previous maneuvers. I'll gladly *give* you my boots, if you'll let me stay as your prisoner. Believe me, there's no way I'll escape and leave that ice water and that chow truck and cook. No way!" He had a laugh, but I was as serious as I had ever been. He knew he was listening to one sincere trooper who had found a home in his prison.

The maneuver lasted just one day after our jump. Having retrieved our drunks from the local jails, we then loaded up on trains again for the trip to our next permanent station in Alliance, Nebraska.

Chapter Seven

RODEO JUMP:
ALLIANCE, NEBRASKA,
AUGUST 1943

We arrived in the hills of northwestern Nebraska on March 23, 1943, where we were stationed with Army Air Force troop carrier units at the Alliance Army Air Base. This was our home until late November when we shipped out for overseas. Because our wild paratroopers resisted the area military police, refusing to let the MPs arrest them, Colonel Millett established his own city patrol in Alliance. We had 507th PIR NCOs walking the streets watching for troopers who might get out of line.

It was in this capacity that I met and promptly fell in love with Elizabeth, the gorgeous blonde ticket salesgirl at the local theater. For days, I just hung around the theater and swooned over this beauty, then walked her home every evening when she got off work. Strangely, her family seemed to approve of me.

I had just gotten a "Dear Bob" letter from my high school love back in Dallas. Without ever really asking Doris if she was interested in marrying a character like me, I'd bought an engagement ring in an Alliance jewelry store. When I received her letter saying that she was marrying an "older" Adamson

High School graduate, I took the ring back, got some of my money back, and threw one big drunk in Scotts Bluff, Nebraska. By the time I met Elizabeth, I was ready for another "real" love affair.

In those days, as I've said before, dating almost never included a sexual relationship. Whenever a paratrooper found a decent girl he cared about, he guarded her like a prisoner to keep her from being exposed to his drunken buddies. You just didn't take a "good girl" out in the company of your friends. For sure, they would act up before the night was over, and bang! there went your newest romance. So I kept Elizabeth to myself, not realizing that she was engaged to an officer pilot. She may have told me this, but I was so much in love I was in denial.

It was while visiting Beth's home that I met the Youngbloods, a ranching family from outside Alliance—a father, mother, and son. The father, Herb, was thirty-six, but because he was the only person to run the farm, he had not been drafted into the military.

In time, I started going out to their ranch every weekend I was not out training in the Nebraska boondocks. I worked like a dog at various farm chores, which was like play compared to my military training. Frequently, I would take some military weapons out to the ranch with me, usually broken down and hidden in a barracks bag.

Herb loved weapons and really liked shooting the various guns I brought. One time, I took out a big slug .45-caliber Thompson submachine gun. I warned Herb to be very careful with how he fired the gun, because it would do crazy things. If you didn't hang on to some of them, they would rise up and spread .45-caliber shells all over the place.

Herb aimed the gun at a four-by-four wooden post that supported the water tower and pulled the trigger. Well, the gun took off. Herb sprayed bullets through the post, through the old wooden barn door, and through the hood on his farm truck, and then cracked the truck's engine block—all in his first pull of the trigger. He was very philosophical about the whole affair and apologized for not being more careful. There may still be farmers with adjoining property who are wondering who or what killed their cows.

Now, Herb thought that a Texan could do anything, and whatever a Texan couldn't do, a paratrooper certainly could. I had told him that animals didn't like me, especially horses, but that was not good enough. With the Alliance Rodeo coming up, he insisted on putting up the ten-dollar entrance fee for me to ride a bull. He knew I'd make some real money. Maybe it was Herb's home brew, but I got to thinking he was right and that perhaps being a rodeo cowboy was to be my calling after the war.

To open the Alliance Rodeo, the 507th Parachute Infantry was going to supply a company-sized unit to make a jump at the rodeo grounds. To clear the air, it must be stated that I never made a parachute jump that I liked. Every time I got in a plane for a jump, I'd swear that this was it. I couldn't refuse to jump— that would have been too embarrassing. No matter how scared I was, the very idea of going back to the barracks and packing my bags was unthinkable. So I'd go ahead and make the jump.

As soon as I was safe on the ground again, I instantly became this bad paratrooper, the Invincible One. I would run to the orderly room and put my name on the sign-up list for the next volunteer jump. This crazy cycle continued until I jumped on D-Day, which ended my jumping experience.

When the day finally arrived for the rodeo, I had two major issues to deal with—a jump *and* a bull ride. Each could get a body hurt or killed. But again, I had agreed to both of these dumb endeavors.

The rodeo was to start about 2 p.m. on Saturday afternoon. Herb gave me some chaps, and I was to borrow his Western hat and wear my Corcoran jump boots to ride the bull. The big opening event was the 507th jump right above the rodeo grounds. Whoever did the planning for that drop did a very poor job. I don't know where the other jumpers landed, but once I was out of the plane, I could see my landing was to be another "experience."

A gravel road, connected to a larger, paved road not too far away, surrounded the rodeo grounds. There were ample barbed wire fences all over the place. Nearing the ground, but perhaps still fifty feet in the air, I saw an all-American looking family walking toward the grandstands on the gravel road: a good-looking daughter, younger son, mother, and father, all decked out and heading for the rodeo. Instantly, still fifty feet in the air, I was in love. Once again I was fearless, now that my chute had opened and I was almost on the ground.

I fixed my eyes on the teenage girl as I neared the sandy ground. A fence separated me from the road on which the family was walking. On the far side of this road, a line of cars was parked near the rodeo entrance.

The first time I hit the ground, I was going forward fast. I went sailing through the air, turned over on my back, and hit the gravel. I skidded across the road and slid under the front bumper of a car with a crash, my helmet clanging like a gong.

I was probably too goofy to be hurt, but it sure looked like I had been seriously injured. I immediately recalled the good-looking girl and started struggling to get to my feet and greet the family. I didn't see any other troopers nearby and, frankly, wasn't interested in anyone but my newest love.

Right on cue, she came running over crying out, "Are you hurt? Are you hurt?" I'm sure I told her that troopers went through this sort of drill every morning before chow. I laid it on thick. I was a bit wobbly, having banged my head on the car bumper pretty hard. The family all spent some time going over my dented helmet and my weapon and equipment.

I assured them I would win all the money in the bull riding event, not knowing, in reality, which end of the bull to face when I got on. After bleeding my crash landing for all it was worth, I learned that my heroics were to no avail with the girl—the family was from out of town. I gathered up my chute, turned in my equipment, and went looking for Herb.

My one and only rodeo experience was short lived. They put me on a very large, very ugly red bull that had bad things in mind for me from the start.

There was a four-by-four wooden bar across the top of the bullpens just over the gate, which would open for the bull to do his thing. With Herb's hat firmly pulled down over my ears, and all my paratrooper buddies roaring their approval, I was just about to nod for the gatekeepers to open the gate, when suddenly, the bull, with a mind of his own, threw me straight up in the air. Once again, my head took all the action, banging up against the four-by-four. It knocked me out cold as a turkey.

They gave me smelling salts and threw water in my face, and I came to readily. I protested that I should get another chance, praying silently for the Lord please to spare me another trip on that or any other bull. Finally, reluctantly, I agreed that I would not ride again.

And so it is that anyone who missed my attempt at bull riding on that sunny August Saturday afternoon in Alliance, Nebraska, 1943, missed my entire rodeo career.

Chapter Eight

The Jumping Mascot

After a very arduous training week out in the boondocks of northwestern Nebraska, every 507th PIR trooper really needed R&R. September in Nebraska is beautiful, with ideal temperatures—the best time of year for field training. This always meant long marches carrying full field packs and all of our weapons, and we were frequently required to run instead of walk. The bottom line was that we all were looking forward to some time away from Alliance Army Air Base.

When my gunner, Duck, came to propose a weekend trip to Scottsbluff, Nebraska, I knew some excitement was in store. That word *excitement* had a variety of connotations. It could involve meeting pretty young ladies at a dance, or it might infer a night in the Scottsbluff county jail for fighting or other mischievous conduct.

We left on Saturday morning, after the usual company inspection accompanied by some sort of parade. The trip of an hour or so sounded like a school bus full of high school kids en route to a big football game. More jabbering than you can imagine, about nothing. Duck and I ran from the military bus in downtown Alliance to the civilian bus station, where we caught a bus that would take us about sixty miles west to Scottsbluff. There were far more soldiers and airmen than seats. Another race ensued from the bus station in Scottsbluff to the hotel, to be first in line to register for a room. There was no such thing as a reservation in those days. It was first come, first served.

Scottsbluff actually had a multistory hotel, where we enjoyed staying in real luxury. There was a nice restaurant, where we ate off fine china and could order just about any food you could imagine. The large, comfortable rooms had first-class bathrooms. We'd been squatting over a slit trench out in the field and bathing with water in a helmet for weeks, so this was a feature we most appreciated.

Despite the lure of these comforts, we could not wait to drop off our bags and head out the front door of the hotel. We never had a plan of activity, such as where we would visit or what movie we would see. The first order of business was always to head for a favorite restaurant. Most of us, being in our late teens or early twenties, had rarely eaten out. We had been raised during the depression, when families seldom ate in restaurants, except on an automobile trip, which was also a rare experience for the typical American family in the 1930s or 1940s.

After dining like kings, in our minds at least, any movie would do. By the time we had enjoyed a double feature, the Pathe current event news, a serial, or one of the thrillers that was continued from week to week, and at least one cartoon, we were ready for another meal.

Once we'd completed our second meal, it was time to start looking for a dance. There were several public dance spots where live music was available, and where local girls came to enjoy the paratroopers and airmen. The airmen were mostly training to be crewmen on bombers—gunners, for the most part, on .50-caliber machine guns. Most would soon be firing at German fighter planes in combat over England, France, Italy, and Germany. No soft touch for sure, but if you did not wear the wings of a paratrooper, in our minds you were missing something.

On one particular evening of dancing, I met a new young lady who was just out of high school and had a job as a secretary in Scottsbluff. She was of such character and beauty that you would not want to introduce her to your paratrooper buddies. Before the night was over, they were sure to have had too much to drink and would be wanting to prove how tough they were—an attitude that was always accompanied by a big, loud mouth.

The girls that evening were very good dancers, and just plain fine young ladies. We were standing on the raised dance floor waiting for the next tune, when my date met a female school friend and introduced her to me. The friend then introduced her dance partner, an airman stationed in Scottsbluff. An interesting and very friendly conversation ensued among the four of us. My new friends were standing below the dance floor, which was lower than us by six to eight inches. Being five foot eight, I was just about as tall as the airman, which meant he must have been more than six feet. This, you understand, is just an observation!

We paratroopers frequently acted much like pit bulls. We wanted to fight—and this meant anybody and for no particular reason. I really did not like this attitude, though I had manifested the same on a number of occasions since I had received my wings. This night, I was acting like a gentleman in an effort to impress my "nice" date, and in hopes of getting to meet her family the following day. That meant no crude behavior, no cursing, and certainly, no fighting. Just good manners.

Well, after we'd visited with the other couple, Joe, a drunken 507th trooper I knew from back in Company F of the 144th

Infantry, National Guard, wandered up. Soon he was challenging me to punch this new friend. I discovered after a few minutes of this stupid harangue that I was actually making a fist and considering hitting the airman. It never occurred to me that this man was obviously much taller than me and probably outweighed me by thirty pounds. I must say that paratroopers were probably in better shape than any of the country's other military. We worked so hard every day that the only possible outcome was outstanding, physically fit bodies.

Finally, it occurred to me that Joe's dumb encouragement was causing me to consider hitting the airman for absolutely no reason. I thought, *This dummy is turning me into a creature who is just as dumb as he is.* Whereupon, I decked Joe, knocking him halfway across the dance floor. I went over to where he lay, and asked, "What the hell were you trying to do to me?" Joe mumbled something, got up, and wandered over to the men's room to wash the blood off his face. We remained friends until we loaded up for D-Day, at which point I never saw him again.

Duck, who was in another part of the dance hall, came over to tell me how proud he was of me for not going for the crazy behavior Joe had suggested. He had recently spent a week in a Denver hospital, having taken a beating from the local police and MPs when he was drunk at Elitche's Garden.

The next day in Scottsbluff started about 11 a.m., with breakfast at a little diner we had discovered on our last visit. On that occasion, we had taken the cafe apart. Afterward, Bill Stoler had volunteered to mop the floor for the young female waitress. This is the same Stoler, the number one rifleman in the regiment, whose body had crashed through our latrine wall in a parachute jump next to our company street in Alabama.

The waitress had no idea Bill was going to mop the cafe floor with catsup. He spread the catsup all over the floor from bottles sitting on the tables and proceeded to mop with a regular mop. Needless to say, Bill wound up in jail and Company

```
        HEADQUARTERS 3RD BATTALION
        507TH PARACHUTE INFANTRY
        AAB, ALLIANCE? NEBRASKA

                                    6 September 1943

SUBJECT:  Restriction of Co. "H" 3rd Bn., 507th Prcht Inf

TO     :  All personnel, Co. "H"
```

1. Due to the increasing number of delinquencies in your company, namely wrecking of Eggle Cafe, Scottsbluff, Nebr., large number of AWOL's, fighting with MP's and civilian authorites in Scottsbluff, Nebr., accident in which a soldier is badly cut and in an exeeedingly drunken condition, with cognizance of the above, Co. "H" 507th Prcht Inf is placed in restriction to the regimental area of the 507th Prcht Inf.

2. This restriction includes all personnel and Officers.

3   a. A disciplinary guard of three men will be posted about the barracks of Co. "H". These men will be posted as follows: one to walk post in front of the Co. "H" barracks. One man to walk post in the rear of The Co. "H" barracks. The third man to walk completely around the Co. "H" barracks. This guard will commence duty at 1900 each evening and will be relieved at 0600 each morning. This duty will not release any one from drill during the day.
     b. All officers will stay in the company area during the period 1900 to 0600 each night and will be responsible for one barracks per each officer. An officer must be on duty at all times during the period 1900 to 0600 each night and will check this disciplinary guard. Other company officers are restricted to the regimental area.
     c. A bed check will be made at 2200 each night by an officer appointed by the company commander.

3. Platoon leaders will conduct evening classes for their respective platoons on the subject of "Leadership and Morale,"

4. This restriction takes effect at 1730, 6 Sept 1943, and will be lifted 2400 12 Sept 1943, providing the company warrants resumtion of their privileges.

```
                        WILLIAM A KUHN, Major
```

Military document putting all of Company H on restriction.

H, officers and all, ended up confined to the company area with a guard posted. No passes, no nothing for what seemed like a month, but was really only six days. The official document that set out the terms of establishing a guard post around the company noted details of the "sentence." More of the officers than the enlisted men were married, so there were some very hot campers among the officers, none of whom were involved in taking apart the cafe.

On another occasion, Bill had offered to help the maid at the hotel by taking all the linens from an upper floor to the basement. Must have been a hundred sheets and pillowcases. The maid had assumed that Bill would take them to the basement by elevator. Not Bill! She went on with her room cleaning while he proceeded to take the linens out onto the fire escape that overlooked the alley ten floors up off the street. There must have been a twenty mile an hour wind blowing down the alley that day. When those linens went over the side of the fire escape, they began flying all over the telephone poles, rooftops, and streets below.

On another occasion, after a late Sunday breakfast, the drinking started. There was nothing doing in Scottsbluff of interest to us, so we just hung around the hotel until check-out time. An insufficient amount of booze was left from our Saturday bash, so for Duck and me, replenishing our whiskey stock became a matter of importance.

After questioning the hotel staff about where one might buy some whiskey on a Sunday, we headed for a taxi stand and a ride to the roughest part of Scottsbluff, where we located yet one more nasty bootleg joint full of tough-looking drunks. We cut our deal for a jug of killer bootleg whiskey and made our way out into the back lot of the crummy place, fully intending to start working on our bottle of booze.

Once outside, we found ourselves among automobile tires, car parts, and old engines. No need to start looking for the usual junkyard dog. Right out in the middle of all the trash, attached by a heavy metal chain that was hooked to a long auto driveshaft anchored in the oil-soaked ground, was the ugliest, meanest, sixty-pound baboon on earth. With his huge, slick, fire engine red butt glowing in the sun, he patrolled the length of his big chain with vigor and passion, clearly seeking out something or someone to eat. This was a baboon with a mission to kill. He had a real attitude problem. Squinting his eyes, he pondered whether he would have Duck, me, or both of us for lunch.

Without saying a word, Duck and I both had an identical thought. What a great jumping mascot this angry critter would make when we got him back to Alliance! One 507th unit had Geronimo, a jumping German shepherd dog. Another had a troubled billy goat with a jumping harness. Surely, a jumping baboon would trump them both. What a terrific mascot for Company H! Captain Taylor would really be proud of us!

The only problem was getting "Booze, the jumping baboon" back to the air base. Our solution was a burlap bag lying right next to the metal anchor pole. Booze had walked around that pole the full length of his chain for so many laps that there was nothing left but hard, oil-saturated dirt. We agreed that Duck would attract Booze's attention to one side of the circle, and I would slip up behind him and grab his heavy leather collar right next to his neck. While I held him, Duck would pull the burlap bag over his head—and presto! He would soon be en route to Alliance.

It never occurred to us to include Booze in the planning, so he was not privy to our ideas. We had observed, however, that he had long fangs on each side of his jaw and rather worn nails on each foot and hand. Unfortunately, it appeared that this was one baboon that some other drunks had already tried to kidnap.

Well, Duck got Booze's attention to the point that all of his fangs were exposed. He had stretched his chain to the maximum length. I slipped into the circle and grabbed the unsuspecting baboon's collar right behind his head, and all hell broke loose. I didn't know a baboon could talk, but Booze was really saying things to Duck and me. He could not decide which of us he wanted the most. Duck, charging into the ring gathering up the burlap bag, certainly had his full attention, until he suddenly realized that someone had him by the neck. This made him start turning in circles, winding up his chain around my jump boots.

As I began to see the folly of this adventure, I started yelling for Duck to abandon the project and get the hell out of his reach. Duck yelled back that he almost had the animal in the bag. In fact, though, he hadn't gotten so much as a finger-nail of that baboon in the bag. For sure, I was just about to go down on that hard, oily surface with a sixty-pound baboon for company.

One more time I screamed, "Duck, he's winding me up with the chain! I'm turning him loose!" And, once more, Duck said, "Hang on just a minute. He's almost in the bag!" At this point, I threw ol' Booze as far as I could and clambered for the end of his chain. He saw I was out of his range and headed for Duck.

Three hours later, the medics at the first aid station back at Alliance Army Air Base said, "My God, what the hell happened to this soldier?" I said, "You wouldn't believe it if I told you. Just patch him up and I'll take him back to the barracks."

Who the hell needs a jumping baboon mascot anyway?

Chapter Nine

SEDALIA, MISSOURI JUMP

After some R&R in the Black Hills, a few of us flew out of a bomber air base in South Dakota to Italy, Missouri. From there, I flew south with some other NCOs to Sedalia, Missouri, to examine the Sedalia Army Air Base from the air. We were to jump on this base the next day as a training exercise. Learning how to jump in and capture a given objective, like an air base, was really what paratroops were all about.

Flying over a target on reconnaissance was a huge luxury, and certainly one we would not have on D-Day. But this time we had the privilege of flying low over the target base and observing with our own eyes, out of our open plane door, just what was on and around the air base. We would know the projected wind velocity at the time of our jump as well as the direction of the wind. This would tell us what direction the planes would be flying, and we could see any obstacles that might impede a paratrooper's landing. We were to be over the drop zone (DZ) the next morning at 0700 hours so it would be good daylight.

We made a couple passes over the DZ outside Sedalia, then flew back north to Italy to spend time with our sticks. On the way back, I suddenly had a "great" idea. Actually, it was a brain function failure, which was not unusual for a twenty-year-old paratrooper. We occasionally seemed to disengage our brains, and this was certainly one of those instances. I started wondering, out of the clear blue sky, what it would be like to cut the break cord on my parachute!

To understand just how crazy this was, you have to know that our parachutes opened automatically, and the break cord was crucial to this function. The break cord itself consisted of a few turns of strong cotton that attached the apex of the parachute to the parachute pack cover. When we stood up and got ready to jump, we hooked the pack cover via our static line to a metal cable, or anchor line, which ran down the center of the plane. The static line joined the parachute pack cover and the parachute through the break cord.

So it was, in the final analysis, that when the trooper went out the door, the break cord pulled the parachute out of the frame on his back. If the break cord is properly in place, it will stay there until the entire parachute, canopy, suspension lines, static line, and risers are all strung out to their limits. Then the break cord snaps, and the trooper is free of any attachment to the plane. If the break cord is cut, the parachute pack cover will be pulled off when the trooper leaves the plane, but the parachute will not be deployed or strung out properly to open up. The silk comes out and sort of floats open as the body falls through space. This is information I had to learn the hard way. My brainstorm was to cut the break cord and see how it would affect the opening of my chute.

On arrival back in Italy, Missouri, I quickly looked up a special friend, Ed Hon, a communication man in our platoon. Perhaps I selected Ed because he was a faithful Catholic and always went to communion before a jump. What I needed was a man who knew how to pray.

I said, "Ed, if we jump more than eight hundred feet tomorrow, let's cut our break cords to see what happens." Hon readily agreed to this very stupid and dangerous idea, indicating that he, too, had not engaged his brain when considering the project.

Before daylight the next morning, we lined up to draw our chutes out of the back of two trucks. One truck held our main packs, or the larger, number one chute; the other contained reserve chutes, which were smaller and used only in case the main pack failed to open. I had not used a reserve up to that time, but knew the procedure.

Ordinarily, the first step in making ready a parachute for a jump was to lengthen or shorten the leg straps. On this particular morning, I started my preparation by inserting my fingers inside the pack cover on my main chute and feeling for the break cord. When I located it, I took out my jump knife and cut through the several turns of strong cord. I then took the cord in hand and went looking in the dark for Ed Hon.

When I found Ed, he was busy working on his harness. I asked him to hold out his hand. When he complied, I placed my break cord in his outstretched palm. I really felt like some sort of hero, when, in fact, this was the act of a true dummy. Ed promptly said, "Just a minute and I'll cut mine."

At this moment, some measure of intelligence came forth. I said, "Hell no, Ed, this is the dumbest thing I've ever done. The trucks have already gone toward Sedalia, or I'd ask for another chute and break this one open, so no one else can jump it till it's repacked. Just pray for me."

Ed insisted that a deal is a deal, and he would cut his break cord as well. But better judgment prevailed and we agreed that the deal was off as far as he was concerned. For sure, if I had insisted in the least, Ed would have cut his break cord, and then there would have been two fools to pray for.

With chutes fitted, we took off in our C-47s for Sedalia, Missouri, in the dark of early morning. I kept praying, "Lord

let it get daylight before I jump this chute with no break cord."
I don't know why I thought daylight would help my stupid situation, but that was my prayer.

To make matters worse, I desperately had to pee. Try to
imagine a stick of eighteen paratroopers, sitting in their aluminum bucket seats in a C-47 transport plane in flight to their
drop zone. In anticipation of the jump, I, like every other man
on the plane, had done two things. One, we all stopped by the
latrine to relieve ourselves, because we knew we would have no
reasonable opportunity for the next few hours to do so. Two, we
spent considerable time adjusting the three heavy canvas webbing straps on our parachutes. These three straps ensured that
the opening shock would not knock us out of the rig. One
heavy strap ran across our chest; the other two went between
our legs, ensuring we would not slip down, through, and out of
the harness to our death.

Why would I take so much trouble with the straps, when I
so recklessly cut my break cord? Maybe some of it had to do
with all of the rigorous training we received, repeating the same
actions over and over. There was not all that much adjustment
to be made in the chest strap; we just needed to be certain that
the locking device on each side was snapped together. Once
this was done, we knew it was impossible to fall forward out of
our parachute harness.

The two so-called leg straps were a different and more
involved matter. They also had to be snapped together with
heavy metal rings and similar heavy-duty fasteners. They
required exceptional attention, however, because they had to
be tight—so tight, in fact, that once we snapped them together, it was almost impossible to straighten up. In fact, we could
barely breathe.

The loving care I had taken with this procedure might well
be understood by male readers, but for the ladies, I here explain
that once the leg straps were snapped together between our legs

with the harness rings, they enclosed some very precious male body parts, which, if not protected, could have a trooper singing soprano in the church choir. Although I had cut my break cord, I went down on my knees to snap the leg straps to the harness rings as securely and tightly as possible. Having protected the family jewels, I walked all bent over en route to the plane. Like everyone else, I needed help in boarding the door by way of a very short ladder. And now here I was, sweating out my severed break cord, with a major urge to relieve myself.

Our C-47s had a very small facility for this purpose through the bulkhead at the rear of the plane. Here, a tiny door opened into a tinier room, with a small urinal against a wall. To use it, we had to release one of the leg straps, allowing our jumpsuit zipper to open. Once a trooper released a leg strap, he could raise his leg and place it against one of the walls of the teeny-weeny latrine, while he emptied his bladder—all over the walls and floor, his hand, jumpsuit, and whatever.

The more the plane bounced around in the sky, the more hazardous the peeing process. This predicament always made for many healthy laughs on the part of the seated troopers. I returned to my seat not much in a laughing mood, although I had often joined in the good-natured ridicule.

After about an hour's flight, we had covered the one hundred miles from Italy to Sedalia. Thank God, it was just barely daylight when we started preparing for the jump. I can't recall the lieutenant who was jumping the stick, but as usual, I was bringing up the rear, pushing the stick of nineteen men. I would be the last man out.

The amber light came on over the open plane door, meaning get ready. The familiar instructions, "Stand up and hook up!" rang out from the jumpmaster, and every trooper hit the anchor line with his snap fastener. "Check your equipment!" came the next command, and we all felt over our equipment to see that everything was in place, including our rifles, which would be tucked inside our reserve parachutes, muzzle down. I was jumping with a Thompson submachine gun, or tommy gun, also muzzle down. When I went out, I would turn the gun vertically so as not to catch it on the sides of the door as I exited.

"Sound off for equipment check!" was the next command. Each jumper checked his equipment on his front side, and the man behind checked his rear. Frankly, given the chance, I would probably have cried, I was so fearful, but I was too dumb or proud to tell the jumpmaster what a crazy thing I had done.

Everyone sounded off without a reported problem. The next-to-final command was heard from the front, "Stand in the door and close it up!" That meant for everyone to start pushing hard toward the back of the plane where the door awaited us all. The green light came on and "Go!" resounded. The officer went out the door screaming our favorite battle cry, "Geronimo!" In four to seven seconds, I was out the door and falling through a beautiful morning's fresh air. We were taught to shout, "1,000, 2,000, 3,000," during which time our main parachute was supposed to deploy and open. Shout I did, to no avail.

I was hauling through the air when I heard, in a super Deep South accent, "Sergeant, Sergeant! Pull your reserve! Pull your reserve!" I had been living with that rebel voice night and day for about a year and a half and would have recognized it anywhere. It belonged to Fred Kelley, my assistant gunner from Wetumpka, Alabama, and I knew he was the number three man out of the plane—meaning, I had passed about fifteen men in the free fall—and still no opened parachute.

Strangely, as I was falling with no opened chute, I could see a school bus entering the front gate of the air base. This was, of course, happening in a matter of seconds. But I was getting to where I could almost make out the name on the side of the bus. Fred's advice was well taken, and I placed my left hand over the front of my reserve, per endless instructions for such emergencies, and pulled the red ripcord handle with my right hand.

We were to use our left hand to hold the silk inside the reserve canvas quarters and feed it out a little at a time. This would keep the parachute from blowing all over me, causing me to roll up in the silk and go into the ground a dead man. I had seen that process before on my very first day in Fort Benning, and I would see it again during a jump in England when a Company I man flew by me screaming as he rolled up in his two chutes and died as he landed like a sack of sand. I also put the ripcord in my mouth as I'd been taught. This kept anyone from being hit and killed by a falling object, however light.

Just as I pulled my reserve, I felt a beautiful tug on my shoulders, indicating that my main chute had opened. I looked up and sure enough, there was a perfect canopy ready to lower this crazy paratrooper safely to the ground. Now, what was I going to do with eighteen feet of extra silk, my reserve chute, which I was holding to my belly? If both my parachutes deployed, they could easily get tangled up, causing one to wrap around the other and bring me in hard enough to injure or kill me.

Brilliant idea! *I'll just stuff the silk between my legs, lock my legs tightly around the bundle, and make myself a soft cushion on which to land,* I thought. *Sounds reasonable enough!* So I started stuffing and felt like I had the problem under control, until I started being leaned forward. I was almost nosedown before I discovered that the silk I'd stuck through my legs was gathering wind on my back side. My point of suspension was no longer my shoulders, but in my crotch.

I hurriedly gathered up the extra chute again and restuffed it between my legs, when I noticed ambulances running wildly around the drop zone wondering where I would land. They had been watching my adventure from the safety of Mother Earth.

I came down on a hard surface in what could appropriately be called a "crash landing." As my head came down very hard, my chin banged on the steel butt plate of my tommy gun. The blood flowed, dripping off my chinstrap and onto my jumpsuit jacket.

Once I realized I was alive, I was ready to resume my role as a really bad dude. On maneuvers or training jumps, we each had our particular mission as part of our team or unit. On this particular jump, my squad's mission was to take certain base offices, gather up all the people—mostly pretty young secretaries—in a single building, and leave a guard over them.

We found our target buildings and occupied them, while all the young ladies awed over the bad, heroic paratroopers. They had just been outside watching the jump and were very impressed with their first view of a U.S. Army paratrooper, especially given the recent deluge of media commentary on this new branch of the combat arms.

The impact of dried blood on my helmet chinstrap, and the blood that had dripped down the front of my unique paratrooper jumpsuit, was all it took to create a squealing band of hero-worshipping "prisoner" secretaries. Naturally, I told them we were frequently wounded like this, oftentimes before breakfast, et cetera, et cetera.

After playing my non-injury for all it was worth, I decided to go impress the medics at the base hospital. I arrived at the hospital and located the emergency room, in the certitude that the staff would also make a big fuss over my "terrible wounds."

I threw open the green swinging half doors to the emergency room to be met by the sight of a very blue, very dead paratrooper. To play the training game to its fullest, the air force base staff had hot-wired certain structures, sending electricity through the wires. The base tower was so wired with a line just off the ground, which was wet with early morning dew. Being a well-trained trooper, the lad in question had gotten on his back with his rifle on his belly. He had been pushing with his boot heels, moving under the defensive hot-wire, when his M1 barrel touched the wire and he was electrocuted.

I stood there speechless at the threshold of the emergency room. A nurse turned and asked what they could do for me. I was suddenly so embarrassed by my little "hero" trip that I backed out promptly, muttering "I'm sorry." I went out into the hall, found a water fountain, and cleaned up my chin. I thanked God for sparing this fool once more, praying for the dead fellow trooper, and vowing never, never, to consider cutting my break cord again.

And, every time I shave, I have occasion to remember the Sedalia jump, for once again I look at the scar under my chin caused by the butt-plate of my tommy gun.

Oct 28, '43

Hi Dear Little Ole Mom,

Gee, thanks for the money . It sure came in handy as I was
sorta broke and need something to buy some wool socks with . I
went to Wyo. last week and sure had a swell time . That town is
sure swell for us as the people don't know paratroopers yet . I
stayed there two days and had a real good time as there are lots
of nice places to go and plenty good music to dance to and that
is what I live on . You're right about finally going as I think
this is the real thing and I sure hope so as we are more than
ready . I have a short haircut now and I sure look like a goon
All of the boys are grtting them and we realy look sweet . Some
of the men are having their heads shaved , but I don't think
I will resort to that as I have tried that too many times and it
doesn't work at all . I hadn't heard about those boys in Ga.,
but it was tough and I can't see how paratroopers could be killed
in a plane crash. We have a standard way of leaving a plane that
is about to crack up , so I don't look to have to ride one of them
to the ground . Bert is flying now and he is sure tickled about
it . Gee, I sure would like to see all the gang again and hook
all the food in the icebao at home like weq used to do . Remember?

We have a long march tomarrow and I have to get my beauty
rest so I think I will close for a while . I hope that you find
out about the acct. Tell my Pop hello and write soon .

Love and XXXX ,

Son

Typical letter home from Bob Bearden to his folks in preparation for
overseas assignment.

Chapter Ten

Taking My Exclusive
Furlough to Wyoming

I must have been an excellent charge of quarters, which was the title of the noncom who watched over the orderly room after duty hours. His job was to take phone calls from off post, give messages to the troops, and generally run the first sergeant's office when he had completed his day.

I suppose I was assigned this task often in Alliance because I did not complain when they gave me the unpopular duty. What they did not know was that I used that time alone in the orderly room with access to a typewriter to do a lot of personal writing. Of course, I did not know how to type according to standard methods. I called my system HPCE for "hunt, peck, cuss, and erase," all the while typing with two fingers.

The recipients of my letters ranged from my ex-girlfriend, Doris, to a U.S. congressman and the White House. The subjects ranged from how beautiful and wonderful Doris was to how crummy the army was. I once received a return letter from Eleanor Roosevelt assuring me that we GIs would receive a ten-day furlough before going overseas, if we had not been home within six months of our departure date. Her efforts resulted in some personal turmoil for me, as the rest of this episode will tell.

True to Mrs. Roosevelt's word, we soon heard from official sources that all members of the 507th would be given a furlough if they had not already had one in the past six months. I basked in the knowledge that this was my ticket for a trip to Dallas—not to see my mother, but my true love Doris before I set off to parts unknown.

It was at about this time (as I mentioned earlier) that I discovered that Doris had plans of her own and was about to marry that Adamson High School graduate who was playing professional baseball. The message of her "Dear Bob" letter was plain—it was all over. I sold back the engagement ring I planned to give her when I proposed, took my mortar squad to Scottsbluff for a party, and put in a request for a furlough to visit my mother. Our first sergeant didn't care who I wanted to see, the answer was "No!" There was just too much work to do in preparation for overseas shipment.

Times were rough. Soon after I lost Doris, Elizabeth, the beautiful blonde ticket-seller at the local movie theater, left Alliance to marry her pilot fiancé out on the east coast. He was stationed in Fort Bragg, where his troop carrier unit was flying the 82nd Airborne as they trained to go overseas. "God will bring you back to me," I told her.

In point of fact, Elizabeth was not long gone before I met a young lady in Alliance who worked as a clerk for the railroad. Not that I was fickle! She was one more Nebraska beauty and *soooo* sweet. When this lovely Nebraska girl invited me to visit her at her new home in Casper, Wyoming, my first sergeant's refusal to grant me a furlough took on new importance. It was like telling me, "Find another way, legal or not!" Hadn't Eleanor Roosevelt personally written to me about this very matter?

By this time, every trooper in the 507th had signed a document acknowledging he was aware that he had been alerted for overseas shipment. This meant only one thing to me—we were about to enjoy another venture, even heavier than what we had so far experienced. We were not the least worried about the "big show." The kraut had not been born who could kill us. Going to war was no different than hearing about a fight a mile away, when we were downtown in Columbus or Phenix City. We would run like mad to get into a crazy brawl: cops, MPs, and all. We were bullet-proof.

Little did I realize that document I'd signed made going AWOL, absent without leave, tantamount to desertion. Nor did I know that the penalty for desertion in time of war ranged from company punishment to death by firing squad. I had no idea that a few days AWOL was more than a company punishment matter. I certainly would not have exposed others to a general court-martial, and the idea of losing my chance to go overseas with my 507th would have made me cry. Already, back in the "Frying Pan" (a group of two-story barracks where parachute school students and newly qualified paratroopers lived until assigned to another unit), I had almost cried when I missed going over with the 504th when they left for Fort Bragg with the 505th.

It was payday when my thoughts turned into action. I had broken up a few dice games in our barracks and had a couple hundred dollars. During one of the games, I mentioned I was taking a trip to Casper, wherever that was, to see the pretty railroad employee. "Anyone want to go?" I asked. I had quick takers because I offered to finance the trip with my winnings. It did not occur to me that this was a case of a noncom inviting privates to go over the hill (in other words, desert) with him.

Within an hour or so, three of us were shooting dice along the roadside of the highway leading to Wyoming. I broke up that little game and one of the troopers who'd come with me, Hubert McClain, sensibly chose to go back to camp. He went over to the other side of the road and stuck out his thumb, indicating that he wanted a ride back into Alliance and the air base. Being broke did not affect my other companion, Private Burns, a huge Jewish guy from Brooklyn, who incidentally was not much of a gambler. He'd been telling me for more than a year that when we shipped out through New York, he'd take me into the city and show me the town.

With our AWOL venture down to two participants, what do you know, the first automobile to come by stopped and offered Burns and me a ride. I then discovered that the car was occupied by two MPs, military policemen! I just knew our AWOL trip was over then and there, because the first thing an MP ever asked for was a pass or furlough. Obviously, we had neither.

Instead, they simply asked where we were going, to which I replied, "Casper, Wyoming." You have to realize that MPs knew that paratroopers were not very cooperative. A general officer had recently come from Chicago to speak to the regiment about us throwing "his" MPs off trains while rolling, just for kicks. Then, too, in jump school, we had been assured that once we got our wings we could whip six MPs. Well, as I sit here writing, I can't recall ever whipping *one* MP, let alone six together.

The MPs were, nevertheless, afraid of paratroopers, especially when the troopers had been drinking, as we most certainly had. Maybe that's why these two gave us a ride and let it go at that. With barely a break in their conversation, they agreed to take us to the next town where we could "catch" a train to Casper.

"Catch" my hind foot, I thought. I had spent many an afternoon in the Dallas freight yards hopping freight trains as a high-schooler, riding across the Trinity River bottoms or over to the Fort Worth rail yards and back. So when they dropped us off at the station, we ate at a nearby cafe, bought a cigar for each of us, and went out into the freight yards looking for the train to Casper. The conductor in charge came over and asked, "Are you going to hop this train?" I said, "Yes, sir, we have every intention of riding this freight train to Casper,

Wyoming." He said, "Then get up in the caboose and ride in comfort and safety. We'll be working all the way and won't be needing it."

We thanked him and proceeded to climb up into the caboose, one on each side, light up our cigars, and act like two general officers. The whole ordeal proved to be a real head trip, sitting high up in the caboose, flipping our cigar ashes out the window, and waving at the small-town people as we breezed through en route to Casper.

Upon arrival at about noon, we inquired where we might find the railroad offices. In a matter of minutes, we were visiting with my young female friend, much to her surprise. Then it was off to a local bar for a drink, only to be told by the bartender that some MPs had come in looking for two paratroopers. I supposed correctly that McClain had been threatened by our first sergeant to tell him where we were heading. If we were discovered AWOL, we could be charged with desertion, and even be punished by firing squad.

Burns and I spent the day in Casper wandering around town, waiting for my friend to get off from work. Most of that time we spent in bars where a paratrooper was a hero and the drinks were therefore free. We did take time for one more little chore, getting a barber to shave our heads. Colonel Millett, our 507th regimental commander, had issued a heavy-duty threat to any trooper who went over the hill. He would shave the guy's head, personally. We made sure these were two troopers' heads that the colonel would have hell getting any enjoyment from shaving.

We took our female friend out to dinner and accepted the invitation of a local family to spend the night with them before returning to Alliance the next day. We had a great ranch-style breakfast, which my New York buddy, Burns, thought was the best meal he had ever eaten. As a Jew, Burns never seemed disturbed that he was eating bacon and sausage. Back in Alliance, we frequently kidded our Jewish troopers about the great-tasting "chicken" when the mess hall served pork.

After breakfast we got instructions on how to best get back to Alliance and hustled a ride out to the city limits. Our very first ride was in a smelly cattle truck going to Scottsbluff, Nebraska, about a hundred and eighty miles. I offered to take the wheel, and the driver enjoyed having a little relief. The balance of the trip to Alliance was about sixty miles. The cattle odor almost did Burns in, but it sure beat walking.

When we arrived in Alliance on Tuesday, we went straight out to the base, hoping that we had not been missed. Not so lucky. The word had been passed on to our barracks to report to the first sergeant when we showed up. He delivered us to Captain Taylor, our company commander, who in turn confined us to the company area with the assurance that we would soon be taken to Lieutenant Colonel Kuhn, our battalion commander.

Captain Taylor was a bit amused that we already had our heads shaved to avoid Colonel Millett's shave job. As a private, Burns was dealt with differently than I, a noncommissioned officer. When I went before Lieutenant Colonel Kuhn, he explained what lay before me and asked if I knew the sentence a corporal had received in a recent court-martial. The man had been AWOL for one day. "Thirty years, Sir," I replied.

"And how long have you been gone?" he asked. "Two days, Sir," I told him. Actually, it had been three, but he only knew about two. He said, "Sergeant, I'm going to get you thirty years for every day you were gone." I promptly calculated that to gross out at sixty years in Fort Leavenworth Disciplinary Barracks in Kansas. My response, completely ignoring the potential disaster to my life, was, "Colonel, I'm going to be an old man when I come out of there."

I joined Burns in the Alliance stockade as the 507th was packing to go overseas—putting their equipment in order, getting all their shots caught up, and the likes. We, too, participated in this activity. Everyone in the stockades also went out daily to some clean-up detail. I rode a trash truck around the base, emptying trash containers.

I was on the truck one day when a jeep honked at our driver and told him to pull over. Out of the jeep jumped Captain Taylor. He shouted to me to get in the jeep, referring to me as Sergeant Bearden. From up in the truck bed, I told the driver, "Drive on. I have important work to do collecting trash in the war effort."

Taylor went nuts and began shouting that my mortar squad was to give a demonstration of firing the 60mm mortar. I don't mean to brag, but the fact was, I had been living with the 60mm mortar all my military life, so I was unusually experienced. I actually knew more about this weapon than any officer I ever encountered, and I had personally trained Duck and Kelly, my gunner and his assistant, since the Frying Pan. No other squad had ever been chosen to fire demonstrations for visiting brass.

So there I was, standing in a garbage truck, looking down at my CO, and refusing an order. I told him I was a private and had no squad. I listened to him squeal a little more, then got in the jeep and went off to entertain the general.

This time, however, we did not demonstrate the new system I had invented with George Forte, the rifle squad leader in our platoon who also had a talent for landing on telephone poles. We could fire our 60mm mortar without the base plate, sight, or legs, using nothing but our new sight, the "Forte Sight," and the tube. We had just perfected this for going overseas, but I guess our CO wasn't taking chances. We had previously fired a demonstration for a large group out in the Nebraska fields, when George (not a mortar man) forgot to remove certain propellants from the fins on the demonstration shell. It shot straight up instead of down range and could have killed some of our friends had not George also failed to pull the safety pin on the shell. It did not, therefore, explode, but I aged fifty years.

As it turned out, I was never badly punished for taking my exclusive furlough to Wyoming. I found out later that my squad had gone to Captain Taylor. They could perform just about as well without me as with me—they always came through, and Taylor was proud of them. But they told him they wanted off jump status and out of the paratroops if the authorities took me out of my slot. That revolt was short lived, but serious. Talk about a "band of brothers." No greater love hath any man. . . .

Most of all, though, I owe my narrow escape to an old buddy of mine, Eddie Keehan, a fine older soldier from the 144th Infantry. When I met Eddie, he had just been busted from sergeant, and I was to teach him how to inspect cars that wanted to cross the bridge from Washington to Oregon over the Columbia River. Like others of us, Eddie had left the 144th to go to jump school. He also went to Officer's Candidate School and was now a second lieutenant assigned to the 507th.

Eddie went as a platoon leader to our 3rd Battalion headquarters and pled my case with Lieutenant Colonel Kuhn. As a result, my charges were reduced, and I was tried in a special court-martial, instead of the potential general court-martial where real deserters were tried and given severe penalties. I was "busted" or reduced in rank to private, fined sixty-three dollars and sentenced to from 90 to 120 days of confinement. Burns received about the same punishment as I did, although as a private, he obviously was not reduced in rank.

I was mighty glad to give the lie to Colonel Kuhn, and that he had forgotten his promise to get me sixty years in Leavenworth for desertion. I was so impulsive, I might have done most anything; the term *general court-martial* left a serious impression on me. It reminded me of the Company H guy who went home on furlough to be with his wife who was giving birth, then returned to Alliance and shot and killed a nineteen-year-old Company H kid who'd been dating his local girlfriend. That was the sort of real bum who got a general court-martial—not me. We had to guard that murderer to keep our own from raiding the Alliance jail and killing him.

Because the entire regiment was confined to our area, party time was over for all of us. They never seemed to follow up on my sentence at the personnel office, so my pay was never reduced. The captain threw another fit, telling me to take off my stripes, which I did. Then he came by my barracks and told me to get ready to do a training session on the 60mm mortar. Again I told him I was not a noncom and could not do his bidding, and again, he went nuts. This time he ordered me to go over to the PX and have my stripes sewn back on.

I did so, but asked the lady if she had some sort of little snaps where the stripes could be put on and taken off easily. That she did, and I proudly went to show the captain what I had done. I said, "See, Captain? I can put 'em on and take 'em off anytime you get in a huff."

This demonstration did not set well with Captain Taylor. "Take those damn stripes off!" he screamed. And so it was that I came to be busted three times in one day—a real claim to fame. Incidentally and fortunately, all that my discharge records reflect is that I lost one day under AW 105, company punishment.

Burns and I were under guard on the train from Alliance Army Air Base to Camp Shanks, New York. We were set up in a make-do prison room in a barracks. The first night there, we started gambling with the guards, and I broke up the game, though it did not mean much winnings. The guards were not paratroopers.

Burns had promised to show me New York City so many times that I came up with a plan, forgetting my recent narrow escape from the edicts of martial law. I told the guards that I would give them their money back if they would come with Burns and me off post to the first bar. There they could check their pistols with the bartender, and we would all go into the City by train. Talk about setting up a big-time court-martial!

Well, these guys were going overseas anyway so they figured, "What have we got to lose?" Burns and I and the two guards all went to New York City and had a blast. One thing I discovered was that Burns knew no more about Manhattan than I did. All those times he offered to show me around New York, he failed to tell me he had never been off his block in Brooklyn.

We managed to find our way back to camp after getting lost several times in downtown Manhattan. No one had even missed us. Feeling as if we had gotten away with something one more time, Burns and I boarded the British troop ship HMT *Strathnaver* on December 5, 1943, and set off with the rest of the 507th for England and Northern Ireland.

Chapter Eleven

THE 507th PIR IN NORTHERN IRELAND

It was in the dark of night that HMT Strathnaver docked in Liverpool on December 16. We immediately unloaded onto a much smaller vessel, the American Liberty ship Susan B. Anthony, for the short hop to Northern Ireland, where we would be stationed in Port Rush until about mid-March.

Our eleven-day trip across the ocean had been relatively uneventful. While the crew referred to the sixth largest ship in the British navy as "His Majesty's Transport," or HMT *Strathnaver*, we preferred our own name, "His Majesty's Tub." We were told it was a quarter mile around the big deck and that the ship was propelled by two huge screws. During Atlantic storms these came completely out of the water, and the ship went dark. Seconds later when the lights returned, every trooper had his life jacket on and tightened up.

Probably the worst thing about the voyage from New York to England was sailing past the Statue of Liberty and having to leave her behind. Next was the British chow, which we ate off metal trays that slid back and forth with the rolls of the giant ship as she turned in circles dodging German submarines. Third, were the very tight bunks that hung from walls and posts, stacked six high. I will not go into the plight of the guys on the lower bunks when the guys on the bunks above them got sick, which was frequently. As bad as it was, those of us in bunks were better off than the unlucky troopers who had to sleep in the hammocks that filled the mess halls. Most troops, including Texans, had never slept in a hammock before, and they experienced all sorts of injuries from falling out onto the steel floors.

As we sailed to Northern Ireland, most of us had no idea of where the hostilities concerning Northern and Southern Ireland came from. If our Irish brothers were aware of the never-ending conflict between the British and Irish, they never shared that information with the rest of us. We landed in Northern Ireland in complete ignorance of the hatred that existed between its citizens. We would soon learn to keep our mouths shut, however, when folks began to talk about the House of Orange.

We debarked and boarded railroad cars that transported us to various communities around Northern Ireland. Company H was assigned to live in multistoried stone buildings that had formerly been reserved for tourists in the port city of Port Rush. On the bottom floor of my five-story barracks was a cafe-bar that specialized in the traditional Irish fish and chips. Talk about your greasy meal! We were convinced that the oil used to fry the fish and potatoes had not been replaced in many years, a detail that did not deter our daily purchase of this meal.

It appeared that the area's income came from the production of Irish whiskey, which gave us a great laugh. At long last the army had finally discovered an improved place to station a regiment of crazy paratroopers—right next to an Irish whiskey factory! There was a bar on every other corner, and did these Irish know how to drink. Many a paratrooper

V Mail to Bob's Mom and Pop while at sea en route to Liverpool, England. Although dated December 21, this is most likely a transposition of December 12, while they were still only four days out from Liverpool.

wound up sleeping under a table as he tried to drink with the regular Irish pub patrons.

In Port Rush we received a new first sergeant, Sergeant Pettus. We had heard this name back in Alliance, Nebraska. He was a super-tough Old Army soldier who had been assigned to take a hundred of the regiment's "eight ball troops" to the west coast for shipment to the war in the Pacific. These troopers were real crazies. Moving them by train to the West Coast was a nightmare in the making, but if any human could handle the task, it was First Sergeant Pettus, the absolute "baddest of the bad." He did the job and received much praise for his success.

Pettus had a body like a human wedge. We figured that he must have had a hair cut every week, because his hair was always burred. Most mornings, he could be found at 3 a.m., ironing razor-sharp creases in his fatigues or first class uniform. Then he would be the first man out in the company street for roll call. Then there was his signature weapon. Pettus was the only man we had ever seen who carried a tommy gun with an ammunition cylinder on top, just like the Chicago bad guys in the movies. The story was that he was the sole trooper in the regiment who did not have to carry insurance, because he had no relatives to whom he could leave his money if he was killed. He was the model of the American soldier.

Well, the first thing Sergeant Pettus did was call all of the Company H NCOs together for a conference to tell us how he was going to run the company. We all gathered in the orderly room at company headquarters, which was pretty crowded to say the least. I don't remember much of his speech, but he concluded with the remark, "And I'll beat the hell out of every man in the company if they cross me." That remark was a mistake.

As soon as he uttered his final words, all hell broke loose. About thirty of us beat Pettus to a mass of blood and bruises right there in his orderly room. When, after ten minutes of beating, we let him up, he just took a towel, wiped the blood off his face and out of his hair, and sat down at a table. With a smile on his face, he noted that he appreciated NCOs who would fight for their men and we would get along fine—which we did.

Land was at a premium in Northern Ireland, and we were not allowed to practice military maneuvering tactics such as small unit problems. The only way to get off the roads was to march out on the golf courses, which seemed to be in great supply. Unlike most courses in the States, these were a series of hills and gullies. It was just up and down walking, always carrying our weapons but never getting to fire them.

The southern part of Northern Ireland did have some rifle ranges and areas where tanks could be used. It was here that we were first exposed to small American tanks for training purposes. We learned to drive every German vehicle as well as our own tanks. We never seemed to get along with any tankers, no matter where we met them, so the training they gave us in the operation of their tanks offered the tankers a great opportunity to mess with us legally.

We had dug many a foxhole and slit trench in the field for defensive training, but we were told to dig especially well at this site, because the tankers were going to run over the foxholes *with us in them.* Our instructors had our best attention, and the tankers were assured a great time! Those suckers buried one of our men when they maneuvered one of their tank treads over his foxhole, and then spun the tank tread around. He almost suffocated under three feet of Irish dirt. Fortunately, we dug him out in time to save his life, but he was not a happy camper, and no other trooper was willing to expose his foxhole to that level of testing—certainly not Sergeant Bearden.

This training area also introduced us to a very puzzling sight. From our rifle range, we could look out over a body of water that separated Northern and Southern Ireland. Like the little bit of Liverpool we had seen in port, all of Northern

Ireland was completely blacked out. You could not see even the tiniest glimmer of light coming from homes, businesses, bars, or vehicles, even when the latter were traveling at high rates of speed. There was no light exposed in Northern Ireland. But if we took our field glasses and looked across the water, we saw a completely different sight. Bars, movie houses, autos—it was all lit up like downtown Dallas! Just watching the street cars moving about was a real treat.

Many of us had another unusual experience when the young lass we were dating encouraged us to "come south and live out your life without getting shot at in the war in France." Yep, many of us had an invitation like I had from a pretty and charming twenty-year-old, a native of England who had moved from London with her family to avoid the German air raids. She also had all the associations necessary to facilitate my taking off for the Republic of Ireland with a load of military equipment. There was an established market price for every piece of American equipment, from rifles and ammunition to mortars, machine guns, and grenades. Mines of any sort were particularly valuable. I am confident that some of our men went south where they were "detained" for the war's duration. It sounded tempting, but I had come to kick some German butt and still had that commitment.

Of course, no matter where we were stationed for whatever period of time, our guys immediately became romantically involved with the local female population. The first crazy thing that our guys went nuts over was the fact that Irish girls wore many pairs of bloomers under their outer garments. We never figured out if it was their mothers who insisted on this unusual attire, but it appeared to be universal and was a great source of amusement and frustration to every paratrooper who made this discovery in the dark on a street corner for himself.

Sometimes just locating our particular Irish lassie proved to be a real problem in black-out conditions. More than likely,

if you and your girl did not agree during daylight on a very specific time and place to meet, you were likely to miss her in the
pitch black of night. This often led to some violent shouting on
mistaken street corners, when you started feeling around the
body of a female you did not know and who was not waiting
for you. It was very embarrassing, to say the least. In both
Ireland and England, couples soon learned to establish very
precise meeting places. In England, you might have to put up
with a German air raid as well. The natives did better at han-
dling air raids than did the average GI Joe.

Fighting in the bars in Northern Ireland soon became a
nightly affair. Not only did the Irish like to drink and play
darts, they were also adept at brawls and had no fear of paratroopers, regardless of our tough reputation. I vividly remember one occasion when my close friend, Sergeant George Forte,
got drunk, and in the course of taking on a whole bar full of
Irishmen unintentionally hit a little old gray-headed grandmother type. When I went up to my room that night via the
very tight stairwell, I looked into Forte's small room and saw a
body lying on his little bed. I asked a trooper standing nearby,
"Who is that with his face all messed up?" He said, "That's
Sergeant Forte." I protested mightily, noting that I had been
soldiering with George Forte for years. "Don't tell me I don't
know George when I see him!"

But yes, it was George, who simply could not drink and
associate with human beings without brawling. He had hands
like big hams and was the toughest man I had ever seen, only
this time he had met his match. He had been left to die on the
outskirts of town after having been beaten to a pulp. His face,
beyond recognition, would take weeks for full recovery. Later,
on the D-Day jump, he would have a compound fracture of his
leg, make a splint out of his bayonet and bayonet scabbard,
wrap the leg with his rifle sling, and use his rifle as a crutch to
walk out from his landing site. That's a tough hombre in Texas!

We left Port Rush on March 11 without much notice to the local population, except a couple of waitresses. We were loaded up on buses and sent toward Londonderry en route to fabled Nottingham in the Midlands of England. With the exception of a couple photographs of wives, girlfriends, or family, there was little else, so loading up was not that big a deal. All we had was a duffle bag or two, and perhaps a foot locker, although I do not even recall that luxury. There were no civilian clothes, personal radios, or the like. Probably, a few men had cameras, but they were a minority in the outfit.

Needless to say, we had had ample time to develop any number of relationships, and surely families or at least the makings of families had been started. Those Irish girls were certainly delights and lots of fun. I've sometimes wondered how many of them wound up as war brides in the States. I do not recall any occasions in Northern Ireland where girls with their parents were allowed to walk through the company formation looking for the father of a girl's expected baby. We did have these in England, however, and they were spookier than the ride down to the planes to load up for D-Day.

Chapter Twelve

JOLLY OLDE ENGLAND: FISH AND CHIPS, 507th STYLE

The 507th was ferried from Ireland to Glasgow, Scotland, where we took the train to England. We arrived on March 13 at Tollerton Hall, a tent city just outside of Nottingham, the town of Robin Hood's fabled activity. Our billets were six-man tents arranged in rows along dirt streets topped with a layer of coal dust and coal particles. Officers lived in Tollerton Hall, a four-story castle out in front of the company streets. Enlisted men all ate together in what I believe was a battalion mess hall.

By the time we got to Tollerton Hall, Britain had been waging war against Hitler for four long years, with combat troops in Africa, Italy, and Sicily. England and Northern Ireland were blacked out every night, of course, but this was not the case in the Republic of Ireland. When we had been in Port Rush, we could look across the bay from the rifle range and see the "South Irish" running around with lights on, doing business as usual. Many of our guys were proud to be of Irish extraction, but not being Irish myself, I had personally wondered what the hell we were doing over here, bailing their asses out of a fight of little concern to Texas.

I was not alone in questioning why all of Ireland was not in the war. Cities such as London were taking a major butt-kicking by German bombers and V-2 rockets, which were very bad news. Of course, we knew nothing of the problems between the British and Irish governments. We just saw all the night clubs and movie houses doing a great business right across the water, while there we were on a rifle range, training to fight their battle in France, or wherever it was the army was going to send us.

The U.S. Air Corps was also bombing daily, attempting to blow Germany back into the dark ages. Just down the road from Tollerton Hall was a small emergency landing strip primarily used for disabled fighter planes returning from missions over Europe. One of our 1st Platoon squad leaders had a brother who flew the gorgeous and very fast P-38 twin fuselage fighter plane. This air corps brother would fly to our Company H area and make a 300 mph pass down the company street, shaking our tents—some to the ground. Then he'd do a beautiful roll-over and head down the road to the landing strip. Our 507th member then borrowed a bicycle, peddled down the road, picked up his brother, and brought him back to entertain the guys with fighter pilot stories. To have that P-38 blow past Company H, just off the ground at that incredible speed, was practically a sexual experience for guys like me. This occurred several times during our brief stay in England.

Guard duty in the 507th was never taken lightly. It was serious business for everyone, from the men walking post to the NCOs and officers in charge. So, when I called my new guard detail out for duty at Tollerton Hall, and only one-third of the men showed up, my reputation was suddenly on the line.

This particular guard shift had another peculiar element, in that Company G—I mean the whole damn company—was a guard post. We were to place a guard detail all around the company area for some dumb thing they had done, which had obviously hacked some field-grade officer. Company H had been in a similar dilemma once, when Colonel Kuhn placed us on confinement to the company area and made our company street a guard post for a week or so, officers and all.

I went into a quick boil, storming around the area screaming at everybody and everything. "Where the hell is the guard detail, every damn one of them? I'll have their asses stuck under the guard house, for the duration and six," I shouted.

My raving produced nothing, so I started on another tack, begging privates with whom I had a tight relationship to tell me where these clowns had gone. Finally, my gunner Duck, one of my closest buddies, cautiously mentioned that he had heard that a small commune existed over on one of the creeks traversing the area, where our guys had pitched a few pup tents. This established a comfortable little site for maintaining some local girls, who seemed to be enjoying the arrangement every bit as much as the troopers.

This site was concealed by a sizable clump of trees that prevented anyone from seeing what was going on. Apparently, I was the only man in 3rd Battalion who did not know about this little love nest, where each guard shift took turns at enjoying the company of the girls. All the guys involved made a modest financial contribution, providing something like toothpaste, food, or the like. Fortunately, no sergeants or officers were involved. Had I been a private, I would have bought into the deal in an instant.

This arrangement, as well as our other vigorous sexual activities in England, produced frequent searches for "fathers of my daughter's baby." For the first time, we were lined up in formation on the company street, while an English father, mother, and (alas, all too often) ugly daughter reviewed each trooper, in an effort for the expectant daughter to identify who would be the father of her baby.

As a sergeant, my problem with this routine was not in trying to help the gal find the father of her baby. I knew that all the girls concerned realized that the more stripes a GI had on his sleeve, the more income he made. Let's just say that I stood in ranks several times trying to look as homely, dumb, and unhusband-like as I could. Fortunately, I never recall a 507th loser in any of these find-my-baby's-father formations.

The small, running creeks in the general 507th PIR area also offered other sorts of recreation. The groves of short, bushy trees along their banks were cool and shady, attracting many GIs who wanted to avoid unpleasant duty or just to gold brick and loaf. They soon discovered that the creeks and their water holes were full of excellent fish. Having no sort of fishing tackle certainly was not a hindrance to our resourceful 507th. No, they just appropriated some very deadly fragmentary hand grenades.

The water holes were probably four to five feet deep and eight feet wide in places, with an average width of about five feet. The "fishermen" pulled the pin on a grenade, let the handle fly off, held it armed for a few counts, then threw it into the creek just as it exploded. This blew water and occasionally fish all over the place. I called this venture "scrambled fish," but the guys said the fish were not too seriously damaged to eat. This activity continued until we pulled out for our marshalling bases for D-Day.

In England, as in Northern Ireland, we were mostly restricted to small unit training. Afternoons, we had language lessons in French and German, map reading, and first aid. By now we were attached to the 82nd Airborne. We loved the division and its reputation from the Sicily and Italy campaigns, and we all had friends in the 505th and 504th. It was a great day when we sewed that bright red, white, and blue 82nd Airborne Division patch on the sleeve of our jumpsuit jackets.

Except for the very last days of our stay in England, those of us in the rank and file had no idea of the plans for

Operation Neptune—the invasion of France—which were now in the making. Officers were briefed on the regimental level at the beginning of April, and on the battalion level in early May. Training intensified, and the battalion made two rehearsal jumps, one by daylight and one at night. It is my understanding that a regimental jump also was scheduled, but this did not come off.

We had a real problem getting our aircraft into the British sky. It was almost solid with Allied bombers, twenty-four/seven. There was no room up there for our slow troop transport planes, which were mostly C-47s. While we hung around waiting for practice jumps, we had plenty of time to meet American and British flyboys at air bases and bars. Many paratroopers had sought to be fighter pilots but failed to pass the entrance exam, as was my case back in California. But once we earned our parachute wings, we never looked up to anyone, let alone pilots. We considered ourselves the "baddest of the bad."

Meanwhile, we got air base loafing down to perfection. A time would be set, and then it would change, and we would sit around for days sometimes waiting for another slack in the bomber missions. This left a regiment of two thousand paratroopers with nothing to do but loaf and get into trouble in nearby villages.

The day we found out about "transient mess" we knew we had made a grand discovery. This special dining facility was open twenty-four hours a day for pilots who had made an emergency landing or just returned from a combat mission. The menu read like a short-order diner with steaks, hamburgers, full-course breakfasts, desserts—the works. None of us had ever seen such chow at our home base or, for that matter, in our entire army careers.

At these emergency landing fields, you could see fighter planes parked alongside bombers, many with bullet or flak holes in their sides and wings. Everything about the care of

American air force crew members was outstanding. They ate better, oh, so much better! They dressed better. Even their mattresses on their bunks were hotel quality, compared to the mattress cover filled with straw that served as our bunks. Make no mistake, the U.S. Army Air Corps were the creme de la creme of American military personnel, and they were treated accordingly. But when they got out in the boondocks at some remote air base like those in southern Italy, times were as tough for the elite as for the "doggies"—"dog face" infantry soldiers like us.

The time of our day jump finally did arrive, and the 3rd Battalion lined up in the sky. Company H was to go out first, with Company I coming along immediately after us.

I was concerned to figure out a better way to jump our 60mm mortar sight and case. The leather case was about six inches square, just large enough to break an ankle if we attached it there, and it could break a rib if we jumped the case and sight attached to our belt. I ended up attaching it to my right ankle, but very comfortably. I had a great parachute opening. As I drifted down toward the quiet English countryside, enjoying the view, a feeling of assurance pervaded me. All would be well, I felt, and the sight case would not be a problem.

Suddenly, I heard a terrifying scream from above. Somebody was in trouble and lots of it. I looked up and saw a trooper from Company I in free fall, coming down fast quite some distance above me. The closer he came, the louder the scream, until I wondered just how near he would actually come to me. If he landed on my canopy traveling at fifty miles an hour, less than half of terminal velocity, we were both dead.

In fact, he passed within a hundred feet of my position. My own free fall at the Sedalia Army Air Base flashed into my mind. It scared me so much that I started trying to figure out a better way to land so as not to mess up my ankle with the mortar sight case. I slipped my parachute toward some trees, intending to make a tree landing, which is precisely what I did. This was my only ever tree landing. I came out with barely a scratch, but deep regrets for the trooper who had died.

As it turned out, he had tumbled as he exited the plane door and rolled up in his parachute. When he pulled his reserve chute, it just made matters worse, and he plummeted right past me to his death. I went over to the Company I supply tent, and there were his canteen, mess kit, and helmet. Just as I had been told, the helmet was flat as a pancake.

My one other jump in England was along the Grantham Canal, a narrow waterway in the midst of Midlands farm country. This was my first and only night jump ever, except on D-Day. The best part of this mini-maneuver was hanging out at the air base for a week waiting for the skies to clear of bombers long enough for us to get up and to our drop zone.

When we finally did take off, we still got mixed up in the English skies with huge British bombers flying night missions. There were several "near misses," as we called them. We were flying with the door open, as was our habit for practice jumps. Whenever a bomber's wingtip lights flashed by our open door, we all shouted out appropriate paratrooper comments. Flying was seldom a pleasant experience for us. We were all too conscious that too much could go wrong to have a good time en route to a drop zone.

We had not been in the air more than thirty minutes when our jumpmaster shouted, "Stand up and hook up!" In another fifteen minutes, we were scrambling out the door, having checked our equipment and sounded off for equipment check. I was pushing the stick like mad, yelling, "Go, go, go!"

We must have jumped at no more than five hundred feet, out into the darkness. I had not even checked my canopy yet, when I was startled by the sight of an older gentleman no more than five feet away from me, his features lit by the light of the moon. "Good morning, laddy," he said.

"Where the hell did you come from?" I wondered. "I haven't even landed yet!"

But as a matter of fact, I had landed—right onto some nice, plowed earth. The landing was so soft I didn't even realize my feet had touched the ground! Yet there I was, standing in this farmer's vegetable garden, and there he was, on his way to the outhouse in the wee hours of the morning. This was like no other landing I had ever made, and by my reckoning, I had made twenty-three jumps by then. I was accustomed to bouncing over barbed wire fences and sliding under car bumpers, but a soft touchdown and a warm welcome were new experiences. We chatted a minute, and then I went on playing war games and rounded up the rest of my crew.

England was swarming with U.S. infantry and armored divisions, and the scene was ideal for brawls between tankers and infantry, tankers and paratroopers, blacks and whites, and paratroopers among themselves. There were fights between different PIR units, and plenty of fights within the units, too. Right in our company street at Tollerton Hall, for example, Tom Donahue, who had been raised in the streets of New York City, beat the crap out of John Yates Montgomery. Tom had had considerable fighting experience, and Monty wound up with coal particles from the street embedded in his lip forever. He was older than most of us and a Southerner, while Donahue was tough as nails.

In order to help keep the peace, Colonel Millett declared the nearest village, Plumtree, totally off limits to the regiment. Some of our guys did find a way to sneak out to the pub where they made friends with the locals. I don't think they were ever caught. Otherwise, we went to Nottingham, a large city, to enjoy the company of English girls.

Actually finding your girl, as I mentioned earlier, was another story. As we rarely got to Nottingham in daylight, physically locating our date under black-out conditions in such a big place at night was a real challenge. The only way to arrange it was to agree to meet at a very specific spot, marked by a specific object.

One night I went into Nottingham to meet a girl named Millie. She and her friends chose to meet their dates between the huge cement reclining lions in front of a major government building. That sounded specific enough to me until on date night, in the pitch dark, I discovered that the lions reclined about a city block apart. There were hundreds of girls looking and feeling around for guys, and guys for girls. I just about wore out the cement steps walking back and forth, feeling every girl I touched as I whispered, "Is that you, Millie?" I can hardly believe that I did indeed find her, and we went off to take in a movie—a "flick" as she called it.

My Millie and I were enjoying some high-powered courting in the balcony, when an MP came by looking for jump boots with his flashlight. A riot had taken place, and they were rounding up all the paratroopers in Nottingham. In the couple of moments, we had to say good-bye, Millie gave me the shock of a lifetime. "Robert," she said, turning her sweet face up to me, "when can I expect you to knock me up?"

Now, I had been shocked many times before—when, as a teenager, for example, I tried to sneak a drink of communion wine in the Episcopal church kitchen, but the stuff in the bottle turned out to be bug spray. But this was nothing compared to the shock of having a pretty young British female ask me to knock her up! *Oh, hell yes, your place or mine?* I thought I might be killed on a combat jump and go to Heaven, but this was too much.

Bubbling over with excitement and stumbling over my tongue, I began to seek clarification on this matter. It was then that my joy came to an abrupt end. Millie was asking me to call her on the telephone! To "knock up" was an ordinary English expression and a perfectly respectable activity.

Oh well, win some, lose some, and have some rained out! Breathlessly, I explained that we were pretty busy at Tollerton Hall, and we had no telephones out there, but as soon as we got a break from packing and training, I'd slip off to Plumtree, which had phone service, and get back in touch. The answer seemed to please my charming young Nottingham clerk. And so I regretfully left the theater, escorted by the MP.

All jump boots off the street was the order of the night, which meant he took me to the MP station. I was going to jail! During the four-block walk with me in handcuffs, the MP described the tremendous riot that had taken place that night. Every paratrooper in England must have been in it but me.

At the station I was handed over to the MP colonel, who directed his men to put me in the drunk tank, all because of my jump boots and wings. I pleaded with him that I had not had a single drink, and had not been involved in a fight in months. "Colonel, please don't throw me into that tank with a bunch of drunks," I implored. "If I let you go, will you go straight to your unit truck and not come back on the streets tonight?" he asked. Absolutely! I would be out of Nottingham for sure, and swore it was the truth, believe me.

Cold sober, I started down the blacked-out street to meet the 507th PIR truck for a ride back to camp. As I passed the mouth of an alleyway that intercepted the sidewalk, two punks jumped out and attempted to rob me. I was alone, and all hell broke loose. I would have preferred death to giving up my wings, wallet, and boots to such a couple of dogs.

After rolling around with these jerks for a few minutes, I was really into the affair. I hated this type of punk so much that the fight was a welcome event. I had fought in back alleys as a kid in Dallas, boxed in the Golden Gloves, and learned judo in paratrooper training. I was going to take both their heads off.

The alley stank and was full of coal dust, ashes, and pools

of filthy water. To complete the charming atmosphere, the whores were plying their trade right up against the buildings on either side of the alley. I was bleeding a bit, but on my feet, when two MPs arrived. They broke up the fight, cuffed me, and took me back to the MP station looking a total mess.

One of the MPs had seen me there earlier in the evening. "Do you want to see the colonel again?" he asked. "Hell no," I said. "He'll never believe what happened to me." And that is the only night I spent in an English jail.

Shortly before we left Tollerton Hall for our marshalling airdromes, we had one last poker game in our squad tent. Most of the major payers in Company H were in the game, along with a few heavy hitters from Company I and maybe a guy from Company G. We started playing just after evening chow. From the way our training had intensified, we were all aware that this was *it*—our last chance to gamble before the Big Trip.

We didn't have much respect for British currency. First off, it was huge and looked and felt different than the money we used back home. It just did not represent real money to most GIs. I don't remember what the exchange rate was, but it did not impress us with the value of the stuff. We gambled with it just like it was play money.

The game progressed much like most of our games, with certain unfortunate players going broke or deciding they had had enough, or that this was just not their night. They simply rose, gathered up whatever was left, if anything, and headed out the tent and toward their bunks.

About 3 a.m., we had a long run where no one opened the draw. Jacks or better was always the word on opening hands. Well, hand after hand, for perhaps an hour at least, no one opened. Each time, we would ante up again, until the pot became a small fortune. There must have been five hundred dollars in cash or junk money lying out there on that GI blanket.

Now, we were making about a hundred and twenty bucks a month, jump pay and rank included, so the pot was equivalent to four months' pay. Sure as hell, no one was going to open with the bare minimum, surely not me. Then there was my old nemesis, Chet Gunka, looking holes right through my weak heart. Those bushy eyebrows hid a pair of eyes that could cut you in little pieces and scare the hell out of you, no matter what cards you held.

A number of the losers who had gone broke stayed around to see who would win this one last game until we returned from "wherever!" I had passed with jacks several times as the pot grew larger and larger. Finally, as I sweated the cards and just about wore the numbers off the card stock, I saw two queens.

No way in hell could a man pass opening with two queens in his hand. Why, I reckon a man could go to hell for such a violation of poker wisdom. Of course, Chet had been playing games with my head throughout the evening, but now we were into the serious business.

So I played an old Chet Gunka trick. I picked up my entire stash of bills and counted them, again and again. I must have had at least three hundred dollars. And, just as I had seen Chet do so many times to freeze his opponents, I shuffled the bills over and over, like maybe I would throw them *all* in as opening money, or maybe not. The small-time gamblers who did not know the Gunka treatment were sweating like their lives were on the line, which in fact they would be shortly, as we headed for the jump on D-Day.

Finally, looking Chet right in the eye, as he had done to me so many times, teaching me the game the hard way, I tossed the stack of bills out into the pile on the blanket. A couple of gasps came from the audience of losers as the bills covered the present ante.

Now we were subjected to the famous Chet Gunka sweat.

He counted out a like amount of British pound notes, squared them up, counted them again, and patted them into an orderly stack over and over for about an hour. The whole time, I was drawing on the Gunka system with remarks like, "With no more guts than you have, how in the hell did they ever get your ass out of a C-47 with just two parachutes?" Or, "You know that's too much money for you to be messing with. Why don't you just go to bed?"

In time, most of the other players got tired of waiting for Chet's decision. Finally, he called and dropped his bundle in the pot, as did two others. My two beautiful queens stood all the challenges around that table, and after another hour of the players drawing from one to four cards, my pair of queens stood tall and mighty and sent me to bed with about eight hundred dollars in play money.

I agreed to take all the players to Nottingham for one last bash, which I did. I spent the evening needling my very best friend and leader, Chet Gunka, about his being the best poker teacher in this man's army. Before we left for our marshalling fields, I sent home a stack of money. It did indeed make a nice little nest egg when I got back to Killeen.

Although we had no idea of when or where our mission would be, we knew we soon would get the chance to make the Germans squeal "Onkel." I personally felt like the 507th were the best trained, if not overtrained, soldiers in the world, and I was itching to prove that my own team was the best 60mm mortar squad in the army.

We were told daily that "even the walls have ears"; the krauts knew just about everything we were doing. Little leaks went in all directions, it seemed—waitresses, cabbies, aides, every one was privy to bits of information. Just before we left Northern Ireland, for example, we first got news of our immanent departure from one of the girls a guy in our squad was dating. She had the news from her sister, who was dating a junior lieutenant.

Another case in point was a young girl I saw from time to time for about a month at the end of our stay in England. She was what we called a "local girl," from Tollerton, not Nottingham, and there weren't many of them. She was quite young, and our relationship was purely platonic. Less platonically, she also was seeing an air corps general who was old enough to be her father, for sure. I never knew his name, and I am not sure she knew his real name either. Running around with such a young girl would not have been good for his reputation.

The general had given my friend a bicycle to get around on. A bicycle was just next to having a car, which very few people owned or had access to. Of course, in total black-out conditions, you either had to have night vision or risk being run over after dark, especially on a bicycle. And yet, I never saw a wreck or an accident. Looking back, that seems amazing.

My friend said she would let me use the bike if I wanted to, but I seldom had time for biking or even much time for her. All I could think was, *Let's get out of here before the krauts have a man in our stick!*

One day, we got the order to move out—to where, we were not told. I assumed we were having another practice jump somewhere along the Grantham Canal. We were sitting in a bus ready to go, when a GI came to the bus door and called for Sergeant Bearden. He said there was a girl waiting for me down in the meadow below the company street.

I went about two hundred yards from the bus to the edge of the meadow, which was bordered by a narrow dirt road. There was my young friend, waiting with her bicycle. We talked for a moment, and I said I was surprised to see her. "You've never seen me off for our other jumps," I said. "We're just going up the Grantham Canal." She touched me on the arm and said, "No, Robert, you are going to France!"

There were no specifics, but I knew then and there that

this was *it*. "I don't know where you got that false information," I told her, "but you certainly better keep it to yourself." She agreed, and we said our good-byes. And off the 507th went to France.

It was May 28, 1944. The 1st Battalion of the 507th went to the airfield in Fulbeck, and the 2nd and 3rd battalions went to Barkston-Heath. Only after we arrived at the airfield and moved into bomber hangars to sleep on canvas cots were we informed of our mission. I suspect that the army didn't much trust enlisted men. Even for sergeants, all the villages and towns on the sand tables were identified only by their first letters: C-Town for Caen, S-Town for St. Mere-Eglise, and so forth.

Living in our bomber hangar, sealed in and completely surrounded by MPs, we had ample time to listen to the Berlin Bitch on the radio. She was playing some of the best Big Band music I had ever heard, and broadcasting news as a personal FYI directed at the 507th. She said the division welcomed our arrival and reminded us we were in the 82nd as a replacement unit because the 504th had been taken apart by the great German army in Italy. This, unfortunately, was true.

The Berlin Bitch clearly knew more than I would have liked anyone to know about our upcoming venture. She dedicated a song especially to the 507th: "It'll Be a Hot Time in the Old Town Tonight." But we went into France with such vast strength that it did not really matter how much the Germans knew.

Were we concerned about the danger? Yes, but not excessively. Our attitude was more like, "Sic 'em! Let's see if we are as bad as we claim." My squad trusted one another completely, and we knew just what each of us could be expected to do. And we were damned well tired of training, period! Yeah, we were ready for the Wehrmacht. This we proved when we kicked their butts and paid the price by burying Billy, Chet, George, and Mac, and many, many more.

PART II

D-DAY AND
THE BATTLE
FOR NORMANDY

DATE

A/C NO. (TAIL NO.) 42-92842   CHALK NO.   43

PERSONNEL

DROP ORDER	ASN	RANK	NAME AND INITIALS	UNIT
1	O-1295815	1st Lt	Woodward, Thomas M.	Co "H"
2	39379255	Sgt	Willey, Glynn G.	" "
3	O-462474	1st Lt	Rushmore, Forest F. Jr.	" "
4	34702503	Pvt	Woods, Cecil G.	" "
5	11038838	Pvt	Scanlon, Bernard J.	" "
6	37217051	Pvt	Sachen, Albert J.	" "
7	35556546	Pvt	Heaster, John W.	" "
8	12016536	Pfc	Middlemore, Edgert Y.	Med Det
9	32289471	Pvt	Keith, Wilson W.	Co "H"
10	14106030	Pfc	Kelley, Fred G.	" "
11	19013661	Pvt	McClain, Joseph E.	" "
12	15077289	Pvt	Lewis, James (NMN)	" "
13	6861767	Pvt	Ballingrud, Lloyd H.	" "
14	39566765	Pfc	Roman, Jose L.	" "
15	6975484	Pvt	Reilly, James (NMN)	" "
16	7040142	Pvt	Cooper, Carl E.	" "
17	39025458	Cpl	Warwick, John W.	" "
18	20811340	Sgt	Bearden, Robert L.	" "
19				
20				

CONTAINERS

RACK NO.	TYPE CONTENTS	GROSS WEIGHT	PARACHUTE COLOR
1	60MM Comp & Ammo	201	
2	60MM Ammo & 2rds Flare	154	
3	60MM Ammo & 1 roll		
	60M Wire	162	
4	BAR Ammo & 60 MM Ammo	148	
5	ATRL 12rds & 60MM Ammo		
	8 Pannels & 2 flags	158	

Inspection completed _____   Signed _____

I certify this to be a true and correct copy.

JOE A. GUAYANTE
1st Lt. 507th Prcht Inf., Ass't Adj.

Bob's D-Day Jump Roster.

Chapter Thirteen

D-Day Jump
and the
Little French Maid

In years to come in the late 1940s, I would cram all night in a last-minute effort to pass college exams at the University of Texas in Austin. The stakes were important and meaningful, but the greatest, most important "final exam" I was ever to take officially began at one minute to midnight, June 5, 1944, when the 507th Parachute Infantry Regiment flew out of air bases in Barkston-Heath and Fulbeck, England, and headed for Normandy and D-Day.

The stakes involved the future of France, the free world, and the lives of thousands of young men. My long-time friend Howard White would soon have his mangled arm, hanging by shreds of flesh, strapped to his body as he was loaded onto an invasion craft to be rushed back across the English Channel in an attempt to save his life, and perhaps his arm. In a couple of hours, my buddy George Forte, third squad leader in Company H, 3rd Platoon, would be forcing the shattered bone in his right leg back inside his skin. He would use his rifle bayonet as half of a leg brace and the bayonet scabbier as the other half, bound together with his rifle sling. He would then use his rifle as a crutch to depart his personal drop zone.

Chet Gunka would be killed, as would Hubert McClain, from my own squad, who jumped between Kelly and Duck, and First Sergeant Pettus, our tough Old Army burr-headed Superman. Chet, Hubert, and Pettus all reside at the American Cemetery in Normandy—three great soldiers who paid the ultimate price for America's freedoms.

Far from the traditional jostling and kidding around, calm reigned in the C-47 carrying my stick across the English Channel. The absence of joshing and carrying on was almost a shock on this very special trip. An atmosphere of quiet and deep thought prevailed. We had the usual eighteen men in our plane. My guys were all lined up in order of their position in the mortar squad, namely Duck, Fred, McClain, and Bones, right in the middle of the stick. It had been my personal responsibility to see that the six equipment bundles under our belly were properly packed and correctly attached to the under-side canisters of the plane.

This was the first time I had ever taken off from an air base in a C-47 with the door in place and closed. Always in the past, the door had been removed and stored inside the plane prior to takeoff. About thirty minutes into the flight, the air corps crew chief, Tech. Sgt. Clifford Meadows, came back to the rear of the plane and asked us to help him remove the door. He affixed it to the rear bulkhead next to the opening with elastic straps. This occurred about half way across the channel, so from there on, we had perfect sight of the water below and what looked like thousands of ships obviously filled with invasion troops.

All totaled, seventy-two sticks of the 507th had taken off from Barkston-Heath and forty-five from Fulbeck Airfield, preceded by three planes of Pathfinders out of Witham. The flight was as perfect as any I had ever experienced. There was not a ripple in the sky, and the moon glistened on the channel water about a thousand feet below, reflecting like stars off the sea. I appreciated that this was one of the smoothest plane rides of my two-year parachuting career. I did not see a single sick paratrooper, which was highly unusual.

There was quite a bit of praying going on in the aluminum bucket seats of that dark plane. There was also some sleeping, much smoking of cigarettes, and one hell of a lot of sweating. We had never made a combat jump, none of us. Nor had we ever been in combat. Jumping was rough enough on a friendly air base in the States, but we now were likely to encounter some folks who would not be very happy about our flight across that channel.

I was assistant jumpmaster, or "push-out" man, which means that my jump position was number eighteen, or last man out. If someone in our stick was hit by ground fire while we were still in the plane, part of my job as pusher was to make the man jump ready by hooking him up to the anchor line, then shoving him out of the door. The thinking was that he could get medical aid on the ground faster than flying back to England, and if he recovered, we certainly would need him. My buddy Chet Gunka pushed the next plane after ours.

Although my place was at the back of the stick, I sat for a spell with Lieutenant Woodward, Captain Taylor's executive officer and our jumpmaster, who would be the first man out. On maneuvers, both in the States and England, Captain Taylor always jumped as jumpmaster of the stick in the first of the planes assigned to transport Company H. All of our Company H jumpmasters tried to jump on Captain Taylor's exit, after the stand up and hook up. If our pilot saw Taylor jump, he would turn on the green light, signaling Woody to go; if Taylor were out of sight, Woody would lean out the door and observe the other planes, then jump on the exit of any other plane in our formation.

First Sergeant Pettus jumped that night toward the end of Captain Taylor's stick, which also included a number of Company headquarters men. As I found out later, Lieutenant

Colonel Kuhn, our battalion commander, was also in that stick. He would be injured in the jump and get captured by the Germans with his runner or radio operator until he was rescued, hurting pretty bad, on D-plus-2 by a 505th PIR combat patrol near Neuville-au-Plan.

Woody and I sat right across the aisle from the door, where we could see perfectly out into the beautiful sky and down to the awesome scene below. He showed me a letter from his wife in which she described the recent birth of their first baby, a little girl. He tried to show me a picture of the newborn baby, although it was too dark to really see anything. But my, how proud he was—and more than ready to get the job done so he could get back home to his young family. I sort of lost the urgency of what was about to take place, listening to Woody describe his feelings. It was so very peaceful and gentle a conversation, in view of what was about to break loose in an hour or so, when all hell would consume every man on that plane.

Later, from my place at the back of the stick, I visited with the pilot and copilot. I discovered that our pilot, Captain John L. Wood, was from Fort Worth, Texas, where I had spent many years as a kid, just after my mother died when I was seven years old. Given the momentous occasion, that small fact took on great importance for me.

Looking out the small plane windows, I could clearly see we were traveling in groups of three. Each lead plane had another plane off each wing, flying rather close, I thought. Here we were, all of Company H, heading toward our drop zone at 140 miles per hour at an altitude of one thousand feet or more. All in all, 2,004 troopers of the 507th PIR flew over the English Channel that night. It was the biggest, most awesome thing any of us had ever done.

Off the northwest coast of France, the islands of Jersey and Guernsey were in plain view, looking just as I had seen them a hundred times on the maps and sand tables we had studied.

This was the point at which our convoy turned east for the approach to Drop Zone T west of the Merderet River near the village of Amferville. Those islands were almost speaking, "You're just about there, boys." Yet somehow, I had a vision that this awesome thing we were about to do would not happen as long as I continued to talk with the two pilots. Perhaps my attitude was not very healthy for a "leader" in this project, the invasion of Hitler's property, but I honestly was not looking forward to what we had to do—not one bit!

As we crossed over the coast of France, we flew into cloud banks. Then, of even greater concern, we began to encounter all sorts of antiaircraft fire and huge German searchlights. Halfway inside the dark cockpit, standing just behind the pilots, I peered through the windows at the fogbank and anti-aircraft activity ahead. The pilots, if excited at the sight of fog and enemy fire, did not react. They seemed to take it all as part of the job.

Once we entered the fog, all of the pilots started looking out for their individual planes. We had been flying so close that we could easily see one another's wingtip lights. Now the pilots could see nothing, so the scramble was on as the planes went every which way with their human cargo.

Suddenly, I heard a familiar racket, one I had heard twenty-four times before—the shuffling sound of paratroopers heading out the door for a jump. "What's that?" I asked, as if I didn't know. The pilot replied, "They're gone!" Indeed, a couple of men had jumped. I had been so caught up in the cockpit that Woody had the stick standing up, inspected, and ready to go without my even knowing it! I did not hear the jump instructions. I did not see the pilot hit the green light. I did not even participate in the very important, urgent process of equipment check. I was not yet even hooked up, much less pushing the stick!

I charged out of the cockpit with a stream of profanity, grabbing my snap fastener from my shoulder and snapping it onto the anchor line. Just like the old firehouse horses I used to read about, I was out of there in a flash. Charging against the last man in the stick, I started pushing like mad to clear the plane as fast as possible.

Just as I left the cockpit, we entered the field of German fire. Things lit up and the whole plane bounced and rocked like nothing I had ever seen before. Strangely, nothing in this scene disturbed me. I just obeyed the traditional admonishment, "Get the hell out the door!"

One reason for exiting immediately was to preclude any trooper from really thinking about what a foolish thing he was about to do, namely, jumping out of a perfectly good airplane and into the ground fire of two German infantry divisions! One of the air corps crew chiefs in Normandy later told me that paratroopers were literally stacked up in the door of his plane, hit by machine guns as they were going out—a horrible sight for the sergeant.

I shoved hard against the stick for a couple paces and felt the stick bounce back—a sure indication that someone was stuck in the door. Without unhooking my snap fastener, I ran down the length of the plane. There, just above the plane floor, in the middle of the door, was a helmet.

It took me some time to register this sight. A trooper had failed to turn his rifle up as he approached the door. His weapon, extending across his body, had caught in the frame, butt plate on one side and muzzle on the other. His body had slipped on out beneath the rifle, and there he was, hung by his neck, with the top of his helmet showing above the doorsill.

The interior of our plane was completely blacked out, but the light from below clearly revealed his body, banging around outside the plane. His relief did not require the brains of a rocket scientist. I lifted up the muzzle of his gun, and he disappeared into the cool French air. He vanished so fast I wondered, "Where did he go?" The sky was brightly illuminated with bursting artillery shells and machine-gun tracers. Some planes were spotlighted with huge German search lights, coordinated with antiaircraft machine guns. If the lights were on you, so were the enemy guns.

Immediately, I started shouting, "Go, go, go!" which got the stick charging for the door again. I ran to the end of the stick and started pushing with all I had until I found myself literally falling through space, waiting for my chute to open.

From the time the first trooper went out the door, the pilots kept the plane in a modest decline, which raised the tail to preclude our chutes from getting hung up on it. The hapless trooper had been in his hopeless condition for fifty seconds to a minute as the plane descended all the while, picking up speed. By the time I exited, we must have been down to an altitude of 250 feet. When my parachute opened, I guess I was only 100 feet off the ground.

The opening shock was brutal, much heavier than usual. Anyone shooting at me had precious little time, because I was on the ground in a matter of seconds. I was one of the lucky ones; I landed in a clear pasture, not in the flooded Merderet River where so many of our 507th men drowned before they got out of their chutes. Some friends said later that they discovered bullet holes in their parachutes when they examined them on the ground. I left my chute as fast as possible, having no idea of its condition.

As last man out the door, I was separated far from Woody, who had exited in conjunction with the exit of Captain Taylor from his plane. On the brighter side, the time lost with our stuck trooper's unusual exit attempt meant that we had flown out of the heaviest ground fire by the time I jumped, so the scene was much quieter for my descent. I do not even recall how I landed—hard or easy. I was just there on French soil, alone, in an unbelievable silence, with the sound of weapons firing out in the distance.

I looked around that pasture and had no idea where I was. For years, I had thought I missed the drop zone by twenty miles or so. I now realize that I must have landed about three miles from the Merderet, just a few miles off Drop Zone T, maybe even less. Even so, I was completely lost, despite my effort to memorize every blade of grass on Captain Taylor's sand table.

My impulse was to head toward the source of small arms fire. I knew that the machine guns and rifles I was hearing were being used by both Germans and paratroopers, and I prayed that our troopers were not firing at one another, something I had heard was not uncommon among new combat soldiers.

Never in our instructions about the terrain of the Normandy countryside did we ever hear the word *hedgerow*. Yet like many of my fellow troopers, I immediately encountered twenty-foot-high hedges, which were so impassable that not even tanks could penetrate them. Used to divide farming acreage, most often pasturage for cows, the hedgerows had often grown together to form a canopy over somewhat sunken, sandy roadbeds, where no sunlight ever penetrated. These dark, covered settings prompted much fear, and we quickly came by fine-tuned ears able to detect the slightest sound—like the activation of a rifle bolt, or the click of a German MG-42 .30-caliber aluminum machine-gun belt being run through the metallic breech of a gun in preparation for firing.

As I cautiously moved toward the sound of small arms fire, I ran into another paratrooper with an 82nd Airborne Division shoulder patch. He was a private and a rifleman. I don't remember his particular unit, but he was not from the 507th.

I walked up on his back side and scared him half to death. "Hey, soldier!" I said. I know I should have challenged with the password, *thunder*, in use until the beach forces started landing at 6 a.m., and waited for the countersign, *welcome*, but for some reason, it did not seem appropriate. It could have gotten me killed, but it didn't. The trooper was as lost as I was, and really glad to join up with at least a buck sergeant who might know more than he did, which was zip.

We moved out, continuing in the direction from which the small arms fire was coming. We came to a single farmhouse with a very low rock wall around it. There was one small barn out behind the farmhouse. I told the trooper, who was armed with an M1, that I would go up to the front door of the house and see what I could discover. He assured me that he would cover me from out in the yard.

I approached the front door of the house with my tommy gun at the ready, having no confidence in what we were doing. The farmhouse had a "Dutch door," divided in two horizontally. I knocked, and after what I considered too long a period, the top half opened, very slowly, to reveal a pretty, young French lass. She could have died from fright as she laid eyes on what might well have been her killer or rapist. She could see nothing but a gun, grenades hanging from a uniform jacket, and a helmet—everything that symbolized bad times for people who had been under Nazi authority for four years.

Her pretty, large, dark eyes screamed with fear. With no thought as to what my move should be, I immediately turned to the side and pointed to the American flag that we all wore on our upper jumpsuit jacket sleeve. Instantly, that look of horror left her sweet face, and a huge smile spread across it, melting away the fear. With her heart back in place, this beautiful young lady walked back across the room and faded into the darkened house.

"Papa! Papa!" I heard her whisper. Shortly, an old man with a sweet face and a circular patch of snow-white hair outlining his bald head appeared from the darkness. He came up to the still half-opened door and stood there as if to say, "What can I do for you?"

I have never felt so dumb in my life. I knew how to say in French such things as "My friend is hurt, do you have aid?" Or,

"Do you have food?" and the likes, but I did not know why I had come up to this house as I did, taking a chance on getting killed by the enemy. I stood there for a matter of some seconds. Then I just shrugged my shoulders, indicating "I don't know what the hell I'm doing here," and walked back out to my friend, waving back to the two happy Normans.

Chapter Fourteen

ASSEMBLY

Assembling Capt. Allen Taylor's Company H was not according to the book on D-Day, nor was the jump in keeping with all the preparations the company had made back in the States or along the Grantham Canal in England. On maneuvers, Captain Taylor always led Company H as jumpmaster of the number one plane of a three-plane formation, with the rest of the company following in two more identical formations. Ideally, all of Company H would exit the plane in ten seconds and land within a few hundred feet of Captain Taylor. The two planes on either side of Taylor's plane jumped on Taylor's exit, and as the other three-plane groups passed over the spot where Taylor exited, they also went out.

We all exited over the same spot on the ground. Right? Wrong! It just never happened in practice jumps in Georgia, Alabama, Louisiana, South Dakota, Missouri, Colorado, or England—and it certainly did not happen in Operation Overlord on D-Day. In fact, if our practice day jumps were fiascoes when it came to assembling the company on the ground, the night jump on D-Day was even worse. At least in the daytime, we could see the men from Captain Taylor's stick floating down below and try to slip toward where they appeared to be heading.

On D-Day any miss, even a few miles off, meant we were in totally unfamiliar territory. We thought we should be able to match every blade of grass we saw to the sand table presentation of our drop zone. However, after falling through considerable antiaircraft fire, many of our men landed in a flooded area bordered by the Merderet River. We were worse than lost, and off most of our squad leader's maps.

I later learned the reasons for all this foul-up. The 507th had the worst drop of all the regiments in Normandy, partially because we were the last to arrive: our flight, starting from the northernmost English air bases used on D-Day, gave the Germans two extra hours to prepare for our attack, taking the edge off the surprise. By the time we flew over, they were ready—as the heavy antiaircraft artillery we encountered testified.

Add to this the cloudbanks we hit over the coast of France. Each 507th paratrooper's landing spot was determined by the way his pilot turned his plane when he ran into the antiaircraft fire, the clouds, and the other planes that had broken formation. Then there was the pilot's fear of flying too far and dropping us into the ocean—apparently, a few unfortunate troopers actually did end up on the beaches—and the strict order to the pilots not to return to England with any troopers aboard.

Although a few sticks did land on or close to the 507th drop site in Amferville-Gourbesville to the northwest of St. Mere-Eglise, the rest of us were spread out over more than sixty square miles. Our drops ranged from northeast of Valognes (a little south of Cherburg) in the north to Graignes in the south, which received a cluster of twenty-five sticks. From east to west, we were scattered from the beaches and St. Marie-du-Mont to just west of St. Jores.

In roughly our vicinity west of the Merderet River, two other groups of mostly 507th PIR were gathered, although we didn't know this at the time. These were Lt. Col. Charles Timme's group, mostly from the 2nd Battalion, who were in an orchard north of La Fiere causeway, and a group of some two hundred men that Colonel Millett had gathered up, now west of Amferville. Lieutenant Colonel Arthur Maloney, a great 507th PIR executive officer, had taken command of the regiment in the absence of Colonel Millett. Near the river on Hill 30, there was also a fourth ad hoc force, mostly of 508th PIR, under the command of Lt. Col. Thomas J. B. Shanley.

In one sense, it was good that we were so dispersed. The Germans had flooded the marshland all around the Merderet River to preclude us having a nice flat area for landing troops at Drop Zone T. This flooding did not show up on reconnaissance photos, so we came down expecting to find soft pastures under our feet. Normally, the Merderet is about six feet deep and twenty feet wide, and runs very fast. There was now, however, an additional three to four feet of water covering all but the highest ground. Many of our 507th men who did come down on the drop zone, and troopers from other units, too, landed in water over their heads. Heavily weighted down by equipment and supplies, encumbered by their canopies, they drowned before they could get out of their chutes.

I myself was triply fortunate. I made a soft landing about three miles from the flooded Merderet River in a cleared field, I was somewhat away from the sound of fighting, and I also came across my company commander, Captain Taylor, a few hours later, around 8 a.m. Our position was not too far from Amfreville. I was still with the other trooper I'd met up with, but after I encountered Taylor, I left him and resumed my squad leader role.

Throughout France on D-Day morning, there were probably not five solid mortar squads assembled together, after such messed up parachute drops and missed drop zones, but fortunately, our 3rd Squad, 3rd Platoon, Company H, 507th PIR had the essential elements intact. Duck and Kelly, who always jumped next to each other, must have found each other and our equipment bundles shortly upon landing. Captain Taylor had already picked up both men, and they had a mortar and some ammunition by the time I got there. Our gunner, assistant gunner, and squad leader were together as we had prayed. Unfortunately, no Bones was to be found. We regretfully listed him as MIA (missing in action). Otherwise, small bands of troopers were roaming around the drop zone areas, and Taylor began gathering an increasing number of them from assorted outfits.

Chapter Fifteen

THE BATTLE
FOR FRESVILLE

Much deserved praise has been heaped upon our sister regiment, the 505th PIR, for their gallant fight in taking St.
Mere-Eglise on D-Day morning. However, no mention is ever
given to the fight to liberate another village, Fresville, just a few
miles up the road from St. Mere-Eglise. I attended a number of
Taylor's sand table training sessions back in our marshalling area
in England, and there was no mention of a town called Fresville.
I doubt seriously that Taylor had any instructions to capture it
in the first place, but it beat sitting on the side of the flooded
Merderet River, waiting on the German 91st Infantry Division
to swoop down on us, tanks and all.

Believe me, it was not like the German commander in
Fresville had a receiving line set up to welcome our hodge-
podge group of thirty-odd men from assorted parachute units.
First off, we had to move from the dry land on the west side of
the Merderet through the intended 507th drop zone, now sub-
merged. Sloshing across the area, we crossed over railroad
tracks to our east and went in over the short men's heads when

we crossed the river proper. The whole time we were in the water, we were subjected to inaccurate, but deadly, German small arms fire coming from the shores to our right front, as well as a small amount of .88 artillery fire. When we crossed the tracks, which were built up about ten feet high, I chose to go under them, thus avoiding enemy fire.

Several accounts have been written about the danger of crossing this swampy area. The fact is, when we were out in the water, the Germans were so far from us, and such poor shots at that distance, that I did not see a single man fall from enemy fire. The German .88 is a significant weapon against infantry troops, but the Germans were obviously saving their ammunition for a better target. The few rounds they fired were brief and inaccurate. My guess is that if the same units that gave the 36th Infantry hell on the Rapido River in Italy had been firing at us, we would all have been killed. But by June 6, 1944, we were facing a less experienced foe. The Germans were even using captured Russians as replacements, as well as young kids as frontline troops.

Upon arriving on the east bank of the river, Captain Taylor and I discussed how to use our 60mm mortars on the German troops in Fresville, in preparation for taking the village. By that time, I had access to two mortars. We decided to fire them both close to the church in the center of the village, trusting that the civilians would stay inside and not be hit.

Taylor took his thirty to forty men and headed up the two narrow sandy roads leading toward Fresville. Meanwhile, I climbed a tall tree so I could get a good view of the village, which was somewhat uphill from our position down at the edge of the swamp. We set up our mortars in a field below the tree, with Duck and Fred manning them.

We had practiced so many set-up and firing drills in Georgia, Alabama, Louisiana, Nebraska, Ireland, and England that our first mortar rounds were right on target. I used the church steeple as a reference point and tried to keep our rounds on either side of the church. In this we were successful. Duck and Fred were so well trained that getting six rounds of ammunition in the air before the first one landed was no trouble. The first round had no sooner exploded than ten more rounds burst on target.

All across Normandy, German units were trying to figure out if every band of our troops they encountered actually represented an invasion force. During this initial period, the Allies were able to get established on the beaches, and so the operation was successful. It is said that if the Germans had properly freed their great reserves to attack us in the early stages of the landings, we might well have failed. At the least, we would have paid a much greater price for victory than was the painful case. We had been told back in England that casualties would be very high, and we believed it.

As I watched our troops move up the pair of roads leading into Fresville, I determined when we needed to quit firing the mortars to avoid hitting our own men. As soon as that time arrived, I climbed down the tree and our two abbreviated mortar squads raced up the road to get some of the action. I can't believe as I recall this that we would actually hurry to get shot at, but that was the sort of tiger blood that flowed through our veins in those days.

The battle in Fresville involved house to house combat, which is very spooky. The problem with attacking in this type of military operation is that the enemy knows the territory, but you are learning the city as you go. There is not much "pucker time" as you kick open the doors. Fortunately, we had practiced infantry tactics in every form for more than two years, including working from house to house, so our losses were not that bad in view of the potential.

Because we were providing covering fire for Captain Taylor and the rest, Duck, Fred, and I were late in getting into Fresville and the fight. We ran up the left branch into town and had one minor scrap as we came up the road from the river. When we passed the spot we had been shooting at, we discovered two dead Germans. We assumed that they were the only enemy missed by Taylor's group as they passed en route to Fresville.

Our troopers had run into considerable resistance from German infantry soldiers stationed in the village, but by the time we got to the church, the krauts had been run out of town. When we arrived, only scattered small arms fire could be heard in the outskirts of the village.

Left with no specific orders, in typical GI fashion, Duck, Fred, and I started our own personal village patrol to see what we could find. I had been instructed in the dangers of booby traps for which the German army was famous, but I paid no attention to what I had been told. I kicked open every door to every building and shed in the place except the church. A small frame building seemed to be some sort of official building, because there were several vehicles parked out front. In fact, this was the city hall, which had been serving as the German headquarters.

It was in this building, which I believed might have good souvenirs, that I came upon a metal safe with a large lock. At the risk of being hit by flying metal, I blew the lock apart with a rifle shot. There my wondering eyes discovered stacks upon stacks of reichsmarks—so many, I could only assume I had hit the jackpot and this was the German payroll.

Without wasting time for Captain Taylor to show up, I stuffed all the reichsmarks into my jumpsuit blouse, zipped it up, grabbed the German flag off the wall, wrapped it around my waist, and took off. When I next ran into Captain Taylor, he told me to take a detail and go check out a certain two-story farmhouse they had bypassed en route to the village.

Said to be a German barracks, the farmhouse was located on a corner lot. I took Fred and we went to the house and into the courtyard. Hearing activity inside the house, I threw a fragmentary hand grenade through an upper window. As it exploded, Fred and I went into the first floor and dashed into a bedroom to our right. We heard all sorts of scrambling toward the back of the house. We assumed, and rightly so, that the German troops housed in the farmhouse were "heading out of Dodge." I don't recall even going upstairs. Maybe Fred checked out the upper story, I do not know, but for sure the house was clear of Germans. We went back and reported to Taylor that this was the case.

I went into the old cemetery for a moment to rest and secretly count up my booty. I wound up sitting among the ancient tombstones, futilely trying to figure out just how much the huge stash of German reichsmarks represented in real money. All I knew was that it was far too much to be only company funds. I had visions of going back to Texas a rich man.

This happy dream was rudely interrupted when another soldier came into the graveyard from around the front of the churchyard. "Captain Taylor is not up front," he said, "and I don't see anyone else either, but there's a Tiger tank down the street." I had never seen an enemy tank, but we had all heard rumors about the fabled Tigers, the most formidable tank ever made.

The class we'd had back in the States about how we could take on tanks was some bull. The best thing we could do with a tank was run from it. As paratroopers, we were notoriously short on antitank weapons, and we were pretty much limited to the mines and other explosives we could carry in on our bodies. Maybe Audie Murphy could mount a tank and blow it up, but in Normandy, my associates and I found the best way to deal with the problem was to get a few hedgerows between us and the tank. The tanks could not break through the thick hedgerows, which were often lined with ditches on either side—thank God!

I lit out of the Fresville graveyard with the other trooper, looking for Captain Taylor. I did glimpse the tank at the end of the street, and it sure looked like a Tiger to me. I had no way of knowing at the time that the Germans in Normandy had only light, French-made tanks like Renaults. But Tiger or no Tiger, that tank was a frightful sight. It was so huge it almost touched the buildings on either side of the narrow street as it rumbled into town.

Chapter Sixteen

Taylor's Group: Bundle Duty and Ear Injury

To make a long story short, Taylor's group took Fresville by 10 a.m. on D-Day and held the town until about 1 p.m. when the Germans counterattacked with at least one tank. We then moved out of Fresville in haste and back across the railroad tracks and the Merderet through the swamps in what I assumed was a southwesterly direction to defend a hillside near Amferville. The next day, a patrol of 505th troopers came over to Fresville from St. Mere-Eglise. The Germans ambushed them on a road outside the village, and all were killed by MG-42 machine-gun fire. In 2004, a memorial was erected in Fresville to the memory of these ten brave 505th troopers.

By the end of D-plus-1, Taylor's group had taken more than ninety German prisoners, and numbered about two hundred Americans (mostly PIR). Each American had simply attached himself to the nearest unit commander, be he colonel, captain, or sergeant. I doubt that Taylor or anyone else bothered to take an official count. These troops represented just about every American unit jumping into Normandy. To say the jump was a disaster would be a compliment.

I now had occasion to dig my first foxhole in France. Making a sort of a carpeting effect, I lined the bottom with the Swastika flag that had flown over Fresville, and was I ever proud to display that foxhole!

Soon I received the order to take a detail, go down to the flat land near the water's edge, about two hundred yards away, and bring back some equipment bundles, which the air corps had dropped as resupply. We were just about out of ammunition for all our weapons at this point, and we had just begun to fight. Fortunately, I still had Duck and Fred Kelly with me. I also had access to a couple German soldiers we had captured during the day.

I later learned from some airmen I met that after they had dropped us during the dark wee hours of D-Day, they went back to England, picked up some glider infantry troops, then flew them right back across the English Channel. When they had delivered the glider troops, these same planes and crews turned around yet again and started flying equipment drops into our combat zones.

Of course, we ourselves had previously packed six bundles, which were attached to the underside of our jump plane on D-Day. We had plenty of 60mm shells if we could just locate the bundles. This was the reason we were to venture into the flat land below our company position and take on the German troops, who also had desires on the bundles. Even without the Germans, bringing the heavy loads up to the high ground would be no small matter. The ones that I had helped to pack weighed about two hundred pounds each.

The bundles of real interest to us, loaded with 60mm mortar shells and .30-caliber rifle ammunition, had red canopies on the chutes. I went in with the intention of finding some, but soon discovered that we had to fight like hell to secure half a dozen anonymous bundles, with no idea what they might contain. The German troops, well aware of how valuable the bundles were, went after them at the same time we did.

Soon a firefight developed all up and down the swamp, with both sides taking whatever bundles they could manage to drag out of the shallow water or off the wet shores. Fortunately, we did not lose any men. I never saw any dead or wounded krauts either, so I guess everyone was satisfied just to grab some bundles and get the hell out of the exposed area.

None of the bundles we lugged up the hill had any indication of having been packed by our unit. Carrying and dragging them back was a heavy task, but we also felt like kids on Christmas morning getting ready to open our presents. The firefights depleted our ammunition even further, making us critically in need of resupply. I had visions of finding antitank weapons, like a couple of bazookas and their rocketlike shells. Or maybe the bundles would contain machine guns and their ammunition. The excitement was awesome as we struggled to get our six trophies up the hill.

As soon as we arrived back at our position, guys swarmed around and started opening the bundles. Most of them were filled with some sort of unusable military gear. There was a bundle of rifle grenades, but we had no .03 Springfield rifles with attachments for firing the grenades. There was some bazooka ammunition, but we had no bazookas. To top it off, there were two whole bundles of assorted fruit juice. "Duck," I said, "we best drink up, because it looks like we're in for some heavy-duty moving about the countryside."

Later in the day, I got into a serious argument with Captain Taylor. This turned out to be the occasion of my first Purple Heart and a hearing aid in each ear as I write this story.

The captain had set up his headquarters in a barn. Hearing some machine-gun fire coming from the distance, he called me and Lieutenant Bart Hale outside his CP, near a thick hedgerow, and told us to gather up a patrol and find out what the machine-gun fire was. Lieutenant Hale was too good a soldier even to question Taylor's order, but I had to speak right up.

"Sir," I said, "I know what that is; it's Germans firing our [own] LMGs (light machine guns). I'm sure they got them during our fight down by the river this morning." The Germans had retrieved more bundles than we did, and I felt certain that some of them contained automatic weapons, like the machine guns we were hearing.

Taylor continued to insist that we go make contact. I made it clear, having been patrolling steadily since joining the captain and his men, that every time we stepped through a hedgerow we discovered what was on the other side. There was no other way to find out what was there. In my eyes, we were about to get men killed if we went out to investigate the firing.

"Just wait!" I suggested. "If they're coming this way, we'll let them come to the next hedgerow outside our defense and challenge them. If they're GIs, we'll welcome them into our position. If they're krauts, we'll get it on with them from our secure positions. My way, no one gets hurt. We just wait an hour to discover who the hell is firing an American machine gun."

Being a better soldier than I was, Hale just stood there prepared to do this dumb patrol, the whole time I was arguing with the captain. Our heated exchange had gone on for about five minutes when suddenly, right next to my head, a German rifle grenade detonated on the hedge and hit me in the head. The blast knocked me down, knocked the tommy gun out of my hand, and knocked my helmet off.

I was both furious and thankful. Furious, that this officer would risk Hale, my men, and me for no real, valid purpose. It was like we were on some maneuver back in the States, playing war games with referees. All the officers played the games to the hilt, going to great ends to look militarily proper. Nothing was left undone, no stone unturned. The captain's project was

Marietta, Georgia
August 6, 1981

C-E-R-T-I-F-I-C-A-T-E

I certify that I, Captain Bartley E. Hale (then 2nd Lt.), 0-1318426, U.S. Army, was a member of Company "H", 507th Parachute Infantry Regiment, 82nd Airborne Division, when the Division jumped into Normandy, France on 6 June 1944.

On or about June 8, we were engaged in a fire fight with a strong German force near Vic Les Landes, France. At approximately 1800 hours, Captain Allen W. Taylor, Company Commander of Company "H", Sgt. Bob Bearden, Squad Leader, 3rd Platoon, Company "H", and I were standing near a hedgerow discussing the possibility of sending a small patrol out to silence a German machine gun that had become quite troublesome. During our discussion, a German rifle grenade exploded in the hedgerow next to us and Sgt. Bearden, who was nearest the hedgerow, was knocked to the ground by the explosion. When St. Bearden regained his feet, I saw that one of his ears was bleeding.

As I recall, Capt. Taylor told Sgt. Bearden to see if he could find the aid station and then Sgt. Bearden left. I believe it was at this point that Capt. Taylor told me that Col. George V. Millett, the regimental commanger, had recommended Sgt. Bearden for the Distinguished Service Cross for action on D+1, 7 June 1944, near Amferville, France, in which his heroic action had saved the life of an officer.

Col. Millett was later captured and remained a prisoner for the duration and, apparently, the recommendation was lost during the confusion.

Bartley E. Hale
Bartley E. Hale
Captain, U.S..Army (Retired)

Letter confirming Bob Bearden's combat injury and comments on Colonel Millett's recommendation for DSC.

very likely going to get someone hurt or killed, and for what? So he could say he knew the men who shot us were krauts.

Anyway, I learned there and then that it doesn't hurt all that much to get hit. My blessing—for which I was grateful—was that it was a German rifle grenade that hit me. One of our own would have taken my head off for sure. Instead, this grenade had exploded when it hit a heavy hedge, and all I got was lightweight canister particles and powder in my left ear and eyes. I got up off the ground with my tommy gun in hand, then threw it down again. "If you want to know who that is, get your ass out there and see for yourself," I raged. "But don't take our men with you and get them killed too!"

I ran about thirty yards over to my slit trench, lay down, and cried tears of fury. Taylor later acknowledged that he should have listened to a good noncom who had personally been engaged with the Germans and knew what the hell was going on out there. After all, he had been in his command post, not engaged personally. I would later minister first aid to Captain Taylor when he was hit by a single bullet through his side. We actually laughed together as I worked on his injury, with no reference to our previous encounter. He was still my beloved company commander after the war, back in the States.

On D-plus-1, Taylor made radio contact with Colonel Millett, our 507th regimental commander, who directed him to come out deeper into the Cherbourg Peninsula and join him. I heard Taylor talking on the radio to Millett, who was dug in with a couple hundred paratroopers from assorted units and surrounded by a much larger German force. The conversation ended with Millett giving Taylor the grid coordinates on the map so we could find his position. It turned out that Millett had been seriously attacked several times the day before, but had managed to repulse each attack. I don't know if the colonel told Taylor how hopelessly he was surrounded by krauts—but we sure as hell found out, the hard way!

Later in the day, Taylor had a conference with the officers and NCOs in his barn position, when we again heard lots of firing outside. It was like all hell broke loose, but our meeting went on as planned. When it broke up, and we went back out to the hedgerow we were defending, we discovered that the Germans had overrun our position. Our temporary company commander, Private First Class Alcott, an Arizona ranch-hand type, had personally organized a counterattack all on his own and kicked the krauts out of our position. Having lost a number of troops to Alcott, what was left of the Germans must have split.

The next radio contact Taylor had was with an armored (tank) unit that had pushed in from Omaha Beach. The tankers were led by a lieutenant, and Taylor requested that the tanks come to our side of the causeway so we could follow them back across and out of our precarious military position. The officer told Taylor that he had achieved his instructed objective. That was as far as he was taking his troops. Taylor pleaded for about an hour's support, but to no avail.

We had many fights with tankers in the Fort Benning areas of Columbus, Georgia, and Phenix City, Alabama. Some tank high-command type had permitted tankers to wear boots. It was common knowledge that there was no love lost between us. We were so proud of our jump boots that we would have killed to protect our exclusive right to them.

As Taylor finished up on the radio, the tanker was heard to say, "Remember Phenix City!"

As I later found out, Ridgway and Gavin wanted to consolidate the four groups of troopers that were fighting their own little wars west of the Merderet River, cut off from the rest of the division. Our move to join Millett was part of this plan, which was meant to prevent the Germans from destroying each group, one by one. Timmes was told to hold his position in the orchard for the time being. The 508th was also holding on Hill

30, but theirs was a desperate situation, with many wounded and dying, and no medical supplies. Their food and ammunition had also all but run out.

I had mixed feelings about our move to join Millett's group. First, we were leaving behind our wounded, as well as the wounded German soldiers we had, in a barn full of hay. I helped to gather them up and get them settled as well as we could. A couple of medics were going to stay with them. In hopes that the medics could buy some food and fill other needs, I gave one of them the entire German payroll I had stashed in my jumpsuit blouse. There went my vision of starting a large business when I got back to Dallas.

On the one hand, it was true that the Normandy farmers, for the most part, did not need to be bought off. They were very cooperative and supportive. But then again, if we got caught by the Germans, I didn't want that payroll on me, nor the kraut flag I'd stolen from Fresville. So I unloaded all my goodies on the medic and determined that I would not return to Texas a wealthy man.

Secondly, I thought the idea of joining our regimental commander in his perilous position was stupid in and of itself. This was in the direction of Amferville, which was farther away from the beaches and the friendly forces moving out from the invasion landing sites. Of course, I had no idea of the bigger picture at the time so could not know that our move was the first of a series meant to consolidate a number of groups in the hopes of saving all of our skins.

Chapter Seventeen

Millett's Group: My Hottest Day of the War

We set out about dark on D-plus-1, and marched all night toward Millett's position. We came under attack a number of times during the night and early morning hours. I have no idea how far we had moved toward his area, perhaps three miles, when we came to a point where our group had to cross over a road in single file, and go into the field on the other side. I remember so vividly how scared I was when Lieutenant Hale told me to go up that road and stand guard while the rest of the group crossed. The object was to keep the Germans from bushwhacking our men farther up the road. If they caught our people in the middle of it, we could incur heavy losses.

But why send Mrs. Bearden's son Bob up that dark road and all alone? I thought. I had already been jumped a number of times in our brief stay in Normandy, so I was really spooked. But I was more of a good soldier than my fright, so up the road I went, and nothing came of it and the troops crossed safely over.

Just at daylight, we were pinned down by sniper fire, and a number of our people were hit. At the time I did not realize it, but we were just outside Millett's position. During this time, our entire group was lying on the ground, exposed out in the open. It was dangerous for everyone.

Along with any number of others, I shot my M1 rifle at the spot in the tree from which the fire was coming. When the sniper fired, the leaves would shake as the bullets came out, and a tiny bit of smoke also emerged from the branches and leaves. Finally, one of us hit the sniper, who fell out of the tall tree.

When the body hit the ground, one of our guys went over to see what he could take off of it. A pistol was our favorite trophy. Upon rolling the body over, he saw that the sniper was a young woman. This greatly surprised us all at the time. Even now, I can only surmise that she was one of the German women snipers I have occasionally heard about.

No sooner were we freed from the sniper than we ran into a substantial German force. The point, or troops who were out in front of us all, were feeling their way along the route to Millett's position. Theirs was a real anxious adrenaline trip, as they were liable to be fired on at any moment. When the point would hear or see something unusual, they would halt the column and go forth to check it out.

At one of these junctures while our column was halted, word came back for a tommy gun man to come up front. That request frequently meant a shoot-out with a German patrol. For those unfamiliar with weapons, a tommy gun takes a .45-caliber bullet, about the largest bullet fired from any small handheld gun. A .45-caliber slug can literally make a man flip when hit, and might turn the shooter around if he isn't prepared when he pulls the trigger.

I was carrying an M1 .30-caliber Garand rifle at the time, so the word did not apply to me. But as I lay there waiting with nothing happening, I saw a young officer lying about fifty feet away. He was holding a tommy gun and crying softly. The trooper had experienced all he could handle. I knew he was as scared as I had been the night before when Hale had sent me up that road alone, but he wasn't moving. A day or so later, I would reach the same level of brokenness.

I went over to him and asked for his tommy gun, then gave him my rifle and started off toward the front of the column. Suddenly, I realized that I needed more .45-caliber bullets for the tommy gun. He gave me two more clips and off I went, stuffing them down the front of my jumpsuit jacket and not too happy.

When I reached the front of the column, a trooper I had never seen before was squatting down by a three-foot hedgerow overlooking a small, red sandy road cut out of a moderate hill. I didn't notice much about him, except that he was rather short. He whispered to me that two Germans were standing in the middle of the road just to our left. He told me to throw a gammon grenade at them, follow it over the hedge, down into the roadbed perhaps six feet below, and up the hill on the other side of the road. When the gammon grenade, made of composition C-2 explosive, went off, all the force of the blast would go forward, not backward toward the user. The trooper then would follow me, bringing the rest of the men over the embankment and into the field.

This was to be quite a flying experience, clearing the three-foot hedge and descending another six feet to the road below. I could thank God for some awesome physical training back in the States and England that had made us ready for just such situations.

I threw the grenade. By the time it exploded, I was already in the air going over the short hedge and into the roadway. Suddenly, I heard a frantic shout. "Look out below you!" Sure enough, as I fell against the steep embankment on the other side, I turned to see three German soldiers who had all been sleeping right under our position. The two Germans in the middle of the road bed had both keeled over dead, but the others had experienced a rude awakening when the gammon grenade went off. I fired from fifteen to twenty feet into the three of them as they fumbled to bring their rifles into port position and shoot from the hip. I obviously hit each one as my tommy gun clip ran dry, because none of the three got off a round from their weapons.

As any soldier with a tommy gun will tell you, it is not that easy to drop one magazine hurriedly from a T-gun and slip another in place. There are a couple of critically narrow grooves into which the magazine must fit, so making this move successfully was a Godsend for me. Somehow, inexperienced as I was with that gun, I managed to hit the magazine release, drop the empty one, and insert a full one taken from my jumpsuit.

I raked the three German soldiers again, and shouting all sorts of profanity, went up and over the low hedge on the other side of the road, screaming for the man with a plan to get his blankety-blank ass over here!

New issues instantly arose on the other side. I was now in another field occupied by German troops. To my left and about fifty yards away was a ten-foot hedge, beyond which was a house. The first sound I heard sent chills up my spine—a German MG42 machine gun being prepared to fire. They were using aluminum belts, a dreaded sound we were well acquainted with.

In my hyped-up condition, I threw a fragmentation grenade toward the gun crew, who were hidden under the eves between the house and the tall hedge. I threw that grenade so hard that it bounced off the roof. This, as it turned out, was perfect. The grenade rolled off the house and into the middle of the kraut machine-gun team just in time to blow up—and take every member of the gun team with it.

Other Germans now made the mistake of identifying their positions by movement. In my sheer terror, I sprayed everything that moved on that side of the road with the tommy gun. I was locked in a fight with the group of Germans who had Colonel

Millett surrounded, but I had no idea of that fact. This fight took place within three hundred yards of Millett's foxhole and covered one hundred yards as I moved forward. I may not be Audie Murphy, but those krauts knew they had encountered "Airborne!" I kept moving forward, not knowing I was entering Millett's position as the fight ensued, and in a matter of minutes I had breeched the German line.

As I soon discovered, the occasion of my personal "hottest" combat experience, during which I thought I had fought World War II alone, may have been in vain. The Germans ultimately simply moved aside and allowed us to move our troops into the trap with Millett, effectively encircling about two hundred more of us.

When I say "us," you must understand that most of the four hundred troopers or so usually referred to as "Millett's group" were not from the same military units. As with Captain Taylor's men, several different regiments were represented, and some were even from other divisions. Some were not paratroopers, either, but glider infantry troops, for example, who came into France in gliders after daylight on D-Day. Supposedly, we paratroopers were to have secured the landing sites for the gliders, but the fact is, they landed all over that end of France. What real, unheralded heroes these glider infantry men were is also another story. They were usually a good deal older than paratrooper types. They darn sure had unusually hazardous duty and received no flight pay as we did jump pay. They were ripped off for sure.

Later that afternoon, I came across one of the Germans I had shot in the road bed. He was the first enemy I saw that I knew I had shot myself. He was a really fine-looking young man—tall, with blue eyes, blond hair, and a light complexion, wearing the usual gray German infantry uniform.

I stopped and sort of wanted to say something, but I just stared. He was receiving some sort of fluid into his arm, with the bottle hanging from a low-hanging tree limb. I was not proud and wanted to tell him I was sorry. He obviously recognized me because he smiled a tiny smile, which I acknowledged with a shallow smile of my own. It was as if he had said, "It's okay. You just did your job, your really crazy job."

Once we got oriented in our new position, we were happy to encounter Bones, who had somehow managed to hook up with Millett earlier on. That afternoon, I learned something that deeply saddened me. Millett's group had captured a German soldier who had an American tommy gun with an ammunition cylinder on top, just like the Chicago bad guys in the movies. I agreed with the men who showed me the gun that it could only have belonged to Sergeant Pettus. It must have taken a company of Germans and a hell of a firefight to kill Pettus, tough as he was. I talk to George every time I visit the American Cemetery above Omaha Beach in Normandy, where he is buried. A great soldier, First Sergeant George Pettus.

It was later that day that I ran into Lt. Jack Hughes, Company H's 1st Platoon leader, an outstanding Virginia Military Institute graduate and a very popular officer. I had gone to the aid station to get some warm oil in the ear that had taken the rifle grenade back in our position near the Merderet River.

"Congratulations, Sergeant Bearden," Hughes greeted me in his deep Virginia accent.

"For what?" I asked. He said, "Colonel Millett is going to get you a DSC (Distinguished Service Cross) for saving that lieutenant's life this morning."

"Lieutenant?" I said. "What lieutenant?" That's when I learned that the man on top of the road giving me instructions was an officer. I just thought he was a man with a plan. It also turned out that patrols sent out by Colonel Millett talked about twenty dead and wounded German soldiers, and Millett seemed to think most of them had been involved in my frantic firefight. I truly had no idea that I was working with an officer.

As for personal bravery, all I can say is that the Germans, in trying to kill me, inspired me to effectively use that borrowed tommy gun.

"A hell of a lot of good a DSC is going to do anybody in this screwed up operation," I replied. And with that, I left the aid station and went back to managing my foxhole.

Later the lieutenant who had sent me over the road had some nice things to say about my performance. I assured him of how mortally scared I was throughout the affair and apologized for cussing him out. The real heroes are still under white crosses in Normandy today.

Chapter Eighteen

AVOID CROSSING
GOD IN COMBAT

After I left the aid station, I huddled down awhile in my very deep foxhole, sort of licking my emotional wounds. I thanked the Good Lord for his miraculous protection. I had not been hit in this very personal and up-close experience, but the fear from being shot at, eyeball to eyeball, from a distance of twenty feet by three scared German infantry soldiers no doubt remains with me today.

When an infantry soldier is lounging, sitting, sleeping, or just lying back in his deep, comfortable foxhole or trench, he assumes a measure of peace and "at homeness" most people never know. It's like you are protected from all the hostile elements in the world—no one, nothing can "get" you. That includes bombs, enemy artillery, and whatever else might seek to do you harm. This is an experience only infantry soldiers share. It's a relationship, an infantry soldier and his foxhole. It's there to provide protection for sure, but far more than that, this hole in the ground is the infantry soldier's own personal creation.

There is the initial foxhole, when you are trying desperately, and with great haste, to get your fanny below the fire line. That is the line where fragments and bullets are flying. Depending on the ground's firmness, digging this initial home-away-from-home, or basic foxhole, takes twenty to thirty minutes. In this amount of time, all your body parts are below the surface of the earth. As for the time it takes to dig a hole, I'd wager on the speed of a scared infantry soldier over any backhoe I ever saw!

Foxholes improve in style, hominess, comfort, size, depth, and convenience as time allows, and as flying metal objects subdue for a spell. There's a lot of pride to be taken in one's foxhole. Just as you like inviting friends and neighbors over to see your new home back in the States, a GI dogface or Marine grunt likes to brag about his foxhole, his latest creation in earth. Before he leaves it, he may have entered that foxhole feet first, head first, or whatever position you might imagine, depending on the circumstances of the moment. Certainly incoming artillery fire will often find the foxhole occupant diving into the hole and worrying later about how he can extract his body from the depths. The depth itself probably depends on the ground-pounder's height. I suppose, at five feet eight inches tall myself, my foxholes when complete were about six feet six inches deep.

As time allowed, I added a little cubbyhole here, a niche there, along with a shelf-like indentation in the wall of my hole. Each of these, and there might, in time, be half a dozen, was dug out to accommodate cigarettes, some form of food, maybe a metal mirror or a paperback book, or anything else I might have use for.

Short of a streamer on a parachute jump, there was no greater disappointment in life for this particular paratrooper than to get a foxhole in great shape over a period of four hours or so, only to have the word come down: "We're moving out in ten minutes." I could only hope that some other American soldier would later enjoy my creation and not an enemy soldier. I suppose most former infantry troops, when asked, could describe their favorite foxhole. Ask one and see what you hear.

As I was sitting in my foxhole recalling how close I had just come to cashing in my army insurance policy in eye-ball-to-eye-ball, arms-reach combat, Heffner came by. He had heard about the award Colonel Millett was supposedly going to get me and stopped to comment on the deal and ask what happened.

His visit was brief, and as he started to leave, he asked, "Hey, Sergeant, want a sandwich?"

Well, not having eaten a real meal in a couple days, I said, "What kind of sandwich?" like that would affect my answer! He said they had cheese, some assorted meats, and French bread. I requested a Dagwood—a huge stack of everything.

It was then that Heffner told me that they had captured a German chow truck. The Germans used half-tracks for their chow or mess trucks, which sounded just like tanks as they rolled along. We had heard that chow truck the night before, coming into Millett's position, and had been running from it half the night. Having no real weapons to use against heavy German armor, we chose to stay out of tankers' gun sights.

As Heffner departed, he called back, "Do you want a watch?" I said, "Sure," and he left me to continue licking my wounds and improving my earthy home for the meal I was about to receive.

In a short while Heffner, being the good machine gunner that he was, returned with a beautiful sandwich and an old-fashioned silver pocket watch. The watch had elaborate engraving on the outside, front and back. It had the typical large button on top, which opened both the silver cover on the front and the back of the watch.

I thanked him for each, and just as he started to walk off, I punched the release button, which opened the silver cover over the face of the watch. I closed that cover and punched the button again, and the back opened up to reveal an engraved message.

I had learned some German as a child from my German aunts. And although I knew little German grammar, I certainly could decipher the inscription I saw: *Zum Andenken an Dein erste Heilige Kommunion.* Or, *In Memory of Thy First Holy Communion.*

Man, I knew I had blown it for sure. Here I had in my hands a watch belonging to God. I called out to Heffner, "Here, please give this back to the German soldier you took it from. If he's dead, put it back on the body. If he's alive, apologize to him for me." And the sweat broke out on my face as I considered how I could make amends to God for messing with His stuff.

I could hardly wait to have Heffner confirm that he had given the soldier back his God watch. It was really a very frightening experience. The idea of nearly dying a few hours ago, thanking God for getting my butt out of that scrape, and then stealing from Him! At last, I got the word that Heffner had returned it. "Now He has His watch back," I sighed with relief. Only then did I feel that I was back in God's good graces and enjoying His protection again.

Chapter Nineteen

Patrols and Moving Out

Later that day, the Germans began shelling us with a large mortar. They had a 90mm and it was very effective, especially since they were firing it from about one hundred yards from our position, across a sandy, twenty-foot-wide road with hedgerows on either side. The mortar was giving us fits, killing both our prisoners and our own troops. We were holding the prisoners in an open field between two hedgerows, guarded by half a dozen men. Their plight was such that if they ran away from the mortar fire, our guards shot them, and if they stayed put, the mortar shells would likely take them out. It was one hell of a situation for those poor Germans.

I got orders to organize a patrol, go out the back side of our position, move away from the German mortar, then go around in a big circle, where it was hoped that we would come up alongside of the German gun.

We took a four-man patrol out the back of our position and moved in a circle to allow us to come up on the gun as instructed. We had a Browning automatic rifle (BAR) with us, a weapon that is something between a light machine gun and a rifle. It sits on a bi-pod and fires .30-caliber ammunition from a rather large magazine, and it is heavy to carry. None of the men on this weapon team was a regular BAR gunner and, like I said, there were only four of us on the patrol.

After a few minutes, one of our BAR team was hit by a sniper, so now we had an even less-effective operation. But we mushed on toward our 90mm German mortar target. Soon, we came upon two older Germans who were both seemingly stoned. They just sat in a mortar shell hole with a slight smile of surrender on their faces. It appeared that they couldn't even move.

Back at Adamson High School in Dallas, before we all went off to war, our math teacher, Mr. Clement, a veteran officer from World War I, used to tell us, "Never leave a live German soldier behind you." Those words rang in my ears as I looked these two Germans over trying to decide what to do with them. We certainly could not take them with us on this confrontational patrol. But if we left them, would they get their acts together and wind up killing us all?

They looked so pitiful, I just could not think of killing them. They couldn't even defend themselves. It would not be fair. Fair, in a terrible, inhumane war! What could have been crazier?

I decided to go against Mr. Clement's advice and let them live. I took each man's rifle and ammunition and threw them as far as I could into the weeds. As we moved out away from the two of them, each had a faint smile on his face.

We went on toward the position of the 90mm mortar and crossed the road over which the shells were coming into our position. We gingerly slipped up alongside a hedgerow, about a hundred feet from the mortar, which was manned by a squad of four or five Germans. Our replacement gunner laid the gun on the built-up dirt that sustained the hedgerow roots. The Germans were sitting like ducks on a pond, a perfect target.

Aiming the gun and being ever so quiet, our gunner squeezed the trigger. The heavy bolt of the BAR went forward, striking the massive breech of the BAR with a terribly loud clang. No bullets flew at the enemy.

Our substitute gunner had no idea what to do. I said a small prayer, something like, "Oh, shit! Did I sleep through all my BAR classes? Please, God, help me break down this gun!"

I scrambled toward the gun, trying to recall the exact position of the pin you pushed out to take a BAR apart. That much I remembered. But the Germans soon relieved us of the task of messing with the BAR. They slipped up on our flank along the hedge to our left and cut loose right down our hedgerow with an MG42 machine gun. The krauts were on the same side of the hedgerow as we were, and they were looking straight up it toward our position. The tracer bullets coming out of that gun made yet another vivid scene of death.

How I survived that moment, I will never know. At the first burst of fire from the gun, I simply flew up into the air and landed on top of the mound of dirt supporting the hedgerow roots. It was as though a Mighty Hand took me and physically raised me up to land on top of the hedge base, and the gunner's fire went right past and under me. I still think it was a miracle.

By the time the machine gun burst again, I had leaned out of this rather exposed position and was firing my M1 left-handed back down the hedgerow toward the machine-gun position. It is fair to assume our BAR men were firing whatever weapons they had as well.

In face of return fire coming mighty close, the Germans fled. They believed we'd be a perfect target at that range and were even more exposed than I was when I returned their fire. They took off with their machine gun toward their original position, adjacent to the mortar. This gave me the time to run the one hundred yards back to the road, go through the hedgerow alongside it, cross the road, and make one big dive through the hedgerow on "our" side. For a moment, I just lay there inside our position, my heart pounding like a jackhammer. I never saw the two BAR men again and have no idea what happened to them. For that matter, I never did know where they came from or who they were. Neither was from Company H of the 507th.

We later discovered that the German mortar we faced killed more German soldiers than GIs. We were all dug in and could handle their artillery pretty well, so our losses were modest, but our prisoners were lying out in the open under guard, and some of them were also killed. Some of the German shells also went too far, landing on the troops that had us surrounded. This was the fate of the two older German soldiers who I couldn't consider shooting earlier in the day. We let them go, only to find that soon thereafter they were killed by their own mortar fire.

After sunset on D-plus-2, Colonel Millett got orders from General Ridgway to move us out of our position. The object, as I understood it at the time, was to move several miles east from the interior of the Cherbourg Peninsula toward the beaches in hopes of joining up with other parts of 507th PIR, which were on the east bank of the Merderet River.

More precisely, I now understand that Ridgway had instructed us to join up with Timme's position. This was in the so-called "Timme's Orchard," only a couple of miles north of us. Millett's position had been attacked three times during the day and had taken casualties. We had kept our ground and now had 96 prisoners that we would be taking with us. Although no hard statistics exist, by the best available accounts Millett's force was now about 425 men.

Colonel Millett gave Lieutenant Stevens, one of our platoon leaders in Company H, the task of leading us out. To this day, I have no idea why he gave the task to a young officer when he had captains and at least one of the best majors in the army, Maj. Ben

"Red" Pearson, available. I must confess that there were many things I did not understand about our most unusual dilemma. The colonel must have made some good decisions—witness that I am here writing about the events.

I have since read an account of our move by Capt. Paul Smith, the CO of Company F, who states that Millett and Taylor led the way out, and that he and Lt. Roger Whiting acted as the rear guard element. This may have been the case, as I was not privy to the bigger picture, and our group soon became fragmented and disoriented in the pitch-black night. I do know that the leader I personally observed and believed to be in charge was Lieutenant Stevens, whose task was made more difficult by the fact that all of us had been in close combat for days. We were tired, hungry, fearful, confused, and, most important, out of ammunition, grenades, and other equipment we sorely needed to effectively engage such substantial German opposition.

Personally, I was an exhausted piece of humanity. I had patrolled and patrolled for most of the time we had been on the ground. In our situation, every twenty-five to one hundred yards we had to step through another hedgerow. We were often fired upon from ten to twenty feet away by Germans, and frequently with an MG42, one hell of a machine gun. I confess here that I was scared spitless, as those twenty dead German soldiers just outside Amferville could testify.

As I look back, I think I was not officer material. I was too irresponsible and careless about details. But I was a hell of a good infantry soldier. I was well trained, knew my way around in the field, could use maps and a compass very well, and had energy and stamina beyond words. Plus, I was an excellent patrol leader—in short, just the sort of soldier a company commander or platoon leader wants to have in the field.

The fact that, unlike many paratroopers in the Normandy invasion, I wound up with my own 507th regimental commander, my own company commander, and my own assistant platoon leader meant that I was well known to all of my officers. This was far from the case for many of the others in our group, especially those from other units, who were more or less anonymous as far as our leaders were concerned. As a result, whenever anyone wanted to send out a patrol, my name came to mind as patrol leader. I really liked the esteem of being held in such trust, but by D-plus-2, so much steady patrol activity had taken a terrible toll on my being.

It is impossible to overemphasize the stress of combat. Just imagine an inky black night in totally strange territory. You are moving through hedgerow after hedgerow to get to your destination. You discover what is beyond each hedgerow as you step through at the end of each one. Then, too, we had gone for three days without sleep or rest, and I had subsisted on a single sandwich and a couple of D-bars made of bitter chocolate.

I still vividly remember Lieutenant Stevens coming over to where I was lying in my foxhole back in Millett's position. I was wrapped up in my raincoat and literally bouncing off the ground as my body responded to the assault that days of patrolling had produced. When he said, "Sergeant Bearden, go out and bring in the outposts," I realized that I couldn't stand up.

I said, "I can't get up."

"What's wrong with you?" he asked. I replied that I didn't know. It was pitch dark. He asked if I was scared, and I said I didn't think so. Stevens realized that something was wrong. Rather than insist, he just turned around and let me alone. He knew, like all the other officers with Colonel Millett, that the colonel had said he was recommending me for a DSC, the army's second highest award for combat activity. Now, like the lieutenant whose tommy gun I'd borrowed for that action, I, too, was stressed out to the maximum. I had reached my breaking point.

Lieutenant Stevens got the troops moving toward the beach in single file, setting out just after midnight from the south end of Millett's CP, moving across country. I don't know who finally brought in the outpost. Whoever had the job probably had to wake up each soldier, for they, too, had been stretched to their physical and emotional ends.

I managed to get myself rejuvenated and moving along as normally as possible in the dark of night. Colonel Millett and Captain Taylor were toward the head of the column. I was between Lieutenant Hale and Lieutenant Hughes, two of the finest and most popular officers in Company H. Although a very distinct separation existed between officers and enlisted men, I had established a peculiar relationship with these two officers. They were my friends, which was not ordinarily the case with other officers, even my platoon leader, who was rather removed. In my opinion, Jack Hughes, an exceptional officer, should have been a general. He operated much like Gen. Jim Gavin.

Because of our exhausted condition, Colonel Millett and the head of the group where I was walking got separated from the back end of the column. Each time we halted for whatever reason, many men fell asleep. Because we couldn't see a single thing in the dark, whenever we resumed our march, we nudged the next soldier in line to alert him that we were moving again. He then alerted the next man, and so on. Unfortunately, it took a whole lot more than a nudge to wake a lot of us. I'd say that splits in the column occurred like this every thirty minutes or so, and eventually the head of the column split off from the rest. At one point, Captain Smith recounts, he found himself in charge of a separate group of as many as 150 men.

At the head of our column were a couple of scouts who had been assigned their duties by Lieutenant Stevens. I had been in this role when Lieutenant Hale had sent me out ahead as we passed over roads coming into Millett's position, so I had really come to appreciate the fear and anxiety of being placed all alone, and being terribly responsible for your buddies as our scouts were now.

When word came back from the head of the column to send up a tommy gun man, I knew that meant me, somehow.

The German 91st Division was everywhere, so the point of march frequently came in contact with German units and individuals as we moved east, northeast in the general direction of the Merderet. The scouts had come across something that would probably require a firefight in close proximity.

Upon hearing this request whispered down the column, I pulled Hale and Hughes together and said, "You guys stay here, and I'll be right back in a few minutes." It may sound like I was giving orders to men of superior rank, and perhaps I was. After all, they were much more to me than officers—they were my real friends.

I no longer had a tommy gun or any ammunition, but I went up the column and contacted the scouts. The two of them had discovered a German MG team in the process of setting up. We slipped through a small entrance in the hedgerow, single file, and into the field at the opposite end and opposite side from the MG nest. The only thing the three of us had left was phosphorus grenades, an ugly weapon. Once the grenade explodes, the burning phosphorus sticks to whatever it hits, and there is no way to get it off.

There was no thinking, no prior plan between the scouts and me. It was pure unorganized action, with zero coordination. We all just heard the metal machine-gun belt being inserted. All together, the three of us instinctively tossed our phosphorus grenades into the midst of the MG team. The explosion was as loud as the Fourth of July in the midst of the pitch-black hedgerows. It lit up that end of Normandy for a second as the phosphorus spread all over those poor krauts.

We literally fried the gun crew, whose blood-curdling screams and shrieks caused panic throughout our column. A shout went up, "Every man for himself!" and the whole scene came apart. The guys behind us had no way to know what was occurring. They fled every which way, except toward the horrible screaming, breaking the column apart and scattering it in all directions, as each man tried to save his skin.

The column never reorganized from this point on. Most of us ended up disoriented in small groups. Because we had mostly run out of ammunition for our personal weapons, we were using German weapons taken from enemy dead or prisoners, so throughout the night, it was almost impossible to orient ourselves by the sound of the guns. There was no way to tell who was friend or foe.

Chapter Twenty

CAPTURE

In the aftermath of the machine-gun fiasco, I think I must have run almost half a mile. The next thing I remember, I was hiding out in a hedgerow when a German patrol came by searching for paratroopers. It turned out that I was near a site where the enemy was installing a huge artillery piece. Just my luck, a grazing cow calmly wandered over and started to eat the leaves off my hedgerow, right in front of my hiding place.

I prayed the prayer of Jesus in his darkest hour: "My God, why have you forsaken me?" Except I added a flourish of my own: "After all I have done for You, Lord!" Immediately, I felt as though God had poured over my head His peace, love, and security in the form of something like honey. This peace flowed from my head to my boots, and I was relieved of all fear. I simply felt that I had a job to do as an American soldier. As strange as it may seem, I had zero fear of dying—a sensation that had totally possessed me minutes before.

Then suddenly, I heard a big "Boom!" The USS *Texas*, off-shore, had begun to shell the German artillery emplacement with their big guns. Never again would I doubt that God answers prayer. The German patrol lost interest in hunting for troopers, and I took off running again.

I soon rejoined a group of about twenty-five others, including Colonel Millett. I was still with his small group of men when later that night he surrendered to the Germans, a story that no historian has ever recorded. This surrender began my own long journey as a POW, an experience that would take me from Normandy to Paris, then all the way east across Germany to the Oder River and Poland. My incarceration would last until the Russians liberated our prison camp, Stalag IIIC in Kuestrin, at the end of January 1945.

The process of becoming a prisoner of war is humiliating, frightening, tiring, and dangerous. We were never taught how to surrender, only what information to give the enemy—our name, rank, and serial number. No military unit, objective, or such was to be revealed.

I remember thinking that the way our surrender took place was very strange, and I still think so today. Our group was cornered in a field bordered on all four sides by hedgerows. We were facing a German force of unknown size, armed with plenty of MG42s. From the outer side of the hedgerows, the enemy started firing parachute flares. Brightly illuminating everything, they seemed to hang above us for eternity, though each one lasted perhaps a few minutes. As one died out, the Germans fired another into place over our heads. They were bright enough to hurt your eyes if you looked into them. We were literally "on stage" as we lay there hugging the ground.

I am not sure if the krauts were actually able to see us hiding next to the hedgerow, but they continued to rake the pasture with their MG42s. Some were using super-fast-firing, handheld "burp guns," named after the sound the weapon made. We always said that the bullets came out so

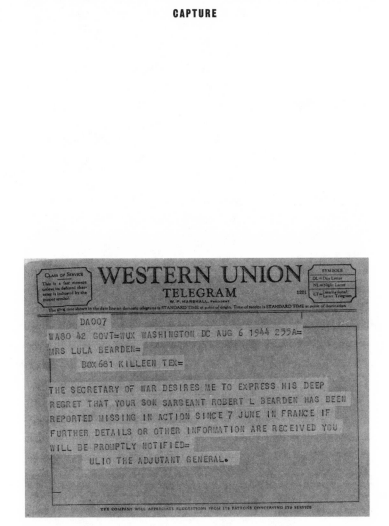

Telegram to Bob Bearden's mother reporting him missing, her first news of him, 2 months after D-Day.

fast they touched one another. The word was, "If you're hit by one bullet, you'll be hit by twenty."

As we lay there under the light of the flares, lit up like targets in a shooting gallery, the Germans remained under cover of darkness on the outer side of the hedgerows. Our only hope of staying alive was to keep low to the ground near the hedgerows, seeking the cover and protection of the overhanging branches. As the machine guns raked the field, one of the troopers just to my rear was hit with a bullet right in the groin. He suffered mightily, but refused to cry out for fear of disclosing our position. What guts!

Every minute seemed like hours as we lay pinned down, trying to pretend we didn't exist. Suddenly, I heard Tom Donahue say, in a fake German accent, "Ve surrender!"

Colonel Millett, lying to my front and just as exposed as the rest of us, responded, "Who said that?"

"I said that!" Tom exclaimed. "Then throw down your rifles and go on out," Millett said.

It was so crazy, a full bird colonel from West Point responding like that to a buck sergeant from Brooklyn, but in doing so the colonel may have saved all of our lives. I was so out of it by this time that I just wandered out into the light with my rifle in hand. A German soldier came up from behind me and just about took my head off with his rifle butt. If I ever have the occasion to surrender again (God forbid), I'll leave my rifle behind!

Just as we had searched our German prisoners the night before, our captors now processed each of us, looking for anything they could use either personally or militarily. I now had occasion to be doubly glad that I had given back the God watch. The first German soldier to search me exclaimed, "Ach, Bibel!" when he located my small New Testament. Like so many other American soldiers, I carried it in an upper front pocket. We had all heard stories about a soldier being hit in the Bible carried right over his heart and living through the wound. Fortunately, neither this German nor any other ever took my Bible.

Our immediate situation was different from most scenes of capture. First of all, it was rather obvious that most of my fellow captives and I were paratroopers because of the jumpsuits we wore, so our captors knew that much about us from the get-go. Besides, only paratroopers and glider men were as far inland as we were at that point in the battle, so the Germans knew we had all participated in the drops and landings on June 6. Rarer still, a full colonel had given us the command to surrender. I believe Colonel Millett was the highest ranking, non–air corps prisoner the Germans had. With the capture of the commander of 507th Parachute Infantry Regiment, they may also have got their first West Pointer in the ETO (European Theater of Operation).

All of us who were captured, officers and enlisted men alike, were surrounded and led away to a structure that had been used as a chicken coop. The small shed-like building had a single metal door, so one German could guard us all. The next morning, we were marched into Gourbesville and once again confined in a small frame structure, but this time with guards all around. It was in front of this building that I met Captain Taylor, who had been wounded in the right side.

"Bob," the captain said to me, "look at my side and see how badly I've been hit."

My response still baffles me. I said, "Captain, back in Nebraska, it was always 'Sergeant Bearden this.' In England, it was always 'Bearden that.' Don't you think this 'Bob' thing is a little too personal? It doesn't show much respect for my rank."

Captain Taylor just rolled over on the grassy knoll and laughed. My examination revealed that a German bullet had passed through the fleshy part of his side. Following instructions I had learned from our medic, I opened the hole and applied our all-purpose sulfa powder. He did not require any medication for the pain.

That was the last time I ever saw my company commander, although he made it back to our unit, wound and all. He lived to fight another day and to receive a promotion to major, U.S. Army. Sixty years later, I continue to seek Captain Taylor's family, so I can tell them personally that he was one great soldier.

As for my DSC, when Colonel Millett was captured and took me with him, all of his records were lost. Colonel Maloney, who took command, made other recommendations for awards based on his personal knowledge, but he had no way of knowing about my action because he was down by La Fiere Bridge getting shot at himself, while we were over around Amferville. While I am still proud to know that Millett had considered me for such an award, I realize it all happened because I was so scared of being caught alone in that pasture. There was nothing but krauts and me with my tommy gun— and they were in trouble!

PART III

TOURING EUROPE 10TH CLASS: MY LIFE AS A POW

Chapter Twenty-one

FROM ST. LO TO ALENCON

Along with hundreds of other paratroopers, Colonel Millett and those of us captured with him began the perilous journey east through German supply lines to prisoner of war camps in Deutschland. The first leg of our long journey would take us from St. Lo south and east through Normandy to a POW camp in Alencon, then on to Chartres for interrogation, and eventually through Paris.

A major concern of the Germans was to get POWs out of the Cherbourg Peninsula, for a primary aim of the invasion forces was to sever the peninsula from the rest of France. This feat was accomplished too late for me and my comrades. We were already approaching Paris when the Cherbourg Peninsula was cut off by American armored units, after the victory in St. Sauveur-le-Vicomte on June 16.

The first city of any size through which we passed was St. Lo, not too far inland from the beaches and the English Channel. One of France's most picturesque cities, St. Lo took the heaviest beating and suffered the most damage of any

French city we saw on our journey. Normally, the Allied troops took great pains in France to lessen the damage that wars naturally bring about, but St. Lo was a major road junction located uncomfortably close to the invasion sites. Similar junctions like Coutances and Valognes also took heavy, systematic bombing as the Allies tried to stop or delay the progress of German reinforcements eastward toward the front.

The huge, lengthy battle for St. Lo required the most powerful weapons available. We used heavy American bombers and the biggest artillery shells and rockets in our inventory. The bombing began on June 6 and continued almost nonstop from June 7 to 13, and even later. Though such ancient stone towns and villages were many hundreds of years old, pounding with that sort of bombardment quickly reduced them to a trash heap.

The heaviest of the bombings in St. Lo had been on June 6 and 8. By the time we got there, which must have been around June 10, it was literally in stacks and piles. It was as if a gargantuan machine had just picked up the city, put it in a bag, shook it real good, and emptied it out onto the ground like a huge pile of rubbish. The walk across St. Lo, west to east, took several hours. Passing through the town meant, literally, crawling through it. We all had to struggle to make our way around, through, and over the huge piles of this ancient and once-beautiful city. Dead animals and human body parts lay jumbled in the ruins of the cobbled stone streets.

Later in our journey toward Paris, we were joined by troops captured in St. Lo, who told us they had had to fight from house to house. By that time, Allied armored and infantry units had broken out of the beach landing positions and rolled along quite rapidly, but they stalled to a halt around June 15, a few miles east of St. Lo. The Germans were well-entrenched, and they defended the terrain with everything they had. A long, bloody war of the hedgerows developed, resulting in a month of combat before St. Lo was finally liberated by the 29th

Infantry Division. Not one building was left standing. The Americans dubbed it the "capital of ruins."

It is hard to imagine how any German vehicles were able to pass through St. Lo. They must have simply gone many miles around the city. It is proper and correct to say that no German vehicles of any sort were able to move about while U.S. Army Air Corps fighter planes roamed over France. The fighter pilots seemed to enjoy a shoot-out with any and all sorts of enemies, be they German fighter planes, infantry troops or 88mm artillery-antiaircraft units. From time to time, they just appeared, often at treetop level, and then all hell broke out.

As POWs watching these fighters from ground positions and railroad boxcars, we all became uncomfortably aware that the pilots were looking for a fight. Air to air, or air to ground, it did not seem to make any difference. Their attitude, often unfortunately for POWs, was "let's get it on." Later in prison we learned that most of the fighters we saw were returning from escorting bombers to ground targets on the continent. When the fighters had gone as far toward the targets as their fuel tanks would allow, they broke off and headed back toward England. None of the pilots wanted to return to their bases with any bombs or, for that matter, any machine-gun ammunition.

Whenever we prisoners were being transported by truck, we were very sensitive to the faintest sound of aircraft engines, no matter how far away they might seem. We knew that, at more than three hundred miles an hour, the planes could be above us in a matter of seconds with eight machine guns belching flames and shells from their wings. The German guards and drivers were even more attuned to the sounds of fighters or bombers than we were. At the slightest indication of American aircraft, day or night, all Germans "abandoned ship," jumping off the truck and heading for any hole in the ground.

Most all of the trucks we rode in had tarpaulins over the truck beds that covered us up completely, prohibiting us to see or be seen. When we heard the planes approaching, we just sat in the truck. If it seemed like the planes were coming after our particular vehicle or convoy, we unloaded post-haste at the last minute, head over heels into the nearest ditch. This procedure happened about ten times on our trip from Normandy to Paris.

We probably walked 30 percent of the distance and were trucked for the rest of the way. Most of the truck moves were at night, but on one occasion when we encountered fighter planes, we had to cross from one side of a sandy road to the other in broad daylight. This way, the fighters could get a shot at us from only one side of the road, as opposed to making a strafing run down the length of it. Of course, the pilots had no idea that the trucks they were strafing housed American POWs and that the bodies racing from one side of the road to the other were GIs.

As we were being moved out of the immediate combat zone, we spent some memorable days in a make-shift prison camp just outside of Alencon. Located to the southeast of *La Manche,* or the Cotentin Peninsula, Alencon lies just inside the border of the Department of Orne in the southernmost part of Normandy. For some reason, the town had become a stopping place for most Americans captured in the early fighting of the D-Day invasion. At the time, I had no idea that it was also the world's headquarters for fine lace, but my female friends would later assure me this was the case.

The camp consisted of a few small frame buildings surrounded by barbed wire and guards. There were two barracks-like structures with no windows and one large door, set up on concrete blocks to preclude rainwater from running through. The barracks were about twenty feet wide and perhaps forty feet long. At the time I was there, we had about fifty prisoners in each of the two buildings. Everyone slept on the floor.

There was no plumbing in the buildings, not even running water. Toilet facilities, as was the case in every prison I occupied, were a series of slit trenches dug into the earth, usually in as remote a spot as possible. The classier latrine or toilet facility had small pieces of thin concrete on each side of the slit trench where we could keep our feet out of the mud. Straddling a slit trench, elbow to elbow with fifty other men, was not my idea of a "comfort station."

There was no such thing as a cooling system in any prison in which I was incarcerated. Fortunately, while I was in the prison in Alencon, it was summer and the weather was excellent—not too hot for a Texan, for sure, though uncomfortable for my Yankee friends, especially given the total absence of any ventilation in our windowless sleeping quarters.

Alencon was rather small and was not considered to be an official camp. It had no designation like Stalag XIIA, for example, the name of the next camp I entered. I do not recall staying in camp during the day. We all went out on work details. We had no roll call, and we ate standard weak soup and sorry kraut bread. Most of our guards were older men who were mainly interested in surviving the war. Again, many were Russians who had been in the fierce fighting on the eastern front. All wore the standard German uniform. Their behavior toward us seemed largely determined by the proximity of watchful SS troops or Nazis.

Because none of us had yet been certified as POWs through the International Red Cross, we were literally "free game." With no official record of who or how many men were prisoners of the Germans, the guards who shot us suffered absolutely no repercussions. So, if old Joe Blow, a GI, was killed by guards, he was buried by some roadside. Later, his grave would be discovered, and his parents or next-of-kin would be informed of his death with no explanation ever of where, or exactly how, he had died.

On the few occasions that I observed these senseless shootings, the prisoner was always killed. These incidents severely raised our stress level. Once we were all unloaded from our boxcars on the side of the tracks. All of a sudden, a guard took out his P38 pistol and summarily shot a GI prisoner dead. It really spooked the rest of us, for we knew this person not to be a troublemaker but rather a quiet sort who never made waves. We all were aware that death could descend on any person at any time and for no reason.

There was a very effective system for keeping us from thinking about escaping. The first day of our capture, we were informed that the guards would shoot one or two other men for every prisoner who escaped. Later, when we were all registered through the International Red Cross in Limburg, Germany, we had German POW numbers and were officially classified as German prisoners of war. Germany and the United States had both signed the Geneva Convention, which dealt with conditions for POWs among many other regulations concerning the behavior of its signatories during war. Red Cross certification assured us at least of certain very marginal standards of living—or so says the Red Cross.

In fact, once we had been certified and had our POW numbers, it is true that we Americans were somewhat free of the intimidation of being shot for no reason. When GIs actually did start escaping, as they did later from Stalag IVB in Muhlburg, Germany, the Germans did not make good their threat to shoot other prisoners in retaliation. Throughout the war, all American and British Krieggies (as we called POWs) thanked God for the Red Cross, and its influence. The Russian prisoners we encountered fared far worse than we, for their country had not signed the Geneva Convention. This the Germans interpreted as giving them free reign in their treatment of Russian POWs.

Chapter Twenty-two

WE LAY TRACKS, DIG BOMBS, AND PLAY NURSE

I myself missed a good opportunity to get shot one day in Alencon. For some reason, the Germans had the delusion that they could really reconstruct damaged facilities blown up by Allied bombers. Frequently we watched medium bombers, B-25s and B-26s, flying rather low-level bombing runs at something like five thousand feet of altitude. The bombers blew up entire railroad yards—trains, tracks, buildings, and all. You could really get a good look at an air raid when it was carried out at this altitude, following the bombs as they fell from the bomb bay all the way to the target or ground.

The British and Canadian bombers always flew at night, but the Americans brought their destruction in daylight raids. It seemed to us that if the British wanted to take out a certain target, say, a railroad marshalling yard, they would make a bomb run extending for a mile or two on one side, to a mile or two on the opposite side of the intended target. This meant that buildings and sometimes open fields ended up full of bomb blast craters. The British usually got the target, but it sure did seem to be at considerable waste. In the back of our minds, we all wondered if one day we might be the victims of such all-inclusive bombings.

The pair of railroad tracks that ran through Alencon was hit big time by air raids. The tracks were blown away, and oftentimes found one hundred yards out of place. The railroad terminal, a two-story, red-brick building, had a small switch engine sticking out of its second story. The tender box, which held the coal fire to create the steam, as well as the crew-operating area, protruded out of the building, just hanging there in mid-air. It really was funny looking, and we all had a good laugh about it.

After the bombing, our job, as prisoners under considerable guard details, was to relay the track so it could be used to deliver German military supplies and troops back and forth to the western front and around eastern Normandy. Our tools consisted of picks, shovels, rakes, and heavy metal bars for lifting track sections. We were to clean up the wreckage and make a bed for laying the tracks back in place. I never saw any new sections of track, so I guess all the repairs were made with the track pieces at hand. The Russians who were converted to German soldiers could not have cared less about anything. They were just trying to survive to the war's end and protect their own rear ends. We could hardly question their attitudes.

One day during this project, fifty or so Germans, many of them high-ranking military officers, gathered around discussing how to get the switch engine out of its second-floor perch. The discussion, typically German, included a lot of loud talk and gestures. Just to needle a guard who had nothing to do with the engineering party considering the dilemma at hand, I told him I knew how to remove the engine with a simple procedure. Trying to make points with the big brass, the guard went over and told them a prisoner had an idea of how to do the task and accomplish it very simply. When they sent for me, all my buddies went crazy laughing, for I had already confided to them my plan for the project and to put it into action.

To the delight of my friends, I was taken up to the ranking officer, who spoke good English. He inquired as to my idea. With as straight a face as I could muster, I said, "Just leave it alone, lay the tracks back in place, and the U.S. Army Air Corps will come by one day, rearrange the tracks, and blow the engine right out of the second floor and into the nearby storage building."

This move, which was not very smart, got me smacked up the side of my head with a pair of beautiful, blue-gray military gloves. The other POWs thought it was wildly hilarious and laughed like mad.

In retrospect, I see I was very lucky to live to tell the tale. Why did I pull pranks like this that could have got me killed? I was no hero, but as far as taking risks go, I had spent my life in that mode. My entire experience as a POW just became a huge extension, an exaggeration, of my natural way of operating. Everything became like a great big game, where risk was the price you paid to play a good joke on a guard, or steal something from the krauts, or make their lives miserable. And I was far from the only one to act in this way. The idea was: If I can't escape or kill or wound you and take you out of this game, at least I will try to make your life tough and unproductive—and I'll take considerable risk to serve that purpose.

Back in America and England, when we had been trained on what to do if captured, the first orders were always to answer any questions with our name, rank, and serial number only. Essentially, the word was to cause the enemy as much grief as possible, short of getting ourselves shot. It always occurred to me at these training sessions that my men would do a magnificent job of following this kind of instructions. If ever a crew could "mess up," it was my mortar squad.

Our training instructors suggested many things we could do to foul things up. One example was to lay a digging tool across something so that a truck could back over it and break the tool. Well, what do you know, Bones, our mortar squad ammunition bearer, had an opportunity one day in Alencon to do just that. The only problem was that a guard was standing right behind him when he laid his pick down perfectly behind a truck as it backed out of the area. Of course, the truck broke the pick handle. Bones was delighted until the huge, angry guard poked him in the face with his rifle and led him off to the commanding officer.

As an example to the rest of us, the commander instructed Bones to start digging an unexploded bomb that had been dropped by U.S. bombers. Frequently, for whatever reason, the bombs would not explode. They just buried themselves deep into the soil and lay there ready to blow. A depression in the earth about eight feet across marked the spot where the bomb had gone into the ground. The bomb itself was supposedly about six feet under. Bones was to dig that six feet out with a pick and shovel, while an armed guard stood nearby. When he reached the bomb, German engineers were supposed to come out and explode the device.

Simply standing over the "hot" five-hundred-pound fragmentary bomb, you could almost hear it ticking away. We knew that when it went off, it would clear out a huge piece of French real estate. To appreciate the power of those bombs, all we had to do was look up at the switch engine sticking out of the second floor of the station house. The sight of that engine continued to be a real morale booster for all of us Krieggies, but we had to be careful about how much we let our joy show.

For sure, we appreciated the power of an U.S. Army Air Corp bomb, and we certainly did not want to participate in setting this one off. As Bones gently put his shovel into the ground and threw out a shovelful of sandy soil, either Duck or I would look around to be sure none of the guards was watching. Then, when the coast was clear, we threw a shovel of soil back into the hole. By the time Bones had been digging for a couple of days, the guards were screaming and cussing him out for being such a stupid, inept American. "No wonder you stupid Americans are losing the war. Your troops can't even dig up a bomb!" To which we would respond, "Yeah, really stupid!"

Bones was not past ankle deep when we were moved out of that area into another major engineering project. I really don't recommend using POWs as road construction crews.

We would do just about anything to avoid a work detail, but one of my worst mistakes occurred when I actually came up with a valid excuse. I asked to go to the hospital, hoping that they would put some warm oil in my injured left ear to relieve the pain. The German military hospital in Alencon was a major medical center for the German army, where amputations were a daily occurrence. I no sooner arrived than I encountered other American GIs, who told me that the kraut doctors used all patients, Germans included, for experimentation.

I had agreed to work in the hospital as a ward hand in exchange for a warm oil treatment for my ear. Before I had a chance to help them on a ward, a medic came over and tried to give me some medication that I did not need. I freaked out, as I was suspicious of their intentions, and split back to the prison.

The guys working the wards would come back to the prison talking about how many times they had bartered with a German patient for his breakfast or his daily fresh fruit allowance for getting the patient a drink of water. I also heard them talk about moving patients from a third floor room to the operating room on the first floor, where they would have one or more limbs removed and be back on the third floor in less than a half hour. The gangrenous odor from these amputation victims was enough to gag a horse. The word was that all of these patients died.

I was glad to take my little issue back to the prison. Sixty years later, I would jerk a tube out of my nose and stomach in a local hospital, when I had a nightmare that a German doctor was about to do some Nazi-style medical procedure on me.

Chapter Twenty-three

GIMME SHELTER

Because air raids were so prevalent around railroad stations, every rail yard I visited had plenty of holes to be used as shelters for passengers during air raids. The train crews made use of the same shelters. In Alencon, the rail line had been laid in a space cut out of a small hill around the station. This resulted in an embankment about fifty feet high on either side of the tracks. The French and Germans had gone up the sides of this embankment and dug caves into the sides of the hill about thirty feet above the tracks to be used as shelters. About ten feet square and six feet high inside, they were entered through a narrow slit about four feet wide and six feet tall. They actually made very good shelters and were deep enough to take in perhaps forty crowded people. Once you were back in those caves, you were pretty secure from bombs and strafing from fighter planes.

POWs and guards alike got to be quality air raid wardens, in that we all could hear the drone of planes long before the planes were in sight. Only by experiencing an American Mustang fighter plane screaming past at three hundred miles per hour with guns blazing can you understand the stark horror that scene projects. Although we POWs were just as scared as anyone else, we did get used to the air raids. It was possible to have a pretty good idea of where the planes would strike and what their target was, as they dropped their leftover bombs and fired off any remaining ammunition from their .50-caliber machine guns or 20mm cannon on their way back to bases in England.

For German guards to see or hear a single fighter plane off in the distance, no matter how far away, spelled panic, big time. At the slightest evidence of an air raid, they all started running for the shelters. They all wore heavy uniforms, carried long World War I rifles with bayonets attached, gas masks, ammunition belts, and large helmets. All this equipment slowed them down as, frightened, they scrambled up the embankments for the caves.

Obviously, with nothing to interfere with our movements as we ran or climbed up the banks, we POWs were able to get to the caves much sooner than any guard. About the time the P-51 or P-47 American fighter plane was making its machine-gun-blasting run down the length of the tracks, the crazed guards would just be reaching the entrance to the shelters. Two or three of us would act like the shelter was already packed by crowding up and filling the entrance. We would scream that it was full and give the guards a shove down the steep hill. They surely thought the fighters would blow them all away, when in fact the planes would usually already be past. Only the sounds of the attack lingered on.

Sometimes, a guard would make several attempts to get into a shelter, only to be shoved back down the hillside. Even today, I can see the mortal fear on the faces of those poor guards as they came clanging up the hillside, canteens and gear banging loudly, only to be shoved back down the hill, head over heels, scattering their equipment over the entire scene. As the planes disappeared in the distance, the guards would, with grateful hearts, gather up their gear and depart the area, licking their emotional wounds.

You ask, rightly so, why the guards did not shoot us for pushing them down the hill. I have no answers, except that after the raid, they were probably so happy to be alive and sharing their experiences with the other guards, that they thought little about what had just taken place. Apparently, our ruse worked: They really thought that the shelters were full, and we were just crazy with fear.

One time, however, we did all come close to being shot by the guards. We arrived back at the confinement area from a work detail just in time to discover ourselves in the midst of a huge dogfight. Some German ME-109s and Focke-Wolfes and several of our P-51s and P-47s were having it out right over the camp. They chased one another all over the French afternoon skies.

It took but a few minutes to discover the rules and tactics of the deadly game. It was a matter of getting in back of an enemy and staying there, following him into a deep dive until the poor soul either crashed or had to pull out of the dive— thus presenting a flat aircraft surface as a target for all his enemy's heavy machine guns, rockets, and cannons. Doing this meant certain sudden death. It was like a huge game of "chicken," with the stakes ratcheted way up. Who would dive their fighter plane closer to the ground before pulling out, and thus avoid becoming part of terra firma?

Almost every POW on our work truck was a paratrooper. As we unloaded, our entire group started cheering our flyboys on, just like we were at an American football game. All of us were screaming at the top of our voices, trying to encourage our "team." Every one of us, even though the guards pointed loaded rifles at us, kept rooting for our pilots.

Frequently a GI would get a German in his gun sights and pull the trigger on some very serious munitions. In an instant, pieces started flying off the enemy plane as we went into a frenzy of screams and shouts, jumping and clapping our hands. All we needed was a couple of cheerleaders.

Needless to say, the krauts took serious offense at this display and tried to herd us into the building, but to no avail. Pretty soon, they started pricking us with bayonets, threatening to shoot. With the score about four to five krauts shot down to only one of our flyboys lost, we decided we better follow orders and get our behinds into our quarters, or we really would get shot. We could hardly go to sleep for all the recapping of the victorious dogfight.

Eventually, some of us Krieggies got even bolder during air raids. We discovered that with one firing pass by the planes, we could tell what they were after. We knew that the pilots all had limited fuel by this stage and would thus not be around long or be picking too many targets, so as soon as the guards headed for the hills, we took off running for whatever interested us. Had our guards been members of the Nazi party, like SS troops, we would have all been dead—shot down like animals. But happily, this was not the case.

One of our discoveries was an Alencon warehouse that had been hit in an air raid some time back. To douse the resultant fire, the French had soaked down a ton of tobacco products stored in the warehouse, including cigars. We ran to this building several times during raids and gathered up anything of interest to eat, wear, or smoke and were never missed by guards. We were under the threat of their killing five men for every escapee.

During one such raid, Duck and I located in the warehouse some pound-sized cans of good fruit jam, slightly damaged by the fire, but edible for sure. We had been issued heavy old military coats, which had a ten-inch lining at the inside bottom. This lining would hold lots of stuff, at least four one-pound cans of jam. Well, Duck and I each loaded as many cans as our lining would hold and took off back to our work sites.

Needless to say, not having eaten a decent meal since the day before we jumped into Normandy, we had lost a lot of weight and could hardly walk, let alone run, with four pounds of jam clanging around at the rear of our coats. When we got back, the guards were loading the Krieggies back onto the trucks. With the help of other prisoners, we clambered aboard to return to camp.

Upon our arrival, wouldn't you know it—another air raid was in progress. The guards were going nuts, screaming and cussing, and some were even crying. "Get off the trucks, get off the trucks! Unload, unload!"

Duck and I had some idea of what we were about to experience when we jumped off the back of the high truck with all that jam weight behind us. Until I took a good look at the German rifle pointed at my head by a scared guard, I refused to jump. But under the circumstances, jump I must. Both Duck and I were quite short, so the shock of bailing out of the truck was a major attack on our joints. My hip problems this very day must be the result of how hard I landed, having leaped from the tail gate of that truck with a year's supply of French jam.

Back at the barracks, the air raid alarm was still going, but no bombs had landed. The bomber formation was only passing overhead—try to tell that to scared and frantic guards who had already been through an Allied air raid.

As we landed and rolled across the road, some of our fellow Krieggies dragged us into the barracks and started examining the goodies in those jam cans. Little attention was paid to the air raid sirens. Everyone broke out what bread he had and passed around the can opener. The jam lasted for weeks because there was so little bread available.

Chapter Twenty-four

BUTTERED FRENCH BREAD

This brings me to the one time in France when I had my fill of good, fresh-baked bread. This occurred when we were sent to perform a cleaning detail. Although I doubt that respect for the Geneva Convention had anything to do with our assignment to this task, it better conformed to the stipulation that officers and noncommissioned officers like myself were not to be subject to the heavy work details imposed on other prisoners.

The chore involved cleaning a mansion from top to bottom—the word was we were preparing it for an upcoming visit by Adolph Hitler. Supposedly, the Fuehrer himself was coming to the western front to see why his super troops were not doing so well against the Allied invasion forces. I hoped he'd get a good look in St. Lo.

The spacious, three-story red-brick home we were to clean had been taken from a local French banker's family. It had a beautiful red tile roof, white frame windows, and white blinds, which prevented any light from shining out of the house at night or during black-outs. The Germans had discovered, as had we infantry soldiers, that the least bit of light at night brought on air raids or artillery bombardments. The front door was the creation of some proud European carpenter or, more likely, a fine cabinet-maker. The brass door fixtures represented the best tradition of craftsmanship and a major investment of funds.

Inside, the rooms were very spacious, with fine hardwood floors. The walls were of plaster, painted white throughout. It seemed like every room had a fireplace. All the windows were large and double hung for easy opening and closing.

In every part of Europe I saw, all the better homes were graced by fine Persian or Turkish rugs. The banker's house in Alencon was no exception. These were no mere throw rugs, as we had known in America. They were so heavy that a ten-by-ten-foot Oriental carpet must have weighed at least one hundred pounds. In our half-starved condition, each of these carpets required half a dozen prisoners to carry it outside for cleaning. Beautiful, antique tapestries also hung on the walls throughout the house, portraying hunting scenes and idealized, wooded areas. They were usually in subdued, yet somehow vivid colors, veritable works of art. I cannot begin to guess how expensive they must have been. Frequently, they were as large as six by eight feet. Grouped together, they occupied very large areas of wall space.

Believe it or not, cleaning this magnificent house and everything in it was to take a single day, start to finish. Twenty of us Krieggies were assigned to the task. We reported to a German army nurse, a veteran of the Russian front who held the rank of captain. She had to have had some real heavy-duty combat experience. No one went to the Russian front for months. It was more like years. As a matter of fact, I never met a German guard who had ever returned from the Russian front at all, unless he had been seriously wounded in combat. These lucky survivors had tons of ribbons on their chest and probably an extra bread ration.

In very respect, Captain Nurse was a large and formidable person. I don't recall her name, but she was physically imposing, with a powerful voice she enjoyed throwing around. She never requested or asked, nor did she merely speak her orders. She barked with a special German quality of authority. I am sure she thought it was a great honor to have been chosen to prepare for Hitler's visit. As far as she was concerned, she might as well have been preparing for the coming of the Lord himself. Incidentally, she knew only about six words in English, none of which assisted her in dealing with her American POW crew.

Needless to say, within a few minutes the POWs had a variety of names for her, none of which are suitable for print. The B, as I more politely referred to her, had planned her cleaning project to the letter. The first step was to remove all the furniture, every stick of it, to the outside yard. Nothing was to be left inside if it was not nailed down. Imagine the weight and number of all those pieces of heavy, overstuffed furniture. On every floor there were also at least a couple of paintings, most of which were large, with heavily gilded frames.

The B decided that I should start on the third floor, scrubbing it down as if someone was going to eat thereon. I liked the idea of being way up there, because the B was stationed in the front yard, supervising the placement of the furniture the other Krieggies were bringing out.

The stairway up to the second floor from the reception area resembled that of a large hotel leading to the mezzanine. They were completely carpeted with fine, deep maroon pile. The stairs going to the third floor were not as fancy, but the carpeting was still of very high quality. The place must have had ten bedrooms, with one huge bath on each of the top floors.

Left by myself, and not having eaten a meal for days, I searched for food like a rat in a kitchen. I soon discovered the bedroom of the German colonel who had occupied these quarters before the new assignment of the building. He had eaten a big breakfast with a couple of other officers. They had bacon and eggs, toast, fresh country butter, and a jar of excellent berry preserves, topped off with a large pot of great coffee with cream and sugar. How do I know what they had for breakfast? Bless their hard heads, each left a portion on his plate and in his cup.

I have an idea just how a king must look and feel while eating breakfast, for that was exactly what I felt like. First, I bolted the bedroom door shut. The meal had been set up royally, with a fine, white linen tablecloth and napkins at each place setting. So, with my private dining room protected from the outside world by a heavily bolted door, I tucked a napkin in my neck, took my place at the fullest plate of breakfast scraps, and started dining as if I were at the Waldorf Astoria. When I had finished, mice would have been disappointed to come upon the scene. Nothing, zip, was left. I stuck a couple pieces of bread in my pocket for Duck, who was not on this detail.

The meal must have taken an hour, during which the B made a couple of appearances, banging on the door and shouting for someone to come out. The king, however, refused to have his breakfast interrupted, so not a sound issued forth. Eventually, she went back down the stairs and shouted some more at the guys who were working their tails off as furniture movers.

To top off this priceless adventure, every one of the German officers whose meals I'd finished were smokers—as was I. I had not had a cigarette since my capture, and I was vitally in need of nicotine. Each officer had left several cigarette butts and half a cup or so of sweetened coffee. The large coffee pot was also about half full. They had even left a couple of books of matches, so my breakfast party had really just got started. I lit up the cigarette butts, poured a cup of coffee in a fine china cup, and topped off my best ever breakfast.

The next time the B appeared at the door to my breakfast room, she brought help—someone to take the door off the hinges, if necessary. I slipped out a window and onto the roof, then down an outside drain pipe to the ground. I walked in the back door of the house, just as if I had been carrying furniture out all the time. The B never knew what hit her.

I began to carry furniture down the back stairwell that connected to the kitchen. Even this functional space was beautiful, the obvious creation of some talented bricklayer, with unusual cabinets of quality wood made by expert cabinetmakers. Carrying furniture down those stairs was very tight, as the stairwell was small and winding. This was fine with me, as in my weakened state, I obviously couldn't carry a very big load.

I had made a few trips up and down the stairs and through the kitchen, when I smelled the glorious scent of fresh French bread baking. A little old lady was cooking for the German officers, preparing for the evening meal, I suppose. She had churned a huge crock of country butter and had a number of large loaves of bread in the brick oven.

This was a sweet little French lady, who obviously had no love for the Germans. Her life and those of her family were riding on the quality of her work. I can imagine that when the officers came into Alencon, they checked out the best baker and commanded her to make their bread.

As I passed through the kitchen, I noticed that the lady would try to get my attention, as if she were telling me something was coming off in the kitchen. In time, the bread came out of the oven, and it was like a scent directly from heaven. I would have killed for a slice of that bread, but I didn't have to. This sweet lady, knowing that we were starving POWs who had fought to set her France free, was ready to risk everything to get a piece of her fresh-baked bread into my hands.

She was slicing the bread to standard thickness, when she saw me entering the back door. She then made a very distinctive motion with the knife to come by her. Just as I walked across the kitchen in her direction, she slid the bread into a position that allowed her to make a giant cut, about one-third, of the large, hot loaf. No rehearsal was necessary for this act. I promptly picked up the chunk of bread and headed out the back door from whence I had just come.

A twenty-gallon crock of freshly churned, French country butter was between me and the door on the right-hand side, sitting on the brick floor. I took my bread in hand and rammed it down into the butter almost up to my armpit. Outside was a two-story frame barn, with many small, compartmented areas formerly used as stalls. I located a quiet place off the beaten path of our work crew and spent another hour relishing the bread and butter. And so I completed my two-course French breakfast, a meal never to be topped and always to be cherished and remembered.

Bob Bearden, Doris Cook Avera, and Robert "Bob" Hughes, Brownwood, Texas, 1941.

From left to right, Howard White, Morris Frost, Bob Bearden, Doris Cook Avera, Bert Smith, Bob's sister, Mary Bearden, Carter and Robert "Bob" Hughes, Brownwood, Texas, 1941.

Corporal Bob Bearden in old Army blue fatigues after an eighteen-mile march, Camp Bowie, Texas, 1941.

Bob with a 30-caliber machine gun, Camp Bowie, Texas, 1941.

Corporal Bob Bearden in front of a squad tent, Camp Bowie, Texas, 1941.

Howard White, Bob, and unnamed platoon sergeant, Camp Bowie, Texas, 1941.

Corporal Bob Bearden, Brownwood, Texas, 1941.

Corporal Bob Bearden, F Company 144th Infantry. Camp Bowie, Texas, 1942, as a 60mm mortar squad leader.

Bob smoking a pipe while stationed on Baldhill out of Fort Bragg, California, on the North California coast, August 1942.

Billy Blansett and Howard White in Columbus, Georgia, on leave in 1942.

Manual Allen Deaton, alias "The Cobra," at squad tent, Camp Bowie, Brownwood, Texas, 1941.

Billy Blansett, Stinson Beach, California (KIA, March, 1945).

Eddie Keehan, Point Reyes, California, 1942.

Sergeant Bob Bearden,
Alliance, Nebraska,
1943.

H Company picture taken on Army Air Base Alliance, Nebraska, 1943.
Bob is second row from the bottom, fifth from the right.

Standing, left to right, Fred Kelley, William Stoler, Chester Gunka, Bob Bearden, and William Wolfinger (kneeling is in an unknown paratrooper), Alliance, Nebraska, 1943.

Air Base Alliance, Nebraska. Hackbart, Vermillion, Hebe, Lewis "Bones," and Keith "Duck." About to take a non-jump flight, 1943.

Clarence Hughart, Alliance, Nebraska, 1943.

Private Bradford, Private Ballingrude, and Sergeant Bob Bearden, Army Air Base, Alliance, Nebraska, 1943.

Bob and Hubert McClain, England, 1944, just prior to D-Day. McClain is buried in American Cemetery, Omaha Beach.

European boxcar, same as used to transport German POWs, 1944. Also referred to as a "40 or 8," meaning forty men or eight horses.

Furlough in Dallas, 1945: left to right, Virginia (Tencie) White Skelton, Bob Bearden and Chuck Carrell with unknown female. Both women were dance instructors for Arthur Murray.

Chuck Carrell with Bob Bearden holding his nephew, Johnny Carter, while in Dallas, on their first furlough after the war, 1945.

Bob Kelley, Alliance, Nebraska, 1943.

Bob in 1994 at the cross of his platoon sergeant, good friend, and poker instructor, Chet Gunka, in the American Cemetery, Omaha Beach.

Bob Bearden in the jeep of a World War II reenactor, near Normandy, France, 2002.

Bob and Debbie Bearden with French friends Clement and Mimi
Mouchel, Fresville, France, 2002.

Ceremony for President's Child Safety Partnership Award, 1987.
Attorney General Neese, Bob Bearden, and Ronald Reagan.

Bob in Fresville, France, 2002, with French woman, Denise Leboulanger, who was sixteen when paratroopers landed in her backyard on D-Day.

Eric Mouchel and Bob Bearden at the unveiling ceremony of the 507th PIR Monument near Amfreville, France, 2002.

507th PIR Monument unveiling, June 2002.

Bob Bearden and wife of sixteen years, Debbie.

Bob and Debbie Bearden at banquet after 60th anniversary of D-Day celebration, Amfreville, France, June 2004.

Left to right, Grandson John Bearden, Great Grandson Ian Osborn, Bob Bearden, and Grandson Tommy Bearden at the American Cemetery, Omaha Beach, June 7, 2004.

Bob and his children in 2003: back row, left to right, Tim, Perk, David; front row, left to right, Terry, Bob, Brenda.

In 2004, Bob stands in front of the house where he threw a grenade in the upstairs window sixty years earlier, June 1944.

Bob Bearden and Desire Duchemin, Fresville, France, 2002.

Chapter Twenty-five

Alencon-Paris
and a Meeting with
the Berlin Bitch

I guess we'd been at Alencon close to a couple of weeks when the guards got word that they should be ready to move out immediately upon receipt of orders from German high command. Things were not looking too progressive on the western front, and a few nights of heavy bomber raids by the British and Canadians had left massive, deep bomb craters all over that end of France.

Unfortunately for the German command, some of the roads vital to their projected hurried departure from Alencon were heavily damaged and loaded with craters. We assured the krauts that some of our men had been in road construction back home in America and that we could repair those serious potholes in short order with little or no equipment and supplies. The "little or no equipment or supplies" really interested the command, and off to the road sites we went.

The guys who made this proposal really knew what they were talking about. Their foul-up plan was so expert that some of them must have studied engineering. The craters were often twenty feet deep and at least fifteen feet across the top—really serious holes in vital highways. With picks, shovels, and axes, and under the supervision of our clever GIs, we went to work.

About four feet from the bottom of the crater, we laid large logs from one side of the hole to the other, perhaps a foot apart. We cut down all sorts of nearby trees, laying smaller tree branches across the larger limbs, then covered the smaller branches with leaves. We threw in the reddish Alencon dirt for the next few feet, and then applied more heavy logs across the expanse, before once again laying smaller branches, followed by leaves across them. This process was repeated until we reached the top of the road surface, where the new smoothed-out dirt joined the rest of the road and made a decent patch job—at least on the surface of it. The end result looked great and properly done.

It was an eternal blessing that we had all been moved to Paris, loaded onto railroad boxcars, and shipped out to prisons in Germany before the first heavy rain came to Alencon. Unfortunately for the Germans, just as the rains came along, the high command ordered all the local troops to head out. The Americans were coming! The order to evacuate included every-thing and everyone, the military hospital and all, and it all took place during the heaviest rainfall in ages.

Well, what do you know, the road repair job had a flaw. The supervisor of this little reconstruction job knew that with the first rain, the filler dirt would start dropping through the leaves toward the bottom of the hole, for the leaves were unable to contain the wet dirt and accompanying water. Soon, every smooth repair job on those twenty- to thirty-foot holes turned into a ten-foot crater.

We learned of the fate of our road job through POWs who followed us through Alencon several months later. No trucks had been able to pass over the road until very major repairs were made. Our plan also had unintentional consequences. The

German military ambulances had been lined up out on the highway, loaded with hospital patients hoping to avoid capture by the Allies, but they were unable to pass by our so-called "repair jobs." Little did we know that we also would prevent hospital patients from being transferred out of the path of the oncoming American forces.

We were grateful to be several hundred miles east of Alencon when we got the interesting news about the road caving in. I don't like to think what would have happened to us if it had collapsed while we were still at the camp. In retrospect, life in Alencon was not nearly as bad as it could have been. In fact, the days of labor we spent along the rail yard there provided about the only entertainment we would have for the next nine months. I never saw a train move over the rails we laid and cannot imagine that any train ever did pass over them.

It is hard to say exactly how long we were kept in Alencon, perhaps ten days to two weeks. From there, we were moved to Paris in German trucks that carried about twenty prisoners each. Along the way, we stopped once, possibly twice, for interrogation. The one place I am sure of was Chartres, home of the famous cathedral, where we were briefly held in a temporary prison. We were housed like cattle, or worse, with between five hundred and a thousand men jammed into a single concrete room about sixty feet square. We had the traditional fifty-five-gallon barrel for sewage, and of course it ran over. The conditions were as bad as if we'd been in a boxcar, and it was impossible to lay down without our legs hanging over another prisoner's body.

On one occasion, the guards came into the hot, stuffy room and advised our senior noncom that any paratrooper who wanted to could come out into the sunshine for a while to listen to Axis Sally. Sally, better known to us as the "Berlin Bitch," had a radio show that played all the great Big Band music we loved, interspersed with taunts against the Allies.

Before the invasion, she was a favorite source of entertainment, and her Big Band music brought me more pleasure than anything else during my time in Europe. After D-Day, I could have shot her just as dead as any other enemy I killed.

We had not seen the sun for a while, and so the vote was a quick "yes." Sally only wanted to see paratroopers, so most of us went outside and sat and listened to this dog for perhaps thirty minutes, enjoying the sunshine greatly. She looked to be about forty or forty-five years old, was about average weight, had short brown hair, and was wearing a flowery, modest dress. She addressed us in perfect English with the modest accent we had so often heard when drawn to listen to her great selection of music.

Finally Sally said, "Because I respect you paratroopers so much, I want to give each of you an opportunity to talk to your parents. You will have the chance to make a record that we will send back home to your families." After she'd gone on like this for a few minutes, the senior sergeant stood up and said, "You sorry traitor bitch, take your great offer and stuff it where the sun don't shine." Then he got nasty. He gave her a cussing out like you never heard before. All of us were of the opinion that the Germans would alter any tapes we made. We joined in, booing and cussing, and she walked off the platform. The guards started jabbing us with their bayonets and herding us back to the crowded, concrete room, and that gig was over.

At one point, also in Chartres if I recall, I was interrogated by a German colonel in civilian clothes. He was a very large man, supposedly highly decorated, who had been wounded on the Russian front. He offered me a cigarette, and we started talking about American sports, especially big league baseball, about which I knew very little. In no time, I was chain-smoking his cigarettes and saying more than I should have, going far beyond name, rank, and serial number.

He started asking me about Colonel Millett and various other senior officers in the 507th, and who they dated back in

Alliance, Nebraska. I assured him that we sergeants did not run with the regimental CO. In fact, a buck sergeant like myself never associated socially with officers, let alone senior officers, nor did they confide in enlisted men about their personal lives, unless one of them had a fight with a flyboy and threw him into the lake at the officers' club.

The most significant topic concerned the fact that the colonel and I both appreciated "good soldiers." After about an hour of visiting like this, he asked, "How many equipment bundles did you carry under your plane?" I responded, "Colonel, would you expect a good soldier to answer that question?" He literally threw my starved butt out of his office and across the hall, where I bounced off the wall with a large grin on my face. From there, a guard dragged me out of the building before I could regain my balance and walk, and it was back to the crowded cement room with the overflowing fifty-five-gallon barrel.

Chapter Twenty-six

Victory Is Sweet

The Germans kept us in Chartres for a few days, and then we headed off for Paris. For part of this journey we walked, for the rest we were trucked. We unloaded near the Arc de Triumph. The object of this stop was to expose us to public ridicule in a long march through the Paris streets. Starting with the Champs Elysees, the major thoroughfare, we moved through the city until we came to the freight yard at the Gare de l'Est. From there we would travel in boxcars to prison camps in Germany and Poland.

The overwhelming majority of the men in the columns were either paratroopers or rangers. I was still with Duck, who'd been with me all the way from the time of our capture, but we had lost Bones back at Alencon. He must have loaded onto a different truck than ours, and we had not seen him since, although I am certain he was in the Paris march.

The Champs Elysees was broad, comparable to a multilane highway. I had never in my life seen such a huge boulevard. Many of our fellow prisoners suffered from various sorts of combat wounds. Having eaten little or no food for several days, many of the men were barely able to walk. I know I half-carried a red-headed Company H trooper for one whole day and night, and he carried me the next morning when we arrived in Paris.

Tens of thousands of men, women, and children lined the thoroughfare for as far as the eye could see. As the guards started pushing us around to get the column moving, we filled the street to within ten feet of either side of the curb. I do not know how many of us there were, but we must have numbered between five hundred and one thousand, clumsily arranged in a group about twenty men wide.

By the time we got to Paris, it was obvious to all informed observers that the Wehrmacht had suffered a crushing defeat in Normandy. The beaches had been taken, the peninsula cut off, and the Allies were pushing toward Cherburg. Our captors were all the more determined to exhibit us as battered losers in a cruel and pompous public display of false superiority.

Thousands of people lined the streets jeering, swearing, and spitting at us, throwing sticks, rocks, dirt, and such from the curbs on both sides. They called us murderers, killers, and many other names. Tom Donahue from New York, a member of my company, spoke French well and reported to the rest of us the meaning of their words. This was to be the greatest hurt any of us would feel in our experience as POWs.

I wish to make perfectly clear that I felt then, as I feel now and always will, very differently toward the wonderful people of Normandy than I felt toward the people jamming those Parisian streets. Having jumped into Normandy and fought our hearts out in an effort to set these very people free from Hitler's tyranny, we could not have imagined that the German army could muster this many French to ridicule and harm us. But here they were. I have requested an apology from the French government, to no avail.

I do not know to this day who those folks represented. I just know it hurt. It was especially hard to take as we were already exhausted, physically, morally, and spiritually, especially those of us who had been wounded. We must have looked like the "spirit of '76." None of us had bathed, shaved, or combed our hair for many days, some of us had bloody bandages wound around our heads, and many were limping badly. Some were literally carried along by their buddies as we slowly moved down the huge street and through the continuous lines of Parisian hecklers.

And so we marched for several miles until we came to the freight yard at the Gare de l'Est. The only redeeming act of that entire miserable experience came toward the end, and it saved me from a broken heart.

The column stopped from time to time, as do most columns of troops. Slow down, catch up, stop, and hurry to catch up again. Waiting at one point in the midst of the shouting crowds, I glanced over at a beautiful building to my right. It was a fine structure; it looked as if it could have been an office building or even a government headquarters. The wall just above street level, raised a little to form a balcony area, contained a series of long French windows lined with lace curtains. I saw a man's face as he pulled the lace aside and looked down at the battered prisoners. It was obvious that we were paratroopers, because of our unusual jumpsuit uniforms. The American flag and the red, white, and blue AA patch, or the Screaming Eagle we wore on our shoulders, identified many of us as 82nd or 101st Airborne.

Civilian and military police were everywhere. The man peered both ways, looking guardedly left and right, trying to see if anyone might be observing him. Then, for just an instant, he gave Winston Churchill's V for Victory sign, promptly let the curtain fall, and disappeared behind it. A sensation of pride welled up in me and every other man in that dispirited column who witnessed this courageous act. In this brief moment, that Frenchman told us, in effect, "We shall over-come." My heart's wounds were substantially healed.

Chapter Twenty-seven

A Boxcar Ride to Stalag XIIA: Horrors by Day or Night

When we finally arrived in the Paris freight yards, many of us were literally carried along by one or more of our fellow prisoners. During our long journey, we had been fed whatever the German guards could scrounge from farmers along the road. Since I had jumped into Normandy, my single decent meal consisted of the leftovers I had scrounged from the officers' breakfast table on my cleaning detail back in Alencon. I was not alone in my pitiful state and was better off than many of my companions. The overwhelming majority of us were malnourished, severely underweight, and suffering from heavy fatigue and emotional stress. There were many walking wounded.

We encountered a means of travel that unfortunately would soon become all too familiar to us, boxcars called "40&8s," which could accommodate forty men or eight horses. Some of us had read about 40&8s in high school history classes on World War I. The ones we rode in looked like they had been in hard use hauling cargo for many years. About two-thirds the size of American freight cars, they were thirty-one feet long and seven or so feet wide. I never could understand how 140 Holocaust victims could be packed into one of these cars, as I have heard was the case. When the door slid shut on forty POWs, we could not lie down without our bodies overlapping, much like snakes in the zoo.

The cars were made of hardwood and painted a faded red. Our single source of meager light was two high windows located at either end of the car, about six and a half feet off the floor. They measured about twenty-four by eight inches and were covered with metal bars. There was a sliding door on each side of the boxcar, but one was permanently locked. I never saw but one door on any car opened, even after air raids. The floors of the cars were rife with splinters. Metal straps throughout held the ancient boards in place.

We soon learned that our army's traditional "hurry up and wait" concept had been adopted by the Germans as well. We loaded into the boxcars, the doors were closed and locked, and the stifling heat treatment began. It was mid-summer, so the temperature was hot. The fact that nobody had "his" space, that everyone was forced to lie with arms, legs, and bodies crossed over other prisoners' limbs, made the suffocating temperature all the worse. In the middle of the never-opened door was a metal drum that could hold about thirty-five gallons. This was to be our toilet. It would be emptied upon arrival at our destination, several days hence, never before. Regardless of how little water or food we were given, the barrels were full and running over at the end of the first day of this and all other train trips I took as a POW. The only place where the urine and excrement could go was through the boxcar, exiting via the cracks in the sliding doors or floors. When the train lurched forward, the sewage ran toward the back of the car. When the engine braked, the filth flowed toward the front. There was no dry place in the entire boxcar: front or back, we were caught in the changing tide. I thought this was the worst thing I had experienced since becoming a prisoner of war—but I'd only seen the beginning.

As we all sat crowded in our boxcar, waiting for the trip to start, a guard unlocked the door and started pushing more men into the car. We did not see how we could possibly survive the trip with forty men in there, but now the guards shoved ten more prisoners in on top of us. In the car next to ours, some young trooper had taken a little pocket knife and proceeded to whittle away a hole in the bottom of the wooden floor. The guards' answer was to split up the men in that car, dividing the group among four others. As one of the "lucky" cars, we now had fifty men.

Hopelessly locked in our forty-year-old boxcars, we were sent down the battered railroad tracks toward our unknown destination. Food was scarce. I do not remember exactly what we were given to eat, but no doubt it was mostly bread. When we were being shipped to the interior of Germany, the usual POW allotment for a five-day train trip was about six ounces of cheese, green around the edges from mold, the same amount of German sausage, and about half a loaf of sawdust bread. And you had best drink all the water you could hold, because the next drink would not be until the end of the line. Any time our train stopped where German military or civilians could be seen, "Vasser, Vasser," meaning "water, water," could be heard from every boxcar. We begged for water for as long as we stood still in the freight yard. All night long we issued the chant and heard the voices of other prisoners begging, "Vasser, Vasser," never to any avail.

This lack of water was the cause of our greatest suffering and pain, except for one other factor. We once again came under fire by the same Allied pilots we had risked our lives to cheer in the Alencon freight yard. Defended by perhaps fifty German riflemen-guards, the trains were "easy pickin's" for the fighter planes with their high-powered machine guns and cannons. Our only defense in these raids was small, .30-caliber arms fire from properly scared German guards who rode in a small frame enclosure attached to the end of each boxcar. It did not appear that there was enough room for the guards to sit in these attached guard boxes, so I assumed they stood between train stops.

We had also become the targets for the pilots' additional weapons—the six 250-pound fragmentation bombs that they never considered taking back to England. Some target, real or imagined, always caught literal hell. The motto seemed to be, "Drop the bombs on an empty hen house rather than take them back to England and have to land with live bombs hanging under each wing. Better yet, find a German locomotive smoking along some rail line and blow it to kingdom come!"

The accuracy of these fighter pilots was beyond words. They never left a column of enemy vehicles without it looking like a junkyard. The guards could do nothing but run for cover, leaving us to enjoy the train wrecking, courtesy of the U.S. Air Corps. At the first sight or sound of American planes, the engineers slammed on the brakes , jumped off, and dived into the three-foot-deep ditches that lined most railroad tracks. We prisoners could see this from the tiny window in our locked boxcars. Some of the roofs and sides of our boxcars were shredded with .50-caliber bullet holes and 20mm cannon damage.

Fortunately, each time I was in a raid, the fighter pilots mainly contented themselves with blowing up the engines into little pieces. The coal-fired steam engine boilers represented tons of pressure, so when penetrated by bullets they exploded into scrap metal. This way, no other train could pass through in either direction until repair crews could clear the tracks. This usually precluded any railroad traffic in the area for several days. In some cases after an air raid, the Germans unlocked the boxcars and the surviving prisoners were required to lay the dead and wounded along the tracks in hopes they could get medical treatment or be buried nearby.

On our trip out of Paris, I believe the pilots were aware that the cars contained POWs. It may be that our train had a red cross with a white background painted on the tops of the boxcars to indicate that prisoners were confined in them. Frequently in such cases, the Germans would load every other boxcar with POWs, alternating their human cargo with military equipment or ammunition like artillery shells.

Or maybe the pilots were too far from their base in England and did not have the fuel to hang around our train and still make it back home. After all, such a mistake could find a pilot shot down and promptly joining us in a German prison camp, eating our meager POW diet until the war's end. What a letdown, I thought, from the fantastic meals those flyboys had at their transient mess halls back in England—great chow to no chow. Years later, I would hear tapes of these really courageous guys, as they described how they lined up to blast away at a German train, having no idea that it might be full of American POWs as well as equipment and supplies.

After a long and harrowing ride, we finally unloaded just outside of Limburg, Germany, a town on the Lahn River, located about thirty miles as the crow flies northwest of Frankfurt am Main. We must have arrived at Limburg sometime in the first week of August. Here I, like most of the POWs I associated with over my nine months of prison life, were processed by the Red Cross at Stalag XIIA. I officially weighed in at 98 pounds, down from my D-Day weight of 163. Like numerous other paratroopers in our group, I had already been a prisoner for ten weeks.

We had our official POW photos taken and received our prison dog tags. This official status offered us some small measure of security against being yanked out of line and shot for no reason. Such accountability hardly seemed serious when a camp commandant's wife could have lamp shades made from a POW's tattooed skin.

For my official photograph, I had to hold a sign up in front of me with my POW number written on it. It was August 20, 1944, my twenty-second birthday. Talk about a rite of passage!

My POW number was 82-927. To this day I cannot repeat the number in English without translating it from German first. I suppose I must have repeated it a thousand times as a POW and could rattle it off perfectly in German, but I never had occasion to give this number to anyone in English.

Stalag XIIA was a transfer camp used for administrative purposes. We "Krieggies"—short for *Kriegsgefangene,* or prisoners of war—were housed in a huge German desert tent, under which about one thousand men slept on the sawdust-covered ground. We did have a bath at XIIA and were deloused, clothes and all. They must not have wanted to transfer the quality lice of XIIA to the next prison we were headed for. Through the whole of my captivity, I had only two baths, and the barracks were never deloused either time. At Stalag XIIA, I think the bath must have been a show for the Red Cross. There again, how could you delouse a huge German desert tent, where men were sleeping in sawdust? We just moved the lice around on our bodies and had to wait till we scratched them back into place.

To our delight, in Stalag XIIA, Duck and I again met up with Bones, who had somehow gotten separated when we left Alencon. Our reunion was like meeting up with a long-lost child. Duck and I had mercifully remained together throughout our whole journey, enduring the trip from Paris to Limburg in the same boxcar. That squat little New Hampshire farmer was closer to me than a brother. By the time we got to Limburg, he was so weak he could hardly stand, but he managed to get into a fight with another American over some unimportant issue. Just to think that he still had enough spunk to fight!

Platoon leader Bart Hale's V Mail to Bob's mother, August 23, 1944.

I was starting to come apart as well. I vividly remember coming out of the tent to discover a rabbit six feet tall hopping across the horizon. I knew I was losing it, truly going bonkers. Fearing I was nuts for sure, I went back into the tent and got Duck to come look at this strange thing and tell me if it was real. He went to the back fence, looked up toward the top of the hill where the animal hopped along, and exclaimed, "Bob, no lie, that is a six-foot rabbit." We went back and referred the matter to an English-speaking guard, who laughingly explained that the U.S. Army Air Corps had bombed the nearest zoo. We had just encountered our first and only liberated kangaroo.

Chapter Twenty-eight

Stalag IVB to Stalag IIIC: Learning the Ropes as a POW

We had not been in Limburg for very long before we moved out by boxcar again. We did not know it at the time, but we were headed for Muhlburg, about eighty miles south of Berlin, and internment in Stalag IVB. At the marshalling yard, we were instructed to pair up in twos. One man in each pair was to go to a bread wagon that was stopped beside the railroad tracks. Each pair was to receive one loaf of bread to split for the long trip of several days.

Duck and I always paired up for any such occasion, so I said to him, "I'll go get our bread ration and you stay here." I went through one of the lines formed up on either side of the horse-drawn wagon and was handed a loaf of sawdust bread. I put the loaf in the lower lining in the back of my overcoat and headed back to Duck, who was glad to see that I had made such a quick trip and successfully secured our share of much-needed bread.

It occurred to me that no guard took names or identified recipients when they took their bread, so I said to Duck, "Why don't you go back through the line and see if the guards will give you a loaf too?" Duck thought this was a great idea and well worth the try. If he got caught and the deal failed, he would only get hit in the head with a rifle butt.

Duck went through one of the two lines and, sure enough, to his delight and surprise, they gave him another loaf of sawdust bread. He was beaming when he walked up to where I was reclining on the sandy bank by the tracks. His first remark was, "Hey Bob, it worked."

Another instant flash of brilliance rushed into my hungry soul. What would happen if I went through the line on the other side of the bread wagon? What did I have to lose by trying? Only the top of my head to some kraut's rifle butt. Surely a whole loaf of bread was worth the risk! My little farmer buddy grinned like a man who had gotten one over on the whole world.

I got up and wandered off toward the wagon, which was parked about a hundred yards down the tracks. No one else, I'm surprised to say, had thought about this obvious scam. We had the spoils of this devious little project all to ourselves.

I slid into the line on the opposite side of the bread wagon. No guard seemed to notice me. I was just another starving, faceless Krieggie. The lines were getting shorter, and soon I was again being handed a loaf of great German sawdust bread, which I promptly inserted into the back lining of my coat. Duck really beamed when he realized we had gotten yet another loaf. I had not sat down with my two loaves before he set out for his second trip through the bread line.

By the time we were ready to load into the cars, each of us had made three trips through the bread lines and had a ten-pound stash of sawdust bread in the back lining of his coat. We actually swung from side to side as we walked, from the sheer weight of the bread. There was no such thing as a good trip on a German railroad, but this one was sure going to be better than the last—not only for Duck and me, but for all the other Krieggies in our boxcar. With the assistance of the other prisoners, we were able to climb up into the car with our heavy bread supply, and with no unfortunate events. If only we could have been so lucky as to store up a supply of water!

It is impossible for me to tell just how long we were enclosed in our cramped and filthy conditions, headed we knew not where. Every moment in a locked railroad car feels like an eternity. I do seem to recall that we were strafed by Allied planes less often than we had been on the journey from Paris to Limburg. I guess you could call this the highlight of the trip.

We finally arrived at our destination, and the guards drew open the doors. Emerging from our fetid boxcar, we cleared our lungs with gulps of clean air. We now were prisoners at Stalag IVB at Muhlburg, a large, well-organized camp about eighty miles south of Berlin, run by British noncoms. Stalag IVB was arranged into three compounds. The largest was British, and this was where we were interred. The next in size was for the Russians, who here, as everywhere else in Germany, endured the worst conditions. The smallest was for the airmen, British and American alike. Some of the men in the camp had been POWs for going on three years.

Barbed wire surrounded all the sections, which were protected by guards in towers. Guard dogs patrolled a corridor of wire forming a double exterior fence. We were housed in long, wooden barracks with bunk beds stacked four high. There was so little space between the beds that we could barely sit up. The Brits received Red Cross parcels more or less regularly at Stalag IVB and, for POWs, lived relatively high off the hog, as did I for the short time I was there.

Here Bones, Duck, and I had a joyful reunion with another fellow squad member, Fred Kelly. After feeling much angst about where "poor ole slow Fred Kelly" might be starving, we

POW form to be used for sending correspondence to prisoners in World War II.

discovered that he had been working in the kitchen at Muhlburg and was heavier than we had ever seen him. He was assigned the task of firing the boiler to keep the kraut guards supplied with hot water. He did such a good job that he was allowed the run of the entire IVB kitchen, which he looted on a daily basis. Every prisoner who was sentenced to solitary confinement found he had been promoted to a better diet thanks to Fred Kelly's food service, delivered directly to the holes where the prisoners were confined.

Although we always had access to news one way or another in prison camps, Muhlburg was the only camp I know that had an organized system of distributing daily news. This came from the BBC, and none of us knew where the radio was hidden. I hear tell that the various parts were disassembled and hidden with numerous individuals, then reassembled for the daily news.

At a certain time for each barracks, a Krieggie would come around with the "football scores," which is what we called the news from the front. Someone would come by in advance and say that football scores would be shared in fifteen minutes inside the barracks. The barracks leaders assigned men to guard each entrance, and all the inhabitants would gather in the center of the building. The news-bearer walked in quickly and read the daily news about the war's progress. In a matter of five minutes, he had covered all the significant events, relayed any comments from the camp leadership, and was gone. We could tell from what we learned of the movement of Allied forces on both the eastern and western fronts that the German troops were under great stress.

It was also in Muhlburg that I became familiar with the concept of "muckers," which we learned from old Canadian POWs. A mucker was a fellow prisoner with whom you could relate and share everything from food to cigarettes, blankets, and anything else of value, including mail from home. For sleeping arrangements with a mucker, we never removed any clothes except our overcoats, which went on top of the both of us, along with anything else that might trap body heat. This system of pairing up, also in place at future prisons, saved many a life, especially given the cruel and bitterly cold conditions in the winter of 1944.

Chapter Twenty-nine

STALAG IIIC, KUESTRIN: WILLKOMMEN!

In early September 1944, the German commandant at Stalag IVB advised the American noncommissioned officers that they were to gather up their belongings in preparation for a train ride to another prison. The expression belongings was nothing short of a joke. Again, we did not know our destination, but our new prison was to be Stalag IIIC at Kuestrin, Germany, about forty miles east of Berlin. This small town, called Kostrzyn in Polish, is situated on the east bank of the Oder River in what is Poland today.

This move was not good news for me, for it meant that I would now be separated from Duck, Fred, and Bones. Privates all, they could not accompany me. Each would wind up in a prisoner work project, such as coal mines or other hard labor. This scared me, sort of, because I had come to really love these crazy guys, who perhaps made up the best 60mm mortar squad in the U.S. Army. I can assure the world that there are German 88 crews who believe to this day that there was at least one hell of a 60mm mortar squad in the D-Day invasion—ours!

The day after the notice that we would soon depart from Stalag IVB, depart we did, and with much apprehension. As we loaded up for the dangerous trip under the ubiquitous rifle-bearing guards, I knew I might never see Duck, Bones, or Fred again. Inside the crowded boxcar, I felt the heavy burden of solitude, despite the fact that my arms and legs were intertwined with those of other prisoners.

The train headed out in what we thought was a northeastern direction. The idea that we might be going to Berlin, the number one target of all Allied fighter planes and bombers in Europe, was terrifying to us all. Years later, we would understand that this was part of the price that was paid for the freedom we all cherish. Freedom is not free at all.

The trip was a long and frightful experience that lasted several days. It did, indeed, take us to the dreaded Berlin freight yard, and it was here that we had the most notable experience of our long journey. Our train was deposited on a rail siding in the middle of the freight yards. This was the marshalling yard, where the various trains were made up. Boxcars were switched around to make up a train both day and night, but most of the work was done in the dark. This precluded lighting up the freight yard as "target for the night" for the Allied fighter and bomber pilots.

We must have been parked there for two to three days. We were locked in, left without food or water and no idea of how long we would have to wait. The heat was sweltering. Our toilet barrel was overflowing, flooding the floor with raw sewage.

Here, as any other time we were stopped in a train station, or even on some railroad siding out in the country, people came by just to see what American prisoners looked like. They couldn't actually see us because there were no windows except the high, narrow slots at either end of the boxcars. These would-be onlookers were subjected to the mournful cry of "Vasser, Vasser!" Once again, I never saw anyone get any water from this process. We even begged the guards for a drink from their personal canteens, but neither our effort nor our misery produced a single act of kindness or relief.

Both bomber commands, the Allies and the U.S. Army Air Corps, were bombing Berlin around the clock. We had seen enough of Berlin from our boxcars as we pulled into the city to realize that it was being laid to waste much like St. Lo. Judging from the view from our narrow, barred windows, nothing was left but a huge pile of rubble. Stifling in our stationary boxcars, we knew we were sitting ducks.

The raids could happen at any time: the Americans continued to bomb during daylight, and the British or Canadians at night. The guards, of course, ran for air raid shelters at the first sign of approaching bombers, as we prisoners were securely locked in the boxcars. We, too, could hear the sirens and the planes coming in, but all we could do was scramble thirty-one feet in one direction or seven feet the other way, over slippery floors flooded with several days' sewage. I have never heard so much praying in my life, nor have I seen so much of God's grace. Miraculously, none of us were killed in the freight yards. We all gave thanks when our Berlin experience was over.

Three days parked in a freight yard may not appear to be a long time; nor does an air raid, which lasts about ten to fifteen minutes, seem so long a time. But believe it, just as eight seconds is a very long time to stay on the back of a raging rodeo bull, sixty seconds in the middle of an air raid is an eternity. It is much more fearsome when you can't run and hide or look for some low spot in which to find cover. We kept wondering, "Where is the Red Cross?"

Imagine our excitement one sweltering morning when we felt an engine attached to our train of boxcars. Conditions had now become life-threatening. We surmised we were bound for a camp for NCOs, but we still had no idea of where that might be or how much longer we would have to hang on without food, water, or exercise in the airless dark interior of our boxcar.

Thank God, we did not have far to go. After a relatively short trip, we unloaded from our cramped quarters at Kuestrin, Germany, the prison home of about two thousand U.S. Army noncommissioned officers. We were only a small part of the camp, which housed thousands of other nationals, civilians and soldiers both, who represented almost every country on the continent and every possible political status. Most of the Americans at Stalag IIIC had been captured in the early days of Normandy. As noncommissioned officers, our status according to the Geneva Convention prohibited the Germans from using us as labor for any heavy work details within or outside the camp. To my knowledge, we were the only group in the camp with this privileged status.

The buildings where we were housed were all prefabricated, delivered in sections, and assembled on site. Each frame and tar-paper barracks consisted of three rooms measuring about twenty by thirty feet. In the middle of the room was a small metal stove with a tiny door for stuffing in coal or anything else that would burn. Each Krieggie was issued a weekly ration of one small handful of coal.

Our barracks room had two wooden platforms, one on either side, to be used as sleeping pallets. The upper-level sleeping surface was so low that when you sat up in the bottom section, your head about hit the level above you. Ten men slept on the floor on either side of the room, and ten more prisoners slept up on the top deck or platform. Thus, each room held 30 to 40 prisoners, for a total of up to 120 men in each building.

We were issued old Hungarian army uniforms and overcoats with the letters "KGF" (for *Kriegsgefangene*) written across the back of the coats and both pant legs. A cotton mattress cover stuffed full of hay served as our bed. The daily menu consisted mainly of a cup of watery soup and a slice of sawdust bread. Krieggies lucky enough to discover a little piece of horse meat in their soup would put it on display for an hour or so—it was that rare of an experience.

We used our coal, supplemented with wood chips, to cook potato peelings or anything else we could scrounge, heating them on the metal stove in the middle of the room. Soon we developed a clever system of "blowers" designed from metal cans for firing up coal chips and dust, or wood chips if we were lucky enough to have them. The cans came from the powdered milk, or Klim ("milk" spelled backward), contained in Red Cross parcels.

Our toilet facility or latrine, as we knew it, was a thirty-by-thirty foot frame building set over a series of one-by-two-foot slits in a concrete floor. Under this was a huge hole into which the sewage fell. Each hole had a pair of concrete blocks about two inches off the floor. We squatted down with a foot on each block and did our business. If you wonder why ex-POWs seldom complain about resources available to the average person today, consider this—we had no toilet paper, ever.

Our main guard was known by the name of O.K., after the only word he knew in English. Not much was okay with O.K. He never spoke, only screamed. He was not a happy camper.

If you have ever seen a photograph of a motorcycle policeman of 1935 vintage, or a Greyhound bus driver around 1940 to 1950, when they wore breeches with boots and a billed cap, then you know how O.K. looked. A German senior sergeant and veteran of twenty years, he was about fifty-five years old, and five feet five inches tall. He wore several medals, in which he took great pride, and packed a bad P38 pistol. I never saw him without his bus driver cap or his P38 strapped to his side. He ran that pistol muzzle up my nose so many times, I thought it belonged there!

Chapter Thirty

DAILY LIFE AT
STALAG IIIC:
PALS SO GOOD AND TRUE

Roll call took place every morning and evening, and was organized by room assignment out in the middle of the compound. O.K. showed up with his clipboard and pencil and lined us all up in eight rows, with five men in each line. Starting at the first man on the left hand end of the first row of prisoners, he walked down very slowly, counting each pair of feet as he went along, looking down all the while. I can hear him now, "ein, zwei, drei, vier," counting slowly in German, clipboard in hand.

One of our favorite amusements was to frustrate O.K. and send him into a rage. Three to four times a week, some Krieggie would run around from the back row, first line, and take a spot outside the last man on the front row. Thus, when O.K. got to the end, he had not eight rows of prisoners, but eight rows with one extra man. It was not uncommon for O.K. to go through this process three to four times, getting hotter with every rerun, writing his findings on his clipboard with each trip down the line. Time and time again, he would strut back down to the start and count each pair of feet, until he finally threw the clipboard at someone and went into a literal fit.

Another trick we would use on O.K. was to have a Krieggie in the middle of the group dig both his feet down deep into the sandy soil, until his head could not be seen from the front row. O.K. would think he was missing a man in the ranks and start to boil. Soon, he would yank out his P38 and wave it around in face after face, screaming and threatening to shoot us all. Then we lined up properly and let him finish his body count. Thank God, he never pulled the trigger.

Food, of course, was a major issue. Several weeks before I arrived at Kuestrin, I weighed in at Limburg, Stalag XIIA, at ninety-eight pounds. I had lost sixty-eight pounds of solid muscle built up from years of calisthenics and training runs. Most of the guys in the barracks were in the same condition, down fifty to seventy pounds from their weight on D-Day.

In the mornings, warm ersatz coffee was delivered from the kitchen in a wooden barrel. A few guys tried to drink it, but most just used it to shave with. Our bread ration usually became available about 10 a.m. The most important daily issue at Stalag IIIC was not "how is the war going?" but "how many men on a loaf?"

Usually the answer was six men, meaning that we would draw one loaf of bread for every six prisoners, or about six and a half loaves for forty men. Then came the critical slicing of the bread. One man usually established himself as the best in the room at the awesome chore of cutting the loaf to the day's directive, in five, six, seven, or eight slices, all the exact same size. Absolutely nothing was more important than this process. The man doing the slicing took his personal piece of bread last, which meant that if the slices were not even, he suffered the consequence of a poor job. For his effort, and for using his blanket as a cutting surface, he got to shake the blanket when he finished, and could gather up the crumbs from the cutting of the sawdust bread. This very important daily routine was carefully observed by everyone in the room.

After we took our individual slice, most POWs cut it up into quarter-inch squares, and placed the little cubes in a square piece of cloth that we folded into a pouch to avoid losing any of the bread. We carried this little cloth pouch with us everywhere we went. If we ran into a friend as we moved around the compound on our daily routine, we would sort of pull aside, break out our bread stash, and nibble on it, a morsel at a time, while we were visiting. This way, our bread ration lasted most of the day and helped us to avoid severe hunger. The act was never mentioned, it just happened in the life of a great many of us. It certainly was a major part of my daily activity, a Krieggie tradition, almost like the British having tea.

If for any reason a Krieggie could not be present at the morning bread slicing, the process was monitored by his mucker, who retrieved his absent buddy's bread ration for him. Although we learned the concept of muckers from seasoned POWs at Muhlburg, my one and only mucker was at Stalag IIIC, Kuestrin. Muckers not only slept together, sharing blankets and body heat, they also shared everything else of value, from food to cigarettes to mail from home.

My mucker's name was August Valacallie, from Maryland. Everyone called him Auggie. He was a mama's boy who never left home until the war, a short, balding, round, thirty-five-year-old Italian guy. You wondered who accepted him into a combat infantry outfit.

Auggie and I associated mostly by preparing whatever meal we could come up with, and we shared our bedding on the wooden floor. He tried gambling, which was a favorite pastime in the barracks, but he was a failure at it. Generally speaking, he was just too nice to be a GI, let alone a Krieggie.

Other than his niceness, Auggie had one other outstanding quality: he did not smoke. This meant *we* could use *his* cigarette ration from our shared Red Cross food parcels to trade
for additional food stuff—*and* I could still continue to satisfy
my nicotine habit by smoking my own cigarettes.

We were all continually on the lookout to get anything we
could that was fit to eat or drink. One day, when the kitchen
truck came into our compound to bring our daily bread ration,
a young POW was so anxious to steal something that he ran
along beside the truck, then jumped up, and tried to grab some
extra bread. The road was surfaced in cobblestones and not very
stable for running. This coupled with the fact that the Krieggie,
like most of us, weighed only about one hundred pounds and
was therefore not too steady of foot. The kid lost his balance,
fell under the truck, and was crushed to death. We all wondered what sort of death notice his mother would receive. Most
of us had grown pretty callous since our entry into Europe on
D-Day, but this soldier's death bothered a lot of the men in our
compound. It was just so useless and uncalled for.

Although I had been separated from Duck, Fred, and Bones
when I was sent to Stalag IIIC, I did know at least a few
Company H 507th men at our camp. Among them were John
Montgomery, a communications man, and Tom Donahue, a
squad leader. Then there was George Forte, who had made those
unlucky parachute landings back in Denver and on maneuvers in
Louisiana. Come to think of it, I had not been so lucky on
maneuvers myself. I participated in Louisiana Maneuvers three
times and got captured on every one. Looking back with perfect
hindsight, I can't help wondering if this wasn't a warning about
what was going to happen when I got to the real deal.

Like me, George was a three-stripe buck sergeant and a
squad leader in the 3rd Platoon. Neither of us had any duties
or authority in IIIC. This was not the case for the other

Company H man I knew at the camp, First Sergeant Marco, who was in my barracks. Marco was older and in the line of authority at IIIC, which was determined by rank and date of rank. He was one of the people who had knowledge of the radio and who received word from England as to what we POWs were to be doing and not doing—for example, there were to be no escape attempts late in the game when the Russians were nearing the camp.

Marco was always solid and continually demonstrated a steady hand. He was one of my favorite Krieggies with whom to visit and share the daily bread ration. The fact that my squad had assisted him to re-establish his jump status back in Nebraska helped to form a bond between us. We shared a definite mutual respect.

I also recall several of the guys in my barracks room, although I can't remember all their names. One unforgettable character I'll call "Mickey" was a twenty-year-old ranger, tough as nails, about five feet eight inches tall. He was all steel and ornery as rangers could get. Mickey was never found lying on his back because he had a solid trench across both cheeks of his butt, where he caught a .50-caliber shell while climbing up a rope ladder with Col. Earl Rudder of ranger fame on the D-Day beaches.

We paratroopers always needled the rangers about so many getting hit in the butt, suggesting that they all were hooking it out of Dodge trying to get back to England, but we secretly admired and respected them and their great contribution on D-Day. But compliment them? Hell, no! Nor would they compliment a paratrooper. As a matter of fact, Mickey's favorite paratrooper comment was that all paratroopers jumped in combat with a Red Cross food parcel under one arm and a white flag in the other, looking for a kraut to surrender to.

One night, Mickey was rattling along about his one-of-a-kind girlfriend—she should have been a movie star, she was so beautiful and built like a Broadway dancer. The lights were out in the barracks, and he was on the lower level across the room from me. He kept on talking, even getting into the fact that she had been the youngest contestant ever to win the women's East Coast Amateur Tennis Championship, although he never mentioned her name.

After listening to him ramble on about his great girlfriend tennis player for about an hour, it suddenly became obvious to me that she was my former mixed-doubles partner in Dallas. We had enjoyed much success and fun playing teen-level mixed-doubles tennis tournaments together when we had been about fourteen. Her father, a *Dallas Morning News* printer, had taken a job in Washington, D.C., where he moved the family, and she had resumed her tennis career.

When Mickey finally took a breath in his presentation, I said in a loud voice, "How *is* Marilyn, anyway?"

He screamed, sat bolt upright, and just about got a concussion when he hit his head on the boards of the sleeping pallet above him. "Who said that?" he yelled.

"How was Marilyn when you last saw her?" I asked again.

He came scrambling across the room on all fours. "Who the hell said that?"

From that moment on, I could not get away from him. All he wanted was to keep telling me how great Marilyn was in every respect. Incidentally, she was all he had suggested and more. She went on to tennis fame in that end of the country, but I'm sorry to say, I never saw her again.

And how could I ever forget Dom, short for Dominick—a real live American hobo who came from who knew where into Stalag IIIC. Dom was attired in entirely appropriate hobo garb. Rather than a military uniform, he wore a tattered, super-large sports coat and very baggy pants with GI brogan shoes.

The really interesting thing is that Dom had a voice like an opera singer. Within a few days of his arrival, he was regularly entertaining our end of the prison with his beautiful rendition of classic songs. His singing was just as impressive to the guards as to the prisoners. We all especially appreciated his concerts as the season wore on into winter, approaching Christmas.

Dom said he developed his powerful voice by singing above the noise of a freight train going down the tracks as he wandered back and forth across the country. His most request-ed song went something like this:

> With someone like you,
> A pal so good and true,
> I'd like to leave it all behind
> And go and find
> Some place that's known to God alone—
> Just a place to call our own.
> We'll find perfect peace,
> Where joy will never cease,
> And leave the rest of the world behind.

By this time, we were all so lonesome for home and fami-ly and friends that tears were not far behind, even for the toughest among us.

Chapter Thirty-one

RED CROSS TO THE RESCUE

Almost every day at one of our roll call formations, several men would pass out and fall over in the sand. You would hear a klunk; it was really no big deal—just another Krieggie hitting the dust! Initially, it did get our attention, but roll call was never interrupted just because someone passed out from malnutrition. Fortunately, the sand was soft, and no one ever seemed to get hurt from the fall. Roll call lasted perhaps thirty minutes, depending upon how much hassle we heaped on poor old O.K., but that was too much time for a starved GI to handle standing in one position.

Personally, I am convinced that death from starvation is not all that bad a way to go. There was no feeling of pain when I weighed ninety-eight pounds. You simply get to where you are so hungry and weak that you can't stand up. I never fell over during roll call, but many times I certainly recognized that I was almost to that point. Those who passed out were simply hauled back into the barracks, where they came to in a little while.

During my months as a POW, I received five or six American Red Cross prisoner of war parcels. Words cannot described the high degree of excitement and anticipation all of us felt on Red Cross parcel days. Some POWs believe that they survived because the parcels, few as they were, gave them the strength to hang on from parcel to parcel. For many, it was literally a question of life or death. We would sit and frequently talk about how big a note we would sign for a Red Cross box. The numbers were astronomical, like two hundred dollars per parcel. I would have eagerly been one of them, for sure. When man is hungry, really hungry, he will do anything, even kill, for food.

American and British Red Cross parcels were significantly different. The Limey packages naturally appealed to their troops' taste, just as the American Red Cross supplied five-pound parcels containing items we ate back home. They contained things such as margarine and Klim, several packs of cigarettes, some form of chocolate bar, and sometimes coffee. Spam, a processed meat in cans, was a parcel staple that we army types were always happy to receive. The air corps people hated Spam because they had been fed so much of it back in England.

Each parcel was usually split between two men who were muckers, although the packages were intended to be issued one per man, once a week. It was common knowledge that as soon as the parcels reached German hands, the stealing began. A large percentage of the food went to German officers, freight handlers, railroad employees, and anyone else who happened to get their hands on the shipments.

Without exception, when we did receive a parcel, we immediately sat down to a real feed—a truly filling meal. That night when the lights were out, the talk would inevitably turn to women. During times of real hunger, all the conversations had to do with food. These tall tales only got taller as the session wore on into the night. No four people could possibly have eaten the food laid out on those tables we imagined.

The talk most often went like this, "Back in Chillicothe, Ohio, where my grandmother lives, I used to visit during the summer when school was out. For breakfast she would always fix me about six slices of bacon, four fried eggs over easy, five slices of toast, a pan of biscuits, and a couple of big glasses of milk. I always also ate at least two bowls of oatmeal or cold cereal. Man, could my grandmother cook."

Another common practice among Krieggies was to take small scraps of paper and write out menus to be prepared when the person got back home. These meals were even more far-fetched than those recalling Grandma's cooking. First, the schedule for a single day usually called for about six meals, to be eaten every few hours from sunup to bedtime. If you wanted a fight on your hands, just challenge the menu preparer with something like, "Hey man, you couldn't possibly eat that much!" This was probably the best way I know of to get into a fight. Personally, I never wasted valuable paper preparing a menu, though I often thought about the voluminous meals I had eaten as a kid at my old German great-aunts' house.

On Red Cross parcel days, the bull sessions were different. As the guys started laying their bodies down in their sacks, one would say something like, "One time I had a layover in Saint Louis on the way home on furlough. I met this beautiful nurse in the train station and it was love at first sight. I immediately forgot that I was going home to become engaged," et cetera, et cetera.

The next character would start his tale with something like, "When I went home on my jump school furlough, my neighbor's cousin was visiting from Oregon. Before I left in two weeks, we were planning our wedding and I made out an allotment to her so we would be able to get married as soon as I get back home." This was also the context in which Mickey revealed his undying love for the truly beautiful tennis star, Marilyn. And so it went, on into the night, getting more vivid about the lovemaking scenes, until we fell asleep with full bellies.

Of course, gambling followed us into POW life. This took place only right after we received an issue of food parcels. The coin of the realm was cigarettes, and every American Red Cross parcel contained several packs. Everything from haircuts to a little bag of oatmeal had a price: it was x amount of cigarettes for x service or x amount of commodity.

As soon as we had eaten, it was "Let the gambling begin!" Some creative prisoner would have hustled up some lightweight cardboard and cut it into small pieces to make a deck of cards. They had no color, were hard to read and easily marked, but suitable for playing poker. Candles were a real luxury, so seldom did we gamble after sundown.

The guy who was the "house man" furnished the blanket and cards. For his service, every half hour or so, he would have every gambler pick up his stash while he shook the blanket and recovered all the tobacco that had fallen out of the much-handled cigarettes. Of course, when he smoked the dregs, he was also smoking wool particles along with the tobacco, which created a terrible stench in the room.

I particularly remember playing poker with a small trooper named Idris Lassiter, a rifleman from Florida, and George Forte. It was with George, also from Company H of 3rd Platoon, that I invented the 60mm mortar sight. He was a near-engineer, but not much of a poker player, and neither was Idris.

Idris was one of the Company H barbers from the 3rd Platoon. He was quite short, about five feet four inches tall, and weighed 130 pounds. He was not formally educated, but he sounded as if he had been to college and was very intelligent. Although he was seldom in a fight, Idris had a temper and would take on a buzz saw if he was drunk. He was slightly bald, and older than the rest of us, about the same age as

Chet Gunka would have been if he had survived, and he always had a wise word for all of us younger crazies. Idris and Chet had been great friends back in Alliance, and I'd been friends with them both. I know I sometimes thought of Chet as I gambled with Auggie's cigarettes and those old marked-up cardboard playing cards. I guess you could say his spirit was with us, even at Stalag IIIC.

To preclude us storing up food for an escape attempt, the Germans tried to punch a hole in every can of food so it would spoil if it were stored. My days of hustling from depression life back in Oak Cliff now prepared me for a major hustle—how to get cans of food from our Red Cross parcels past the kraut guards.

The hustle was a snap, but I really needed an extra five fingers on one hand. One prisoner opened the parcel and took out the cans of food and slid them over to me. I held the can while the unsuspecting guard drove a nail through the top of it with a hammer. Now the can was of no value as a stored item. I then put it into an empty Red Cross box, took another can, and held it in position for the guard.

After the guard had punched about three cans, I started to substitute the cans he had already punched for the fresh cans. I used my fingers to hide the holes, and let the dummy punch a second hole in the same end or, in time, in the opposite end of a can he had already punctured. Then we graduated to side punches, still on the same can. Scoring this game was determined by the number of cans that came back to the barracks with holes in them and how many were hole free. It probably provided as much satisfaction as any event of my life, getting one over on the krauts and being a kraut myself!

The krauts' big mistake was basically a problem of perception. They really thought we GIs were stupid, because we continually messed up everything they gave us to do. In fact, we messed up so well that they never caught on to the scams that we were pulling right under their noses.

Take, for example, the huge hole, four to five feet deep and about eight feet square, that we excavated under the floorboards of our room. All our prison barracks had double walls and floors as protection against the bitterly cold German winter. We had no sooner arrived at Stalag IIIC than the possibilities presented themselves. We cut part of the bottom layer of our floor to slide away and raised a portion of the top layer up, leaning it against the top sleeping platform. The idea was to provide a hiding place for any unauthorized items, including the cans from the Red Cross parcels we managed to salvage from the hole-punching process.

Every one of the forty men in that room probably had something down in the hole. Digging the hole, literally by hand, and hiding the sand from the guards, was another story. The sandy soil was damp from being under ground. We had a team that put the loose, wet sand in their pants pockets, then walked around the prison compound, carefully burying handfuls of wet sand. At first, while the season was still warm, we buried it under the dry sand; later, we shoved it under the snow.

Although we had no precise plans for escape, the general idea was to store up enough food to allow us to make a break for the town of Steteen up the Oder River. Getting to Seteen was a personal goal of mine. The whole idea was nearly impossible, with no better likelihood of succeeding than the success of any of us in speaking passable German. Although we never broke out, our storage hole became more valuable in our chaotic so-called "liberation" by Russian troops in January 1945.

Chapter Thirty-two

Deutsch fur Amerikaner: Swaps and Scams at Stalag IIIC

As winter set in, life went on in Stalag IIIC with many ups and downs. Although we had the privilege of receiving mail, I received no letters during the whole time I was a POW. I later learned that Bart Hale had written my mother in Killeen, Texas, telling her I was a good soldier and that the Germans were treating prisoners well. He also said that Colonel Millett was recommending me for a DSC for action near Amferville. She had written a V-mail to me at Stalag IIIC saying, "Oh, Bobby, we are so proud of you, for Colonel Millett is going to give you a DSC for killing all those Germans." It was returned to her with the censor's remark that "Sergeant Bearden would not want to have his Stalag commandant hand him a letter referring to killing 'all those Germans.'" Somewhere we lost that letter over the years, though we still have the "missing in action" letter that was sent to my mother after I was captured in Normandy as well as Lieutenant Hale's letter to her about Millett's getting me a DSC for the big shootout I had alone with the krauts near Amferville.

To help make up for this dearth of news, a buddy from the 508th PIR generously asked me if I would like to read a letter he had received, as if it were my own news from home. This was an important letter indeed, from his bride back in the States, and he had read it at least fifty times. In this, his first and only communication with his family, she told him about their new baby girl. It was an overwhelmingly kind and considerate act for this trooper to allow me to take his priceless letter and read it as if it were my own.

The worst day of my life, worse even than getting wounded or captured, was when I dropped his letter into the latrine. There it fell, ten feet down into a dark pit of sewage. I almost died with remorse when I had to go and tell my friend what I had done with his once-in-a-lifetime treasure. How he could ever forgive me I do not know, but he did, and without hesitation. He could see how hurt I was, and all was forgiven. We remained friends, but to my knowledge, he never received another letter from home.

I also vividly remember the day that O.K. ordered me to head up a detail to carry out some Red Cross parcel cans that had been piled up for weeks after we'd received a parcel shipment. He told me to bring about six men and gave me a mattress cover full of huge holes in which to collect the cans. The cans were typical grocery-store size, containing things like Spam. They were rather small, certainly much smaller than the holes in the mattress cover that we were to use to carry them.

I gently suggested to O.K. that if we loaded this pile of cans on the hole-filled cover, they would all fall through as soon as we picked it up. He kept insisting that we load up the cans and take them out to the trash heap where, incidentally, the Russians dumped their dead comrades on a daily basis. Much worse off than we, they were freezing to death and dying of starvation and disease at the rate of several each day.

I finally took a can and, holding up the mattress cover with all the holes exposed, I showed O.K. how a can was going to fall through as soon as we raised up the cover. This illustration he rightly took as a reflection on his intelligence, and it warranted a raving, gun-toting fit. For the tenth time I reckon, he stuck that P38 up my nose and just about raised me off the ground. With that, I told the rest of the detail to load the cans and start walking toward the gate. This we did, streaming cans along the way as they fell through the holes. I told the guys to keep walking. We then came back and picked up all the lost cans, a task we performed to O.K.'s satisfaction.

Every time I got one over on the guards, I thought about being left in a locked boxcar during air raids by American fighter-bombers. This was an experience that I, like most American POWs who survived to tell the tale, endured more than once. Although most of our scams were aimed at getting food, any and all rip-offs of the Germans were more than a victory for the stomach.

My hardscrabble life back in the depression, as well as my German background now, combined in my favor. Prior to my mother's death when I was seven, I was made to learn to speak German. At the dinner table, for example, I was compelled to ask for food in German, or go without. I also had exposure to my old German aunts, who spoke nothing but German. In Northern Ireland, when we had been taught how to drill future German prisoners, this childhood vocabulary was refreshed, making me recall words from younger days.

Thus, when I became a POW myself, I soon was speaking a GI's version of the enemy language. I not only understood, but could communicate much better with the guards than most of the other American POWs. I later discovered, in two German classes at the University of Texas, that my German was not acceptable, and I came out with a gift of two Ds in the courses. But grammar or no grammar, I usually managed to get one over on the guards at Stalag IIIC.

When I first arrived, I had almost nothing of value to barter. Some prisoners had managed to hang onto a watch or wedding band, but when my German captors frisked me back in Normandy, they took everything I had, except for a single dollar bill. This I kept hidden in my jumpsuit, in a little compartment right beneath the jacket zipper. I carried that dollar for months and swapped it for bread in time.

The Red Cross parcels I shared with Auggie, however, soon provided me with more than nourishment; some of the items, like coffee, cigarettes, and chocolate, made for excellent trading with the guards. The barter varied from prison to prison and time to time, but always depended on the strength of the local market. At Stalag IIIC, a small can of coffee might bring in one and a half loaves of bread and half a pound of oatmeal. You might even get a spoonful of margarine.

This matter of swapping our goods for goods the guards could provide was not a simple matter. For one, it was strictly *verboten* for any German to traffic with a prisoner. A guard caught dealing with a POW immediately went to the Russian front—a death sentence for all practical purposes. Most importantly, this meant that the guard was not going to snitch on you if you ripped him off. He could not even afford to let the other guards on his shift know a prisoner had beaten him out.

How well I knew this jewel of information. Because no guard was free to reveal if or when he was burned in a trade, I was free to be an aggressive dealer in every transaction with the guards.

Typically, your average GI would inflate the market by settling quickly and not bargaining to get the best deal on his parcel items in exchange for German bread, salami, butter, oatmeal, and so forth. A large can of coffee might bring two and a half loaves of bread, five pounds of oatmeal, or maybe a vegetable of some sort. The bread represented a guard's bread ration as well as that of a couple of his buddies. They would pool their rations just to get something to sell on the black market.

Dealing with a guard went something like this. You go out and walk along the fence line while a guard is walking his post, rifle slung over his shoulder. You talk about his wife and kids back home in Bavaria or over on the Elbe River someplace. Walking along the inside of the fence and talking, you get to be his friend.

In time, you take the conversation to items you have to swap for bread, *et cetera*. After walking his post with him twice or so, for a total of four to six hours, you have made a deal to give him a small can of coffee for one and a half loaves of bread, with maybe a little flour thrown in. The deal is made, to be consummated on his next tour of duty—always at night, of course.

You arrive at the rendezvous, and the guard is happy to see you. He checks to make sure the guard tower is closed; this has three wooden shutters that can spring open at any moment, exposing a machine gun at each port. There is no safe place for a prisoner at night outside of his barracks, except on the path to the latrine. Everything else is suspect by diligent guards. As for the guard caught trading with a prisoner—it's good-bye *Heimat*, hello *Russland*.

Verifying that all is safe, the mark is ready to make the swap—his bread for your coffee. He hands the bread through the barbed wire fence, you take it, hand him the coffee can, and hustle back in the dark to your barracks. Soon, you hear a painful cry, "*Soldat, Soldat!*" The guard is begging you to come back and replace the can of coal dust you have given him for coffee. "*Soldat, Soldat!*" he wails. Needless to say, you stay in your room and go to sleep.

Two nights later, you might take the same, identical guard and deal with him again. First, you explain how hungry you are, that you are sorry to have ripped him off, and that you would never do that to him again. He buys your apologetic story of hardship, and you make another deal, this time for a larger can of coffee, through which he can redeem himself to his buddies back in his barracks. He may even be representing a German cook.

He shows up with his bread, to be exchanged for the agreed-upon large can of coffee. Can you believe he doesn't trust you and insists upon touching his damp finger into the can to be sure this is real coffee? You hold the can, lid off, just at the end of his reach, so he can't grab the can. When he is satisfied that you have real coffee, the deal is completed. He has his large coffee and you have his bread, and head back to your barracks, lest the guard tower swing open.

The wailing begins again as the guard discovers that his coffee is actually coal dust with a thin layer of coffee spread over the top. Twice he has been ripped off, and by now his buddies probably think he is ripping them off. This process worked for me perhaps five times at Stalag IIIC, but only a couple times to its full course.

If you can believe it, the most gullible guard is so into the deal by the second rip-off that he has no course but to talk to me some more, in hopes of salvaging something. At least he hasn't been caught. From his standpoint, there is such a large margin of profit from coffee to bread that he can still come out after being ripped off twice. His problem is that I know this as well.

So, we walk and talk some more, and I'm still convincing him that I'm just a good German who happened to be born in America. I'm only trying to stay alive, not meaning any harm to my fellow Germans. I just came along for the ride on D-Day and am trying to get back to Texas in one piece.

I agree to help him redeem himself with his buddies. I have located a prisoner in another barracks who actually has a large can of coffee, but he wants two loaves of bread and some oat-meal for the can. After much bargaining, it is agreed that he will trade one and a half loaves for the large can of coffee. We meet again on his next shift, actually expressing feelings of sorrow for each other. He really, really doesn't trust me now and tries to stick his finger through the bottom of the coffee tin, which he can barely reach through the fence.

After an aggressive finger treatment of the coffee can, he tries to hand me a loaf and a half of bread, and I insist that the deal was for two loaves. We argue quietly as we walk his post, and I finally agree that he is right, and we make the swap. Only, you guessed it, I have swapped the "tested" coffee for another can of coal dust. This is only possible due to the darkness and quickly switching cans. I'm gone, never to do business on that guard post again, until another unit takes over the guard. I turn my attention to the other side of the compound, which employs a totally different group of guards.

Maybe the next deal will be a trade for a chocolate bar from a Red Cross parcel. This, too, I can trade for bread or oat-meal—except the manila paper wrapping the bar actually conceals a block of wood smeared with chocolate milk, or maybe a thin layer of real melted chocolate. Got to have the smell! Finding a piece of wood is no easy task either, and it is necessary to put the little grooves in it, as the guard may want to rub his fingers over the package to verify.

The cigarette scam is the simplest of all. Just ease open the pack on the bottom. Replace the cigarettes with a little cardboard from a prison parcel box, and seal it back up with paste made from your can of Klim. The guards would go for that, every one of them, until you burned them all.

One day at Stalag IIIC, the word came down in the American sector that the International Red Cross was coming for an inspection. The purpose was to verify that the camp was treating POWs according to the rules of the Geneva Convention.

Needless to say, the rules were not being followed when most of the prisoners weighed one hundred pounds and were receiving, at most, one-quarter of their parcels.

As far as we were concerned, the inspection served a very good purpose. I can't really say that the Germans actually cared about what the Red Cross thought or said, in view of the fact that the German government had slaughtered so many men, women, and children over the years. But the announced inspection nevertheless gave us our first taste of leverage since our capture.

The German commandant personally came down to tell us that we were to receive extra rations during the inspection period. Also, our meals on inspection days would not be our traditional, watery "rudibaker" soup; we would receive an extra portion of real pea soup. If you are sitting in an average American home today, having just eaten a traditional evening meal, it is very hard to imagine the significance of this piece of news to a group of starving prisoners. To some, the promise of a full belly of pea soup was no less than the promise of new life.

Not only were we to get this unusual meal of pea soup, but the commandant promised us a recreation room. This was an obvious joke, given that every time we stood roll call, men were dropping like flies, passing out from malnutrition. The most obvious purpose of such a facility was to impress the Red Cross folks coming from Berlin. An extra portion of bread was also to be forthcoming. This meant we would have something like four men to a loaf, instead of the usual six to eight.

The Russians were brought into our compound to assemble the recreation room. The building was just like our barracks, but without partitions. Once again, it was double-walled and double-floored to keep out the subzero temperatures of northeastern Germany.

The building of this structure immediately ignited interest among the American inmates, which had nothing to do with the real or supposed function of the recreation room. The temperature was falling, showing signs of what would soon become one of the coldest winters in recorded European history. Any small piece of wood that could be burned for warmth or used for baking vegetable slices on the side of our wood-burning stove was worth stealing. As a practice, every piece of wood that could be removed from anything inside the compound was so removed.

The evening the Russians finished assembling the recreation building, there was high speculation about the fate of all that wood. When the whistle sounded the next morning for roll call, we had our answer. The amazing Krieggie termite team had been at work all night. Relying on tools no larger than kitchen knives, they had removed so much of the major support system from the inside of the building that it literally sagged. The Red Cross was scheduled to arrive within hours, and the roof of the commandant's impressive new structure rested on the building floor.

Who knows how many POWs had been busy all night cutting up the large wooden ceiling joists? As good a thief as I had become, this was one event I missed. There was, however, no problem identifying at least one of the rooms from which the thieves had come. Some Krieggie had hauled out a piece of lumber about six feet longer than his room. There it was, a long two feet by twelve feet, protruding from one of the windows. He had thought, *Surely I can dice this lumber up in small enough pieces to get it in under the floorboards.* But there was no way that huge piece of timber was going to be cut up by daylight!

Everyone from that room was scared about what would happen, because obviously no one would own up to the theft. Such an admission could easily get a Krieggie shot. As tragic as the possible consequences were, the sight of that timber sticking out that window provoked us all to side-breaking laughter.

I don't recall what happened to the guys living in that room, but you can bet that someone caught a hitch in solitary confinement. To my knowledge, no one was shot over the incident, and some men got a great stash of firewood until the Russian army arrived to free us all.

Incidentally, the Red Cross did come by to interview us. Would you believe it, some of the prisoners still complained, even after they were served two cups of pea soup in one day, and generously allotted by the German government an entire loaf of delectable sawdust bread to be shared among four men.

Chapter Thirty-three

LIFE AND DEATH (MOSTLY DEATH): THE FRENCH AND RUSSIAN COMPOUNDS

As bad as we had it in Stalag IIIC, as Americans and noncommissioned officers, we were better off than anyone else in the camp. A case in point was the treatment of the French. As the weather turned truly wicked, the Germans continued to force their French women prisoners to work in the fields, in spite of the bitter cold and the fact that it was pouring rain like crazy. Many of these women, about sixty in all, had babies or small children. The women themselves were mostly young, about twenty to forty years old as I recall, but forced to do heavy farm labor in the absence of regular German farm hands, who all were off to war.

Oftentimes, work details were supervised or guarded by Polish or French guards who were not too cruel in their treatment of prisoners—for they, too, in a sense, shared a prisoner status. However, these guards were frequently overseen by a German party member, who was, perhaps, a Gestapo soldier. In that case, the heat was on.

The women first tried taking the babies along to the fields, wrapped up in blankets and burlap bags to preclude their freezing. They placed the babies, wrapped as they were, at the end of the crop rows and progressed down the muddy rows, working on their hands and knees. Then they tucked the babies inside their own clothing to warm them with their body heat for a couple of rows. And so it went. Finally, the women revolted. They insisted that at least one of them be allowed to stay back with the little ones each day, in order to keep them from getting cold and sick from exposure to the terrible weather. The German guards did not agree to the terms, so the women simply refused to go into the field. Soon after, they and their babies were mercilessly all killed. We received this information from prisoners outside our compound, so I cannot personally attest to its accuracy, although I had heard of similar incidents at other labor camps.

I can attest that this was the first time I ever saw the French male prisoners at Stalag IIIC get angry. For the first time, they agreed to help us with assorted projects that required unavailable resources that their knowledge and status could help us to procure. It was not uncommon for French male prisoners to work outside the prison confines, and many of them were married to local German women. They could not be trusted by any regular prisoner but could be a source of almost anything we needed from the outside, provided we had resources to trade, such as cigarettes and coffee.

It was a month after the massacre before the Frenchmen settled down. Meanwhile, no one paid much attention to the daily scene of dead Russian prisoners carted by wheelbarrow out to the dump, a pit where their emaciated bodies were covered with lime, much like the practice we had back home of putting lime on the waste from a farmer's outhouse.

Those of us in the American compound awaited a violent revolt among the French male prisoners, but it never occurred. We then went back to waiting on the arrival of the Russian army from the east, which our clandestine news sources told us was inevitable.

It is easy to condemn the Frenchmen for their apparent inactivity, but they had long experience with the German army, and knew, much better than we, how to extract a price for German brutality. Somehow, someplace, it is possible and even probable, that the French got their pound of flesh in revenge.

It may seem hard to believe, but the Russians had it even worse at Stalag IIIC. The Russian compound, just across one of our fence boundaries and separated by the usual guard walkway, must have contained five hundred Russian prisoners. I got the impression that they were not all military POWs, but political prisoners as well. If we were deprived, I don't know what you would call these poor creatures. The long-standing hatred between the Russians and the Germans, the rampage of savage destruction by the German army in Russia, and the fact that Russia had not signed the Geneva Convention, all combined to assure that Russian POWs were given the most ragged clothes, the smallest food rations, and the heaviest, filthiest, most degrading work.

The one advantage of being worked, albeit like slaves, was that their details often took them outside the prison gates, where they could come by assorted contraband items. We heard that one time the Russians brought into IIIC a baby grand piano, a piece at a time. When the American noncom compound was established right next to theirs, we became the finest market for their goods. These ran from snakes to a "live chicken auction," an event that occurred several times while we were at IIIC.

I here use the expression *live* loosely. For a few days prior to the auction of the illegally imported chicken, the Russians would get a crowd of Americans up to the fence to display the bird. The starving chicken was on the same diet as the starving Russkis and could seldom hold its head up as it was displayed to the American audience. The chicken's head would fall over to one side, and the owner would reach over, straighten its head up, and encourage the fowl to act alive. This display would go on for a half hour, as the Americans howled at the sight of the pitiful Russian dealing with his half-dead chicken. When the silent auction was completed, some goofy GI got a half-pound, half-dead bird, with the challenge of figuring a way to make a meal out of it.

Other details the Russians were forced to do, within the confines of the camp itself, had no redeeming features or advantages whatsoever. The huge latrine for the American compound of about two thousand POWs is a case in point. This was not overly comfortable for the American noncoms who used it, but it was a considerable improvement over the thirty-five-gallon barrels that served as toilets in the boxcars.

Beneath this latrine was a very large pit, which frequently required pumping out. The Russians were assigned to pump out the raw sewage, haul it across from the prison, and dump it on the vegetable garden site. This process really fertilized a mean garden.

The sewage was sucked up with an ancient fire department pump. This consisted of a one-hundred-gallon metal tank and was laid horizontally on a wagon pulled by ten Russians. On each side of the tank was a wooden bar about as long as the tank itself. Six Russians on one side of the tank pressed down on the bar, and six on the other raised the bar up, creating a great deal of suction, which pulled the sewage out from the pit under the latrine.

Unfortunately, there was always a substantial leak in the pump. The suction propelled a large stream of raw sewage into the air, which came down right on top of the Russian POWs. The bitter cold caused the sewage to freeze on the Russians' heads, forming long icicles off the poor guys' ears, noses, hair, and beards. This latrine detail took about three hours to complete. All the while, the fountain of sewage rained down on the crew, causing them to smell just like the latrine pit, with no way to bathe or clean either their body or clothes.

As little respect as I had for the Russians, knowing of their brutal crimes against the Germans, I still felt sorry for these poor guys as they suffered through the worst labor detail I ever saw in my life. War is hell, indeed. I soon was to witness the reason for the Germans' hostility toward the Russians, when I saw with my own eyes the indiscriminate Russian display of animal cruelty against German men, women, and children in Poland and eastern Germany.

Unlike Muhlburg's Stalag IVB, the dissemination of news at Stalag IIIC was not highly organized. The news drifted down from barracks to barracks, but the system, such as it was, worked well. None of us were ever interested in knowing where the radio was kept or who was responsible for it. What we did know was the location of the eastern front and how it was going. We knew that things were not looking good for the Germans in December 1944 and that the Russians were hell-bent on approaching the Oder River, about 550 yards west of Stalag IIIC, and might well overrun our position.

At the same time, the Allies were approaching Berlin from the west, subjecting the German capital to intensive bombing night and day. Viewing the heaviest air raids of World War II at Kuestrin, from a distance of about forty miles away, was a pleasure, knowing that the Berliners were catching hell, while we were far enough from the target not to be victim to the Allied pounding.

The Germans nevertheless took precautions against air raids at the camp. Russian prisoners were sent into our compound to dig trenches that were about one hundred feet long, six feet deep, and five feet wide. On each side, they erected heavy, rough lumber timbers from the top to the bottom of the trench in order to keep the sandy walls from caving in. In case of need, these trenches were to be used as shelters for German guards and POWs both.

As soon as the project was complete, our fantastic GI termites started taking apart the support boards with any tool they could beg, borrow, steal, or fabricate. Cutting off slivers of wood to feed our undernourished stoves, they worked late at night, when the guards in the towers were less attentive, or maybe even asleep. When the camp commandant discovered the damage, he sent word that guard dogs, trained to kill, would be released into the trenches every night.

To be perfectly honest, we never gave a big rat's fanny what the Germans thought, wanted, or said. It was not worth the chance for me personally to be eaten by a German guard dog, but for others, the risk was worth the possible supply of a handful of wood slivers. The first night of the dog patrol, two American POWs went out, jumped into the trenches, and were indeed killed by the dogs. Needless to say, the trench boards were safe after that incident.

Chapter Thirty-four

THE RUSSIANS ARE COMING! THE RUSSIANS ARE COMING!

In the grim conditions of December 1944, prisoners suffered more than ever from lack of heat and nourishment. Also more than ever, every humorous event added to our ability to withstand prison life and all its stresses. So it was when one of the guards asked me to teach him English.

The man was huge, at least 250 pounds, and looked like a tank wrapped up in his heavy overcoat. His job was to operate the twenty-foot tower surrounded by barbed wire fences in a corner of our compound. One of the fences was about eight feet high, and the other ran inside it about two feet off the ground. Guards were free to shoot prisoners who crossed the limits. Go beyond the short wire and you were history.

The tower was equipped with a large searchlight and wooden doors, behind which my "student" sat with a machine gun. Weather permitting, he opened up the tower and visited with other guards as they walked their posts, approaching the tower from three directions, then turning around beneath it.

I stood on safe ground under the tower and visited in both English and broken German.

In a week or so, I had half of our compound laughing their heads off while my kraut friend bragged to his fellow guards: "Me big fat-head—kraut!" The other guards all wanted to enroll in my English class and roared as Krauty pounded himself on the chest, shouting from his open tower: "Me big fat-head—kraut!" Thank God for me, the Russians arrived before Krauty discovered what he was saying.

Meanwhile, the scarcity of food in December 1944 led me to encounter the one inhabitant of Stalag IIIC that never bought my scam. This was a little calico kitten that played just outside the guard tower, next to the latrine. The kitten kept to the outer side of the two barbed wire fences that ran around our compound. Between the fences, the Germans had placed rolled-up barbed wire. Any POW who tried to escape would have to go over both fences as well as through the solid application of barbed concertina wire unfolded and stretched around the area.

One day, George Forte and Idris Lassiter came to me with a proposal. If I could figure out how to get my hands on the kitten, Idris would do it in and clean it, and George would cook it for dinner. Many of our fellow inmates thought we had gone nuts, but we were hungry enough to give the idea a try.

None of us had actually ever tasted kitten. But George had been raised in the swamps in Florida and had eaten just about every other animal imaginable, so his suggestion was in earnest. Idris took the project to be just another crazy paratrooper idea. My mucker, Auggie, included in any dinner plans I made, wanted no part of catching, killing, skinning, cooking, or eating a little kitten. So the deal was just among George, Idris, and me.

I was chosen to catch the kitten because of my skills in linguistics. Because I spoke a passable GI version of German, it was thought that I could communicate with the cat. I had done really well with the German guards, so why not try talking the little kraut kitten into coming inside the barbed wire fence? The German cat did not respond to "Here kitty, kitty." I was, therefore, forced to enlarge my communication repertoire.

Our family always had a pet cat when I was a kid, so I knew all the tricks to get a cat to play. I dragged a string along the ground as the kitten watched from the distance between the fences. It was interested, for sure, but not enough to come through the maze of barbed wire. I had to figure out how to make it more enticing. The rest of our compound went nuts laughing at my antics as I tried to coax that kitten to "supper!" Once, the little thing actually came in past the outside fence. I could almost taste a meat dish for the first time in months. I must have had a look in my eye, because the critter turned around and went back to its business outside the fences. Another day, it brought along a litter-mate to play. I suppose the cats belonged to someone from a German kitchen someplace in the prison grounds.

Idris and George started making fun of me because I could not carry out my part of the deal. I was really serious about my end, but I just couldn't perform. The deal between me and the kitten became a sort of game, with the animal somehow know-ing that I had something in mind for it. The calico played me along, acting from time to time like it might come through to my side of the fences. Never happened!

Would I have eaten my share of the kitten? You bet I would have. Looking back, however, and considering just how much—or little—there is to a small cat, we were just as apt to get a piece of "real" meat in our daily cup of watery soup—and that would have been a miracle. When we were released by the Russian army, a few weeks later, I didn't go looking for that kitten, though I was right where the cat had been, outside the fences. I looted the potato bins instead. It was a lot less effort for a lot more reward.

The violence from the air raids became more frightening by the day, increasing in intensity. The planes would take off from Britain with maxed-out B-24 and B-17 bomb bays full of bombs up to two thousand pounds each. The bizarre sight of daylight raids by our own American bombers played out like a thrilling movie. Every day, thousands of planes were dumping thousands of tons of bombs on Berlin, and we loved the scene. I later learned that the reason that more human casualties were not incurred was because many children had been taken to the countryside to live on farms, keeping them and many nonessential civilians out of the target zones.

At night, during the raids by British Lancester bombers, we could hear and feel the size of the bombs falling on the Berliners. The British air force finally started referring to these larger bombs as "blockbusters," because of the damage they inflicted on the neighborhoods where they landed.

In the midst of this escalation, on a very bitter December evening in 1944, about two hundred mostly female political prisoners came limping into Stalag IIIC. There were also a few old men and many children, including some babies. They had been on the road for weeks, walking all the way to Kuestrin from the Polish interior. As we discovered in our talks with the healthier victims, most of them were Jews.

Without exception, every living creature that had a mind with which to think was fleeing westward to avoid being run over by the Russians. This group had been sleeping in ice-cold barns, taking shelter where they could find it, moving west in front of the approaching Russian armored units, which were followed closely by the Russian infantry. You didn't have to have much experience with the Russian troops to realize the Jews and their German guards had ample reason for fear.

When the German armies advanced to the east across Poland and into Russia, the Russians and Poles fled eastward to avoid being captured by the German armed forces. I myself would soon encounter the sickening sights of German brutality in Poland and Russia—little children with arms and legs cut off by victorious German troops, females terribly abused. The revolting signs were in every community I entered, and the Russians now rolling west toward the Oder River were fueled up on vodka and hell-bent on revenge. All throughout Poland and on into Germany, they pillaged, raped, burned, and murdered in a rampage of indiscriminate violence.

The bedraggled Jewish arrivals that came into Stalag IIIC had been fed little on their march toward the west. A few German guards had been assigned to the column of battered prisoners, who were moved into the compound right next to ours. No sooner did the gates close behind these poor creatures, than we began to throw them everything we had—blankets, jackets, food. Most of the new arrivals spoke German, so we were able to communicate with them. They had been abused in every possible way and had lost many of their number on the long march from their prison somewhere in Poland. I do not remember where they had been interned.

The walkway between our compound and the adjacent one that housed the Jewish arrivals was patrolled by an older guard who was always accompanied by a police dog; I was more afraid of his furry friend than I was of him. There were always a few caring guards, so we could get things done outside the ears and eyes of the ones who were less humane. This was the case that bitter December night, so we were not prevented from helping our new neighbors bed down and get warm. We had nothing of traditional value individually, but compared to these ill-clad, frozen, starving specimens, we were comfortable and well off.

I was proud of my Krieggie buddies. Some cried at the condition of these distressed souls, and without exception they parted with their meager belongings to assist fellow humans more deprived than they. The new arrivals stayed only a few days before departing to the west across the Oder River and deeper into Germany, where the survivors no doubt worked out the rest of the war in coal mines, farms, or factories.

Part IV

THE RUSSIAN EXPERIENCE: OR, HEADING EAST TO GO WEST

Chapter Thirty-five

VODKA, VODKA,
EVERYWHERE, AND PLENTY
OF IT TO DRINK

There was never a bombing of Stalag IIIC, but in the last days, we witnessed hits on the planes of our GI brothers. We often saw parts fly off when the planes were hit by German antiaircraft artillery. Frequently the crew, given the command to jump from the disabled plane, would start leaping from different openings in the fuselage. Sometimes the commander would rescind the command to jump after some of the crew had bailed out, and in such a case, three or so lonely parachutes would float down over the Oder River.

These crew members knew nothing about parachutes and had no idea how to influence the direction the chutes would take them. Their dilemma was that if they landed on the west side of the Oder River, they became POWs of the Germans. If they were fortunate enough to land on the east side, they were in Russian territory and were free to be sent back to England and another bombing mission.

Frequently, the bombers flew at an altitude of twenty thousand feet. If they jumped from something like ten thousand feet, they would drift for perhaps ten minutes. It was not uncommon for one thousand prisoners of many nationalities to be out in the compound cheering the drifting crew members on to a safe landing in Russian territory.

For several weeks, as the Russians moved closer to Berlin from the eastern front, our captors had been moving Stalag IIIC prisoners across the Oder River and deeper into Germany, where POWs would be more secure and manageable. The prisoners were moved west by nationality and in the order that they posed a threat to the Germans. Russian prisoners were the first to be moved across the Oder, the last natural defensive barrier before Berlin.

The Russians had such a hatred of Germans that it would have been folly to keep Russian POWs in any area where the approaching Russian army might be able to unleash them. European prisoners, many of whom were political noncombatants, were also much more hostile toward the Germans than were Americans, Canadians, and the British. Of the ten or so different nationalities held at Stalag IIIC, these last three were considered the least likely to kill German guards and staff if released. Those of us in the American compound were therefore among the last to be evacuated from the camp.

About two days before the Russians arrived, we heard artillery firing in the distance. We could not get accurate, detailed daily information from the BBC on our secret radio, but we did have information on the approximate location of the German and Russian forces. We knew the Russians were perhaps within twenty-five miles of us and moving westerly every day as they continued to beat the German armored forces.

In preparation for the Russians' arrival, we decided that a few of us would stay behind when the Germans attempted to evacuate the prisoners still remaining in camp. Everyone in the barracks drew straws, with the idea that three of us would go into the hole we had been digging under our floorboards since August. The idea was to stay under the barracks until the Russians had taken the prison, then come out and tell them whatever information they desired about Stalag IIIC and its prisoners.

I was among the Krieggies who drew a short straw. It would be crowded down there in our hole, but we figured we would have to stay hidden for only a couple days. Our "safe place" was now full of contraband items, including provisions that could last our three-man team for a couple of weeks, and "blowers," a contraption we had devised to cook any food requiring a fire.

One consideration did give us pause. It occurred to us that the German commandant might decide to torch the prison to keep the Russians from having access to such good quarters for their troops. What would we do if they set fire to all the wood frame buildings? We decided to cross that bridge if and when we got to it. The plan was still on!

Finally, the German guards came through the compound, shouting at us to get ready to move out with all our equipment, everything we had. "You will not be returning to this camp, ever!" We were to get out onto the road and head north, up the Oder River to the nearest bridge several miles away, where we would cross over and trek toward Berlin.

We had seen the move coming for quite some time. Our leadership told us to stall, and stall we did, to the point where the guards attached their bayonets to their rifles and started poking us. Obviously, our goal was to stay put as long as possible, waiting for the Russian tanks. Six months earlier, this sort of resistance would have gotten us all shot. However, the guards now knew that they themselves could soon become prisoners of the Allies, and so we got away with it.

Early on the morning of January 31, while we were doing our best to stall, a single-engine German spotter plane started flying low over the prison, circling around and around. The pilot and only occupant kept excitedly pointing east, where the big gun sounds had been coming from, indicating that the Russian tanks were not too far away. The guards became increasingly anxious to get out. They all knew what their fate would be were they to fall into the hands of the Russian troops. A horrible death for sure.

I had come down with an attack of dysentery, which prevented me from staying back in the hole as planned. Another Krieggie took my place beneath the boards, and I started to bundle up my nothing, getting ready to move out when the bayonet action became too serious. Finally, the guards became desperate. Our leadership gave the word to go, and we all moved out onto the road running in front of the prison.

We still were wearing our tattered Hungarian army uniforms with KGF across the back of our coats and pants. Some Krieggies had made sleds out of tabletops to help drag their possessions through the snow. They loaded so much crap onto them that you would have thought they had been living there for years.

At last we were all out of the camp, walking north on each side of the deep-snow-covered road. The way we saw it, it couldn't get much worse than we had had it there. Our attitude was, "Let's get on with whatever!"

We had trudged about a mile, when we heard the loud horn of the camp commandant's beautiful, four-door, gray convertible sedan. As he flew past with the top up, we wondered where he was taking us. His driver had no sooner rounded the first curve past our column of prisoners than there was a tremendous artillery explosion. A Stalin tank parked just around the bend, about a quarter mile to our immediate front, had center-punched the CO's car and blew it all to pieces, him included.

The tank then roared around the corner and blasted a round across the front of our column, killing about two hundred

POWs. Seeing our Hungarian uniforms, the tanker thought we were enemy troops. The blast sent all of us at the rear of the column racing back toward camp, while the guards went nuts trying to regain control. It was one big wild Krieggie stampede nightmare.

Within minutes, I was back in the barracks explaining to the guys who had stayed behind what had happened out on the road. With the guards now hoofing it out of Dodge toward Berlin, we newly liberated Krieggies started breaking into every office and warehouse in the camp. First, we were looking for anything to eat, and next for anything to wear against the freezing weather we knew we were soon to experience. One Krieggie said he found my photo while roving through the German headquarters. He promised to give it to me, but disappeared before I could get it, and I never saw him again.

In the midst of the chaos, some of the guards came back, shouting in desperation that the German air force was coming to strafe and bomb the camp and that we should all get back out on the road. The word from our own leadership was still to obey German orders and not to try to escape. Nevertheless, it must have taken them an hour to get a handle on us again. It was about noon, I guess, when we headed out of camp for the second time.

In the meantime, Russian tanks had circled around the camp and the location of the initial action. As we went out the gate, I saw a fellow Krieggie lying dead beside the road, whose body had not been there before. From his wrists up to his armpits, both arms were loaded with watches. I had never seen him, but I was told he was a German-speaking Jew from Brooklyn and the biggest trader in the camp. Speculation was that he had burned some POW on a deal, and death had been his reward.

We now headed in a more southerly direction, as opposed to our initial northern route up the road to the Oder. In no more than twenty minutes, a Russian tank spotted us and again fired another round right across the front of our column. One Polish-speaking American GI was heroic enough to run straight toward the tank, screaming *"Americanski! Americanski!"* He was not shot, nor was any other GI shot by the Russians after that. Whoever that Polish-speaking GI was, he should have been awarded a major medal for the lives he saved that morning.

All authority now completely disintegrated, and it was every man for himself. I high-tailed it back to the relative safety of our hidden hole to await the momentous tank battle I knew was about to take place with the baddest tanks in the world, as German tanks began to cross the Oder. We huddled at the bottom of our hole under the floorboards, listening to one hell of a tank fight going on right over our heads. These tanks were no more than a few hundred yards from one another, which in tank terms is right in your face.

I had already had my first contact with a Russian soldier-tanker on the way back to the barracks. The tank commander, a young female, had one of her tank team fetch any German guards he could find. She was sitting on the front fender of her tank when the driver returned with a couple of Germans.

She stood up and positioned the two Germans in front of her, one facing her, the other facing away. Her crew member stood behind the German facing her. She pulled out her pistol and put it up to the head of the German facing away from her, while the tanker put his gun up against the head of the German facing her. Each German could see that the other was about to be shot. She barked an order and pulled her trigger, putting a bullet into the head of one of the Germans, as did the other tanker to his victim. Both men dropped dead and were run over by the tank as it drove on into camp.

As soon as they got through the gate, the first bit of information the Russians wanted to know was which guards had been hard on prisoners, and especially on Russian prisoners.

These guards were executed immediately. As many times as O.K. had stuck his P38 pistol up my nose while screaming *"rouse"* at me, I decided to hide him. He was one of a very few guards who we protected until they could be slipped out under cover of night and across the Oder into the safety of the German lines. We managed to get him out of the camp, but I never knew if he made it across the river or not.

As the camp descended into chaos, one of the grizzliest scenes took place in the IIIC delouser. If you ever had a bath, this was the place where they took your clothes to rid them of lice. It did the job with steam and was a simple room. The Russians started gathering up Germans and forcing them into the delouser, locking the doors, and turning the steam up to max. *Enough horror* is enough, I thought, and this exceeded my craziest limits, even beyond the nastiest horror movies I had ever seen as a kid. I heard others say that when they opened the doors of those chambers, the Germans' bodies had shrunk to the size of pygmies. I certainly never went over to check the matter out.

Russians and Germans both paid a dear price at the great armored battle of the Oder River, which included some of the fiercest tank warfare of World War II. The biggest tanks in the world were lined up hubcap to hubcap for miles on end. The opposing forces were not fifty miles apart, but a few city blocks. It was like holding hands and blowing one another away with pistols at point-blank range.

We prisoners forcibly witnessed the battle between German Royal Tiger tanks with their exceptional 88mm artillery and Russian Stalinsky tanks. The Stalinsky had huge guns mounted on what looked like a building. I have seen a tanker try to turn one of those big suckers around in the middle of a German frontier village and knock down structures on both sides of the street before making the turn. The gun took out every building in its way.

As it turned out, the Russians were so disorganized in their race west across the frozen tundra that they had no idea that they would run smack into Stalag IIIC, a camp with a population of some twenty thousand POWs, right on the bank of the Oder. Throughout the whole process of our so-called liberation, I stayed wired. We were all in such an excited state that it is a wonder that any of us survived physically or emotionally. We literally knew not if we would be alive in the next thirty minutes. I got hold of a German P38 pistol and was never found without it stuck down under my belt. It was one more major scramble for life.

The Germans must have withdrawn back across the river within hours, because the Russians started trying to cross over. I knew that the Americans were coming from the west toward Berlin, moving pretty fast. Initially, my thinking was that if I could fight with the Russians and cross the Oder, then move on with them west through Berlin, I would soon meet up with my own forces.

Two or three days of observing the Russkis in combat convinced me that I needed to go to plan B. We were told that their fuel trucks brought up tank fuel in one load with the next load being vodka, and I could believe it. It was vodka, vodka, everywhere, and plenty of it to drink—and high-powered vodka at that. Every day, and sometimes at night, another freed GI would be killed in a freak "accident" involving Russian soldiers. I figured I was blessed to be alive at this point, but I could see all of us dead through the sheer stupidity of the Russians, who handled all their weapons alike, as if they were toys. I had no desire to be around this combination of booze, artillery, tanks, and automatic weapons. Actually, I wanted my mama!

When the Russkis dropped a couple tanks through the ice-covered Oder, leaving their infantry stranded and doomed on the enemy side, I became convinced that they would never cross that river and make it stick. This certitude was countered by my daily experience with drunken Russians who, when asked "What is your unit?" would respond, "Berlin!" "Who is your commander?" "Berlin!" For once in my life, however, I was correct. I left that scene on February 2, 1945, and, indeed, was enrolled in the University of Texas the following August before the Russians crossed the Oder for good.

Plan B consisted of going east. A group of us decided to follow the Russian supply lines and get as far away as possible from frontline combat. At the time, I really believed that if I went east long enough, I would eventually pass Texas and be home. I agreed to provide the leadership for the long trek.

We did not take our decision lightly. The matter of heading east was almost as dangerous as hanging around the Russians trying to cross the Oder. I understood enough geography to know that getting back to American control any way except straight west through Berlin was going to be a very long trip through country I knew nothing about, and with very modest knowledge of the languages I would encounter. I also knew from Russian senior officers that bandit groups followed the Russian troops. These barbarians robbed, stole, raped, and killed at will, with zero consequences for any behavior, however cruel.

So, on the night of February 2, with all hell breaking loose among vodka-soaked Russians and spooked German tankers, a band of twenty or so American ex-POWs headed east down a snow-covered sandy road. In preparation for our long journey, any of us who could find shoes or boots had added these luxuries to our wardrobe. I started out with Dutch wooden shoes, which killed my feet after walking even a brief distance. I soon jumped on an offer to swap them with an air force bomber crewmember, who had hit the ground seeking someone with whom to trade his heavy-duty fleece-lined boots. The boots looked great, but unknown to me, they had been conceived for use at freezing altitudes and were so warm that they would burn up a wearer's feet in twenty minutes of walking. Within a day, my feet started sweating, blistering, and peeling. Soon I was hustling local leather boots with rags for socks.

It was about midnight when we departed the Stalag IIIC prison grounds with the meager belongings we each had gathered by hook or crook. Initially, I improvised a sled and loaded all sorts of junk on it, but after stumbling into a couple of deep snow banks, I decided that such a traveling system would never get me to Moscow, let alone to Texas.

All of us were emotionally sick to some measure. I have to laugh when I read that some of our leaders wonder where our post-traumatic stress disorder came from and whether it is real today. We lived day after day wondering if we would see the sun in the morning and if we might have to kill the next crazy person we encountered. There was no law of any sort—no police to call, no authority of any kind. I kept my gun in my hand more than I wanted. Most of my decisions were made out of fear.

We had walked for about an hour when we heard a faint crying or wailing out of the distant east. The farther we went down the snow-covered road, the louder the wailing became. It was unlike any weeping I had ever heard. It was as though someone was dying from grief. An increasingly anxious feeling moved within me. I knew in time that I would encounter the scene producing this agony, and I was not at all ready. And yet I knew there was no way around it, so I proceeded on as the cries grew louder.

Perhaps an hour had passed from the time I first heard the faint sound of weeping until I was confronted with the most pitiful sight I had ever seen. Stopped by the roadside was a two-seat wagon drawn by a single horse, with an old gentleman sitting up on the wagon seat. He was staring into space as if he had seen a ghost. He was not making a sound, just sitting and staring. There was absolutely no light beyond the moonlight shining down on the thick blanket of snow.

Next to the old gentleman was an old lady, wearing a bonnet and the modest clothes of a farmer's wife. She was the source of the wailing heard from so great a distance. I had never seen so much pain coming from a human being. As I looked more closely, I saw the reason for her agony.

Just in front of the left front wheel of the wagon was the crumpled body of a young man, who looked to be perhaps twenty years old. He had been shot in the head and was dead. I had already seen the animal-like character of the Russian soldier and had observed the deepest measure of hatred imaginable in my brief stay with the Russian army. At the sight of this woman's grief, I now hated war more than ever.

Sure, we killed people in combat—all around us, people were killing people in an attempt to stay alive—and, for my part, to get back to Texas. But some Russian soldier or small group of soldiers had come along and shot this lad in the head for no obvious reason as his adoring mother looked on in horror.

I felt damn terrible, but could do nothing to relieve the poor soul's pain. So my small group of fellow travelers walked on east, as the painful wailing grew fainter and fainter until it disappeared from the ear and mind of the moment. And yet it lingers. Even now, sixty years later, I hear her cries, I see her grief, I feel her pain.

Postscript

TAKING THE
ANKLE EXPRESS HOME

It was a long, winding road to Texas from Stalag IIIC through Germany, Poland, Russia, Turkey, Greece, Egypt, and Italy, where I finally met up with the U.S. Army in Naples and then shipped out for Boston. I traveled by boxcar, assorted Russian vehicles, horseback, horse and buggy, farm wagon, bicycle, and even by wood-burning Volkswagen bus, but mostly I used the good old "ankle express."

No matter how I try, now, more than sixty years later, I still cannot accurately retrace my route as I loosely followed the Russian supply lines marked by the file of Studebaker trucks twisting along the sandy, snow-covered roads of Germany and Poland. I am convinced that the Russian army would still be back in Leningrad today had it not been for those Studebakers, courtesy of the lend lease program. The trek certainly was my coldest experience, with the exception of some Fort Benning training jumps back in the winter of 1942 that landed us in Uchie Creek and the Chattahoochee River. The ice would form on our jumpsuits, then break off as we fell to the ground during mock attacks. That I lived through either experience says something for God's grace.

In the winter of 1945, it was difficult to distinguish between the eastern German frontier and Poland proper. The Russian armored troops with their huge tanks and female commanders barreled through the countryside somewhat ahead of the infantry. Just as I was warned, groups of bandits, well armed with pistols and rifles, followed close behind every major military unit. Russian army officers on the race to Berlin frankly admitted they had no time to deal with the bandits. All males, and for the most part very young, they ran in packs of four to eight, killing and maiming man, woman, and child in a rampage of murder, robbery, and rape. They were as offensive to regular Russian soldiers as they were to native civilians, liberated POWs, and the hoards of displaced people fleeing east.

After I observed my first display of the bandits' sick behavior, I knew it was "sic 'em time." My German P38, a great little weapon, became my best friend and companion. I'd begun to carry it after my first night on the Oder River, when a Mongolian Russian soldier slipped up on me in camp. I was quite jumpy and had never seen a Mongolian up close before. The last thing I needed was to sense a presence behind my shoulder and turn to find myself suddenly nose to nose with a humungous hulk with tiny slant eyes, who met my surprise with a grunt. I later met many other Mongolians, who turned out to be fun and friendly people as well as fierce combat soldiers.

Because we were behind Russian military lines, you would think we would be free of the threat of German recapture. Not so! Intent on achieving Berlin at all costs, the Russkis bypassed entire cities, frequently leaving large German military units holed up underground. The Russian strategy went like this: they would roll up to a town of considerable size and start shelling it with artillery. Then they invited the city to surrender. If the answer was no, they simply went around it on all sides and continued west toward their objective. With no possibility of receiving supplies, the city would starve and die on the vine, so to speak. Indeed, the Russians tried the same thing on the Americans in Berlin, but failed because of the air lift.

Before our motley group of ex-POWs had gone more than fifty miles from Stalag IIIC, we came upon a village of perhaps two hundred people, which looked like any other farming community near the eastern German frontier. It was not uncommon for isolated areas to remain unexposed to the great world war in process, and such had been the lucky fate of the village up to this point. Neither Russian nor German military forces had moved through the area, and the community had gone right on working the land, harvesting crops, selling produce to larger cities, attending church, marrying, having babies, and sending their children to school.

The entire northern area of Europe was buried in several feet of snow, so our march across country was a struggle, especially for the shorter men like myself. We considered any village as a source of food, so we were excited to come upon the little community, until we suddenly realized that something was very wrong. Only women were coming out to greet us, all of them weeping in deep, grieving pain. They were greatly relieved to discover that we were American ex-POWs and would not do them any harm.

We could not understand what they were trying to tell us, so they began just pointing to a nearby field. As we drew near, we could see the pasture was filled with the bodies of dead men. Eventually, one young woman choked out the story in broken English, clutching her baby all the while she spoke.

Earlier that morning, the Russians had passed through en route to Berlin. When the armored unit roared into the tiny village, they rounded up all the males, young and old, fit and crippled, just as they had gathered up the Germans at IIIC.

They then marched them out into the field and, making it look like a game of some sort, laughing and carrying on in a drunken state, they took out their pistols and used the villagers for target practice. Every single human in that field had been shot at least once in the head.

This was enough to make us cringe in horror, but the grizzly scene before our eyes required the young mother to continue the terrible story. The freshly murdered bodies lying on the ground had all been crushed by the wide tracks of a tank. All of their heads were mashed flat in the snow. You could see what some of the men had looked like before the tanks ran over them, because their impressions were preserved in the snow. Some of them were not yet dead when the tanks had passed over them.

The women had been forced to helplessly stand by, confined inside a building while this travesty took place. We were deeply moved by this little band of survivors, all mothers, widows, sisters, or children of the dead, but there was nothing we could say or do to ease their grief or pain. And so we moved on with very heavy hearts.

We rarely continued for any length of time without encountering obstacles and tragedies. None of us weighed more than a hundred pounds, and many of our members began to fall apart emotionally, physically, or both. All of us were wired to the max, and sometimes a guy would simply lose it, becoming a danger to himself and the group. My own behavior veered toward the paranoid. I was always ready to shoot, even in my sleep. One night, I woke from a fitful dream to discover my arm stretched above my head, my gun in my hand, and my finger on the trigger.

Our numbers were down to around a half dozen when we straggled into a rather large city not too far from the Polish border. The Russians were using the place as a supply depot. The weather had warmed a bit, filling the streets with melting snow, and the heavy traffic had turned the cobblestone streets into a major muddy mess. No traffic control directed the thousands of heavy Russian vehicles, including Russki tanks. There appeared to be no hope of ever clearing the traffic jams.

As we moved on into the city, we came upon a large building several stories high, which had obviously been a luxury hotel. It was the most ornate structure I had seen since the glimpses of Berlin I had spied from the boxcar before we arrived at Stalag IIIC. Russian command and staff vehicles filled the hotel parking lot, and senior military officers were coming and going through the huge, fancy front doors. No, there was no customary attendant to show us to our room.

It seemed that the Russkis were about to move west. I went into the parking lot, where they were loading military luggage, and interrupted a conversation in one of the small gatherings of officers. "Do you mind if we former POWs spend a few days in this hotel?" I asked. "You may stay here as long as you like," said the senior officer. "But when you leave, you must go to the Russian commandant"—and here he pointed to another large office building—"and inform him that you are leaving. We intend to burn the hotel." It apparently was easier to torch the building than search the rooms to ensure no Russian enemies were left behind alive.

I assured the officer that we would inform the commandant of our departure and turned back toward the hotel. On the way, one of my Krieggie companions pointed to a sight that broke my heart. A German boy, perhaps ten years old, had been killed by someone or something. His little body had fallen half off the curb, where his arm had been severed by the endless traffic sloshing through the cobblestone streets. There he lay, an innocent child, his arm out in the middle of the muddy street and his little body covered with dirty, melting snow. In spite of all the unspeakable cruelty we had encountered, this scene tore at my heart. The tears flowed down my cheeks as I screamed a long stream of profanity. How low had we all come to allow this little guy to suffer so indignantly?

Although I was about to vomit, I picked up the small corpse, carried him across the sidewalk, laid him away from the traffic against a building, and covered him with clean snow. With my few Russian words, I borrowed a pick and shovel from one of the Russian trucks, and we dug a grave through the icy turf in the backyard of a nearby house. The unfortunate kid had perhaps the war's most modest funeral. It was hard to leave him like that, but I realized that he was in better hands than I.

Back in the hotel, we began a thorough search of all the rooms. The hotel was many stories high, and everything was first class. I was most impressed with what even I knew to be the finest carpeting money could buy, which ran throughout the building and into all the rooms. The decor throughout was a beautiful gold. Sculpted lion heads protruded from the walls, which were hung with heavy, ornate tapestries. The principal stairway must have been twenty feet wide and was carpeted in deep, lush pile just like the lobby. Halfway up was a wide mezzanine where one could rest on comfortable, over-stuffed furniture.

I was on my way upstairs to check out the other floors, when another paratrooper from the group shouted to me that he was going out to get us a milk cow. Though I had not seen any cows, I did not question his ability to show up with one. I suggested that he house her in the mezzanine. Two hours later, when I returned from my venture of examining the upper rooms, sure enough, a beautiful, large milk cow and a ton of hay occupied the plush mezzanine floor overlooking the even plusher lobby. Our days of Klim were over.

Upstairs, I had discovered a spooky situation. A Jewish family of five hiding in the hotel had somehow wound up left behind by relatives, who thought they were among a large group of locals that had previously fled the city in the effort to escape the Russians. This family had moved several times during the Russian occupation of the hotel. They were hiding on the very top floor in what must have been the coldest room in the building. Of course, there was no heat in the whole structure. German and Russian armored units fighting for control of the city had long eliminated any sort of municipal utilities.

This situation left a couple of us troopers going nuts, trying to figure out how to get this family to some sort of safety. We knew we would be left to watch some drunken group of Russian soldiers slaughter them all if we didn't come up with an idea. Finally, one of the guys, a Polish American, was able to convince a senior Russian army officer to provide the family with transportation in a Russian truck and temporary shelter out in the country, by assuring the officer that the people were Romanian, and hence not enemies of the Soviet Union.

That's where we left it three days later when we hitched a ride out of town with the Russian army. We had enjoyed some real fresh mezzanine milk and plenty of canned vegetables from the homes of German families who had long since fled the city, heading for Berlin in every sort of vehicle imaginable.

The next thing I remember was a pause for a day or so in a small village, probably still near the Polish border. The Russians were stalled in the area, giving the Germans some handy targets. They sent in fighter-bomber planes and started strafing the town with machine guns, running right down the major dirt street with guns blazing. The crazy Russkis ran out into the street and started throwing rocks and chunks of wood at the planes, which were flying perhaps fifty feet off the deck. The .50-caliber bullets rained down, hitting the Russians and flipping them in the air. But they were so goofy, they just kept right on running out into the street. They even mocked us as being weak and scared because we sought cover instead of throwing sticks and stones at the Me-109s that were literally plowing the street up with bullets.

Surely the reader can understand that I thought I was going crazy.

We slept in that village in the basement of a house. I had the guys prop up the cellar roof in case of an air raid at night. I had slept very little at any time on this leg of my journey. Nothing else happened in this small town, and in a day or so we were ready to move back out onto the road and continue our eastward trek. Somewhere out there, there was an American consulate I wanted to meet, seriously!

After all this time on the road with my charges, I realized that I was becoming as fragile as any of my ex-Krieggie crew. I had suffered through one breakdown after another among them, and it was really starting to wear on me. I determined I had a couple of guys who could deal with the issues better than I could. I thought if I stayed that I might crack up and become part of the problem instead of the solution. I'd be better off by myself, seeking help along the way from whoever seemed to give a damn.

I left by cover of darkness and headed east alone. In retrospect, it appears that my decision to do so may have saved more than my sanity. Although I did not then know it, the Russians were sweeping up former Allied POWs and interning them in former German prison camps to be used as pawns in the struggles between Churchill and Stalin. Stalin insisted that Britain and America should forcibly return to the Soviet Union all the Soviet POWs they had liberated, whether or not they wanted to be repatriated. Britain and America did not agree, nor did the Geneva Conventions.

Many desperate former Russian POWs jumped overboard ships returning them to their homeland, rather than suffer their fate under Stalinist rule. Meanwhile, the Soviets started shipping British and American soldiers who fell into their hands to the Soviet Union. Many of these men disappeared. Listed MIA or POW, they never were released or exchanged for Russian solders, but died forgotten in the gulag.

Probably because I was traveling alone, I was able to slide through and wind up in Moscow. No one really wanted to bother with just one ex-POW. My really angry attitude and my gun may also have had something to do with it. Few Russians, including bandits, wanted to waste time fighting with me. I did not hesitate one minute to pull my pistol and wave it around when challenged, though I am not, nor ever was, big and bad—just scared and mad.

As I moved along alone, every living person west of the Russian army was fleeing in a dying effort to escape the Russians. I often came into cities where not a single human being was left. Maybe a few stray dogs, but no people. It was not uncommon to walk into houses and find breakfast or some other meal sitting cold on the table. The family had been surprised by word that the Russians had been sighted, and they had hit the road with all the belongings they could haul. Whole families would be pushing and pulling wagons loaded with their most essential and precious possessions, with an immobile grandmother sitting on the top. It was really a pitiful sight. I often thought, *These poor people never started a war, they are just simple country folks trying to raise their families.*

The first significant Polish town I entered had zero population. It was large enough to have several big stores in the center of town, and I had all these empty, abandoned businesses to myself. I only needed one, the department store. One had to wait on oneself, but the price was right!

I gave my business to a Polish-style Sears and Roebucks, which had everything from ladies' fur coats, which served me well, to real silk hose, which served me even better, to a wood-burning Volkswagen bus. I tried on several wraps in the ladies' department and settled on a couple of fine, knee-length fur coats. I wore the first one inside-out, with the fur against my body, and buttoned up the other one on top of it. My days of suffering in the cold of Europe's coldest winter yet were over.

Perhaps my most valuable loot, though, was the sixty pairs of women's real silk hose that I stuffed down inside my two new beautiful coats. As soon as I laid eyes on them, I remembered my mother talking about not being able to buy "real silk" hose and having to wear all sorts of imitations. That's when I knew I had come by my ticket to Texas. I traded those silk hose for food all the way to Moscow. They were better than any coin of the realm.

The wood-burning bus had a very short lifespan. I found a Russian soldier who showed me how to fuel and start it up. In another building, easily identifiable as a dentist's office, I discovered a couple hundred pounds of dental tools and loaded them in the bus. I had visions that they'd be worth a fortune when I got them back home to Dallas.

I was driving down a back road, not having seen a single vehicle all day, when all of a sudden from out of the blue a Stuka dive-bomber appeared—the dreaded Stuka that made such frightening sounds as it plummeted toward its target. Surely, I thought, this little bus is not a worthy target for the mighty Stuka. Wrong! The pilot rolled that bird over on its side and headed straight down. I drove into a ditch, bailed out, ran for another ditch farther away, and watched as the single bomb he released hit within feet of my brand new bus. The bus and all my dental tools went up in smoke, as did my future dental tool supply business back in Dallas.

I wandered through Poland for an uncertain period, accepting rides on any moving vehicle, especially any train, no matter the direction. That's what headed me north toward Konigsberg for a spell. The city became a target of mine in hopes that I could reach the port and hitch a ride across the sea to the British Isles. I did think big, but this bright idea had a serious flaw, as a Russian officer revealed to me. The city was still held by the German army, with divisions of German troops living in the huge underground tubes used for the drainage system.

In front of every railroad station, the local women set up little tables, displaying homemade food products and warm wraps they had made to sell. I never figured out what sort of money they used, but I discovered immediately that my real silk hose would get me all the meats, breads, and home-canned food stuffs I wanted, all of them good enough to kill for. I did not lose a pound during my travels though Poland and Russia. If I found a sick person, especially a child, I enjoyed sharing my bounty, but I cannot say, other than those occasions, that I was too generous with my chow.

From time to time, I would run for a spell with some other GI the Russians had liberated, but I remained on my own for the most part. I was alone when I got to Krakow, Poland, a place I had heard described as the West Point of Poland. The Russian army had blown through the city a couple of weeks before I arrived, and the fierce fighting, mostly between armored units, had completely destroyed the infrastructure. Once again, there were no municipal utilities, and the back-yards all had slit trenches dug in the earth as toilets.

Someone directed me to the military academy as a good place to stay for a day or so. The barracks consisted of large, red-brick four-story buildings. There was food, if you like boiled fat, and bunks aplenty, because the Russians had moved on west. Some Russian combat casualties were being cared for in the barracks, but medical resources were sorely lacking, certainly compared to what we had in the U.S. Army. Seeing a pregnant female tanker nursing a field-grade Russian officer was a new experience.

On waking from my first night at the barracks, I went outside to the half-acre latrine, an area surrounded by a series of six-foot tarps. Passing through the narrow entranceway, I moved all the way across the latrine to the farthest slit trench, so as not to be disturbed. There was no other sign of life in the place. It was probably 6 a.m., good daylight.

No sooner had I dropped my pants and squatted down to do my business, than a female Russian soldier came through the entrance. She had to be half a city block away upon entering the latrine. I was already embarrassed to see her there, but assuming she would take her place a long distance away, I still felt rather secure. Wrong!

This young woman not only came over to my space, she shared *my* foot-wide trench, squatting right in front of me. She was so close I could smell the cigarettes on her breath. She, too, dropped her pants and went about her business. I didn't know if I was supposed to tip my hat, say "Dobra, Jane," or what. Needless to say, I lost all the urges that had taken me to the site. I tried to slip on out without falling into a slit trench.

I stayed for a day in this facility talking with many soldiers, wounded Russians, and worn-out Polish troops. I had met some Free Polish back in England prior to the invasion, all of them proud Poles. They had some form of army, and a Polish airborne group made the D-Day jump in France. All the Free Poles had a case against the Germans and Russians both. The German army had butchered the Poles going east, and the Russians had butchered them again, going west into Germany.

On the road again, I came upon an abandoned farmhouse. Prospects looked good for some home-canned fruit and vegetables, and, if I was lucky, cured meats. I went in and checked out the kitchen where, sure enough, a large stock of canned goods stood in glass jars high up on the shelves. You talk about dining at the Savoy, wow!

A thick pile of carpeting lay in a mound in front of the shelves, and I stepped up and stood on it. It was unstable, and after nearly slipping off several times, I stepped down to see if I could get a better footing.

When I threw back part of the carpet, I discovered I'd been standing on somebody's grandmother. The old farm lady was quite dead. I cannot describe just how I felt, but it was not good. My instant reaction was to apologize to God for my animal-like pursuits. I certainly lost all interest in that dear old lady's canning products and got the hell out of her kitchen and her house.

Within a mile of that farm, and feeling like I had abused an old lady, I came upon another farm. At first I thought it was completely abandoned. I went to see if the barn had any sort of transportation and discovered an old farmer lying dead in front of the door. He had a thin ring of white hair, a fat belly, and a beautiful face, except for the bullet hole right in the middle of his forehead.

Inside the barn, a Russian soldier was rummaging around for anything of use. In my very broken Russian, I asked him what had happened. He and some other Russians had arrived awhile before and sent the little farmer out to milk his cow for them. He did so and was told to go milk the cow again. This happened several times, and finally the farmer told the dumb Russkis that the cow was dry until the next morning. At this, they shot him in the head. The explanation? "If the cow won't give milk, shoot the farmer." Damn, was I mad—indignant to the max. Before my better judgment prevailed, I pulled my P38, ready to put a bullet in his stupid ugly head.

The Russian took off on a horse he had come by, and I was left to look the place over alone. Out on the back side of the barn, I found the body of a very pretty young woman. By the disarrangement of her clothes, it was obvious she had been raped. I went and got something to cover her body. As I bent down to cover her, I discovered that the animal who had abused her had left her with an artillery shell run up her private parts. I yelled and cursed and stomped out of the farmyard full of rage. There was absolutely nothing else I could do.

I have vivid recollections of entering Warsaw. The entire city was ravaged, nearly razed to the ground. Here, a pitiful Polish general, wearing a tattered uniform, told me how the

Russians had encouraged the Poles to expose their underground combat units. The understanding was that the Russians would then join the fray, crossing the Vistula River into the Polish-held area. The Poles came out of hiding and started a fierce battle with a German force much mightier than they. The Russians did nothing. The old Polish general cried as he told me how the Poles had been slaughtered, losing thousands of men in a matter of hours. He not only lost his family, but many close friends as well. His wife and daughter had both been raped and killed when the Russians later stormed through Warsaw in the drive toward Berlin.

From Warsaw to Moscow, I traveled by freight car. The journey was more than five hundred miles and took a number of days. The floors of most boxcars were covered with straw, which certainly beat the splintered wood my backside had come to know so well. There were usually about twenty-five people in each boxcar, which created enough body heat to preclude freezing, even though there was no heat.

I would settle in a corner of a boxcar where there seemed to be fewer or nicer people, then gather up some hay and literally make me a little nest. There was never any bickering among the adults, and the children behaved beautifully. Obviously, after what these babies had been exposed to, with family members raped and slaughtered before their eyes, the uncomfortable train ride was a vacation.

My real silk hose continued to work their magic on those country-looking ladies selling homemade food to the "affluent" train passengers. I got off at every stop and strolled around their tables, looking at the wares—breads, cakes, boiled eggs, assorted cooked meats, and alcohol. Then I'd pull a single silk stocking out from under my coat and let the ladies start ooing and ahhing, which always gathered a crowd. Finally, I pulled out the other hose and pointed to the items I wanted in exchange. And so I traveled in my fashionable boxcar, always eating like a king.

As the train moved into Russia proper, I started to see the bizarre effects of some of the most brutal man-to-man combat in history. The Germans and Russians had fought from shell hole to shell hole, often using knives and other handheld weapons, and were even said to have fought with their teeth.

I had seen many German guards whose scarred and disfigured bodies reflected the fierceness of the Russian front. I heard many tragic stories from old Russian soldiers, relics of their former selves, beaten to near death not only by combat, but the icy weather in which they fought the Germans. And just as I could testify to the brutal atrocities the Russians committed in Germany and Poland, I saw many Russians, adults and children both, who bore the marks of horrific abuse delivered at the hands of Hitler's army. Frequently, whole Russian towns were literally blown away by air raids or artillery, as the powerful German military pushed forward on the eastern front in the drive to capture major Russian cities. Surely, I thought, the hatred such combat engendered would last for many generations.

At last my long and varied trek found me in the Moscow freight yards. The place was clogged with hundreds of troop trains and thousands of Russian soldiers, probably headed for the western front. Many were missing limbs or a piece of skull from combat on the eastern front a year or so before. By this time, the Americans and Allied air forces had fortunately destroyed the mighty German air force. There no longer was any need to fear that the Germans would fly into Moscow, blowing up trains and buildings as they had done for several years earlier in the war.

Everything in northern Europe was still covered with deep snow, including the railroad cars in the freight yards. And yet the scene was bursting with life. The Russians were dancing everywhere, partying on the flat cars, and drinking vodka like mad. Looked good to me! I hopped from my boxcar, went over to a mixed group of revelers, and presented my drinking credentials.

A young soldier was sitting on a flatcar, playing a little accordion. The music was new to my ears, but suitable for some form of dancing with the tough-as-nails Russian female soldiers. They taught me their style of dancing, and with a little help from a jug of Russian booze, I became the life of the party.

This had gone on for a couple of days, when a young Russian female told her tank commander that she wanted me to teach her how to jitterbug. After a couple vodkas, straight, I would have tried to teach the queen of England to jitterbug, so there I was, sliding around on a snow-covered flatcar to the tune of a squeeze box, swinging a female tank gunner. I kept thinking, *If only my Oak Cliff buddies were here*, or better still, *If only my paratrooper buddies could see me now, I would never live it down*. The little Russian soldier could sure enough jitterbug.

The party lasted until an English-speaking Russian officer, with whom I had indulged in several bottles of vodka, came up and asked me if I had read the bulletin posted on a nearby sign. The answer was no, but I hurried over and read a poster that said something like this: ATTENTION ALL AMERICAN, BRITISH, AND CANADIAN TROOPS: REPORT TO ODESSA BY MARCH 10, 1945. I asked where Odessa was, thinking they were probably not talking about Odessa, Texas, and was told that a nearby train would soon be heading in that direction.

And so I left my dance studio and headed for another boxcar full of men, women, children, and little babies. I gathered some straw from the floor and made me a little den over in a corner. This would be home for the next several days as we bounced down the tracks toward the Black Sea. I still had plenty of pairs of real silk hose, enough to barter all the way to Odessa, 1,200 miles away.

With all the typical Russian delays along the way, we must have taken a week to get to Odessa. On arrival, we immediately became Russian prisoners. We were hustled over to a four-floor structure that already housed about two hundred former

German POWs and were not allowed to leave for any reason. Our view of Odessa came through a series of large windows that opened onto a huge park with wide concrete sidewalks.

A tragic event occurred during our imprisonment. Two Americans, former members of the 36th Infantry Division, my original National Guard outfit, had been captured in North Africa and were sent back to Odessa through the German prisoner lines. They were outside in the walled courtyard making a cup of powdered coffee when one of the brick walls just fell over on top of them, killing them both. Talk about being snake bit.

We had begun sweating out our stay, and as I later learned, we were worried with good reason. Finally, word was passed around the building that a ship had just arrived carrying Russian ex-POWs who had been liberated by Allied ground forces as they pushed across western Europe. If we volunteered to unload the ship, we could take it across the Black Sea and onto Italy where we would rejoin the U.S. Army. Talk about a welcome piece of news!

As number one volunteer, I was part of the detail that was taken down to the wharf to unload the ship. The first soldier to come down the ramp was a Russian lieutenant colonel. A local Russian officer instantly shot him dead at the bottom of the ramp. This freaked all of us out.

We knew nothing of the conflict among Stalin, Roosevelt, and Churchill concerning the repatriation of prisoners of war, many of whom the Allies were in the process of liberating. Stalin was insisting that all Russians so liberated were to be sent back to Russia, whether or not they desired to return to their homeland. He looked upon all Russian prisoners as traitors, with the summary execution of the lieutenant colonel providing brutal evidence.

I wound up in the belly of the ship loading large cardboard boxes onto palletts to be raised up to the top deck and subsequently loaded onto trucks. It was quite dark below deck, but not so dark that I could not identify that I was loading boxes of Hershey bars onto the pallets. In minutes, I had opened some of the large cartons, which in turn contained smaller boxes full of Hershey bars. Soon I was tearing these open too, hastily unwrapping them, and making Hershey Bar sandwiches. I must have wolfed down five pounds of chocolate before I returned to my bunk in the camp building.

The next day, we did indeed take that British ship out of Odessa, across the Black Sea to Istanbul, across the Aegean Sea, and past Athens. For some unknown reason, we went to Cairo, where we stayed overnight. The next day we sailed out to Italy and Naples. As James D. Sanders recounts in *Soldiers of Misfortune,* the ship we left on, the *Tamora,* was the last to reach U.S. forces. The rest of the Allied ex-POWs in Odessa were caught up in Stalin's diabolical requirements for the exchange, or rather non-exchange, of prisoners, and held in ransom for the return of Russians liberated by the Americans and British. The hostages were shipped out to gulags in Siberia, never again to see their homeland.

Our orders to go to the United States from Italy were dated March 22, 1945. I spent a week to ten days in Naples, purchasing canary birds in the open markets and liberating them from their captive state, and eating an assortment of new Italian food. We then boarded the USS *West Point,* a Coast Guard ship that had initially been an ocean liner called the USS *Manhattan.* The ship, unaccompanied by naval vessels, took a circuitous route. President Roosevelt died on April 12, while we were somewhere out on the Atlantic Ocean dodging German submarines.

Two days out to sea, after passing the Rock of Gibraltar, I was walking out on deck when I saw a lieutenant reclining under a lifeboat, reading a comic book. (Later, he claimed it was a classic.) His metal bars and patches told me he was a typical flyboy air force pilot. His face was familiar, but I couldn't quite place him. "Don't I know you?" I asked. He responded, "I'm Charlie Carrell, from Oak Cliff." Fact is, we both had gone to Adamson High School before I left to join the National Guard. Chuck had stayed in school and gotten a year of college before joining the air corps. He had piloted a B-24 bomber, flying combat missions out of Italy up into the oil fields and tightly defended industrial sites of southern Europe.

We visited there in the strong winds of the ocean for a spell, then decided to move out of the weather and into a near-by corridor. We moved down the hall a few feet and were busy catching up on years of separation, when a sailor opened a door next to where we were standing and shouted in a near hostile voice, "Well, if you're coming in, come on in!" Taken aback by the near attack, I said, "For what?" He said, with just as much hostility, "For confession, damn it!" We were standing just out-side the door of the Catholic chaplain's quarters and confes-sional! As neither of us was Catholic, I replied, "Hell, man, we'll be in Boston in ten days. Since we've never been to con-fession before, we won't have time to get that done, so we'll just go back outside and carry on. Thanks for the invite!"

It must have been about April 14 when we arrived in Boston Harbor. We docked next to a huge warehouse and walked off the *West Point* into a building where some nice Red Cross ladies gave us each a small bag of toilet articles, a smile, and good word. At my first opportunity, maybe thirty minutes later, I was in a phone booth calling home to Killeen. I discovered my sister, Mary, had gone through the entire process of marriage, pregnancy, and having a baby since D-Day. She had moved in with our parents in Killeen, Texas, while her husband, John, was serving with the 84th Infantry Division "rail splitters" in the ETO. As John's unit fought across Europe, he had been looking for me in the POW camps they liberated; meanwhile, I had been sailing out the other end of Europe by way of the Black Sea. Mary pinched my nephew, Johnny Carter, so he could cry for me. Little Johnny cried, and so did Sergeant Bearden.

Chuck Carrell and I were soon on a train heading for Texas. At one of our first stops, we went across the street to an army store and loaded up on military ribbons and other stuff that said, "Been there, done that." On arrival at Dallas, we set out for one major party. We quickly learned that the number one caution was not to bounce up on a buddy's front porch, ready to surprise an old friend, unless you could take the news he had just been buried in a military funeral.

All in all, I spent four years, eleven months, and twenty days as a soldier. Looking back, I now realize that from my war experiences I probably learned more about patience than anything else. I also learned that the sign going down into the Adamson High School locker room, "Find a way or make one," was oh so valid. If you had told that seventeen-year-old that he could remove pieces of .88 fragments from a buddy's back, he would have gotten sick. Certainly, if someone had told him that he would be asked to attend to the face of a man who had just had his nose blown off, he would have run away. The thought of taking care of a young officer who had maybe twenty or twenty-five small blue bullet holes in his chest, face, and belly would have been too much for little Bobby back when he was inducted into the National Guard in 1940. Yet all of these serious matters were resolved by that irresponsible little guy whose greatest achievement had been running the mile for Adamson High.

When Chuck and I hit Texas soil, I was just twenty-two. Patience was not on the agenda, and "Find a way or make one" was a recipe for survival. I had kept myself alive through scams, an instinct for hustling, and uncommon good luck. Now here I was, back in the great, wide world of America. The richness of all her possibilities, the great big smorgasbord of life, spread before me. To think that just a few months before, I had been in Stalag IIIC, a POW weighing ninety-eight pounds, wondering if I would ever make it out alive!

Having learned to shoot dice and play poker the hard way, thanks to the late, great Chet Gunka, I now was more than ready to reap the rewards. I had sent home some nice stacks of money after some high stake games. Along with my accumulated POW pay, it added up to five thousand dollars waiting for me in a bank in Killeen. For a guy who went into the service making twelve and a half cents an hour at the local grocery store, I was loaded.

I bought some beautiful clothes, none of which were any shade of green. Powder blue was my color of choice. When Chuck started taking dancing lessons at Arthur Murray's, I went along to dance with the female students for their practice and my pleasure. We went out every night to a Big Band dance hall, came in around daylight, and got up about lunchtime.

It soon got out to our party friends that I had major bucks in the bank. Two entrepreneurs arranged to have lunch with Chuck and me. They had tons of aluminum in every shape and form, and every sort of metal working machine imaginable, purchased for cash from a closed aircraft manufacturing plant in Arlington. They also had an agreement with Neiman Marcus to manufacture a beautiful aluminum cigarette lighter. If I provided $1,500 operating capital, they would repay me before either of them took a dime; I would retain one-third interest in the business and future profits.

Our lunchtime discussion took place at a friend's beer joint. I took a paper napkin, figured out how many beers $1,500 would buy, and declined their offer. Not a great start toward a career in business. Years later, their venture wound up as the Lone Star Boat Company and was sold for a fortune to Chrysler Marine Division.

Chuck and I did go back to Killeen, where we relieved my parents from running the Bearden Army Store so they could take a trip to Dallas. One of the items for sale was a little red, white, and blue flag with a gold star in the middle, indicating that the family had a kid in the service. When my mom returned from Dallas, she was unhappy that her special flag representing me was missing. Chuck or I had sold it, not knowing it was her own personal keepsake.

After a ten-day furlough, Chuck reported to an air force base in San Antonio. As an ex prisoner of war, I had a month of furlough, so I hung around Killeen for a few more days, then reported to Hot Springs, Arkansas, where the army was putting ex-POWs through a rehabilitation program. Lord knows I needed some kind of rehab.

Several months later, in August 1945, I paid a visit to an old fellow Adamson High School athlete, Rip Collins, who was running track for the University of Texas. We spent the night at the Sigma Nu fraternity house near the campus, and the members took me out to a house party. The place was filled with good-looking young co-eds, many from wealthy families from all across Texas.

After a night of considerable drinking, I conked out on the fraternity's sleeping porch. I was awakened the next morning by two of the brothers asking me if I was interested in joining the fraternity. "Just what is a fraternity?" I asked. They started to explain, but I soon interrupted, cutting straight to the chase. "How often do you do what we did last night, and how much does the membership cost?" Their reply was that they partied quite often with beautiful girls, and the whole fraternity thing, room and board included, cost sixty dollars a month. I did the math and decided that my bank account could stand quite a bit of that. Still, I had to ask one more question. "Do you have to be a student?" To which they replied, "It would help!"

Despite having dyslexia, I would go on to complete my BBA degree by correspondence from Texas Tech, and by commuting sixty miles from my home in Killeen for my last two-hour course in report writing. I am now a proud lifetime member of the "Texas

Exes," the Texas Ex-students' Association of the University of Texas. I guess it all just goes to show that with a little willingness to work hard, take a few risks, and persevere, even a trouble-making, sometimes dysfunctional kid can rise to the top. Which brings to mind my favorite Latin phrase: *Non Illegitimus Carborundum*— "Don't Let the Bastards Get You Down!"

In 1957, I got a concessionaire contract with the army and air force PX out at Fort Bliss, Texas, and thought that Duck might like the job as manager. I called and discovered he had been committed to a state mental hospital and could not be released without the approval of those who committed him. With the influence of my friend Ted Connell, who was national commander of the Veterans of Foreign Wars (VFW), Duck was transferred to a Veterans Administration hospital, where he would receive the best treatment available. I was thankful to be able to help my friend and brother in combat.

I later heard that Duck went to visit his sister, fell down a flight of stairs, and died from his injuries. Later still, in an effort to let his children know what a great man and soldier their father had been, I wrote them a letter sharing some of our war experiences. Years later still, his children wrote to say that every time they gather for a family reunion, they get out my letter and read it to the group. Though it has been more than sixty years since we shared those crazy, funny, and dangerous times, I still miss my friend and gunner, Duck, aka Wilson Keith. I hope his children and grandchildren will continue to pass along the story of one great American paratrooper.

On the fiftieth anniversary of D-Day, I gained some important closure with the past when I revisited Normandy with my son Tim. I had never seen anything written about Fresville, which seemed like a village that history had forgotten. I needed to retrace my steps to assure myself that the events I so vividly remembered had, indeed, taken place.

Tim and I discovered a two-story stone farmhouse with a traditional courtyard out front, which I thought might be the Fresville barracks where Fred Kelly and I had our shoot-out with the Germans. I was wearing an exact replica of my 1944 jumpsuit, wondering aloud to Tim if we had found the place, when two well-dressed gentlemen came out of the courtyard. Seeing my jumpsuit, one of them walked over and said in perfect English, "You were here?"

"Yes," I replied.

The man, Mr. Pignot, the present owner of the property, put a hand on my shoulder, directing us toward the door, and said, "The story goes that on D-Day two American paratroopers came into the courtyard of this home, which was being used as a German barracks. The paratroopers threw a grenade through that upstairs window, there." Here he stopped and pointed to the room we had blasted with our grenade.

By this time, we all had arrived at the front door of the house. The owner led us inside as he continued to tell the story of the two American paratroopers. Guiding us upstairs, he took us into the room damaged by the grenade fifty years earlier, and pointed to the scars the blast had caused on the wall. On an overhead beam, the German soldiers had left a message in German: roughly translated, it said "Kiss my ass."

The bare wooden floors, over two hundred years old, were marked with large, dark maroon stains. The owner pointed them out, adding that attempts to remove the blood over the years had been to no avail. Throughout his presentation, Tim and I kept looking at each other. The hairs on our arms were standing up, and tears were welling in our eyes. At the conclusion of our tour, as we walked toward the front gate, I whispered, "I didn't lie to you boys, did I, Tim?" He was unable to respond, caught up in his overwhelming emotions.

The mayor and vice-mayor of Fresville were very kind to Tim and me. They had us over for meals, and gave us a personal, two-day tour of the area. They and their town remember well the day they were liberated from the German Army, June 6, 1944.

I learned many things from my experience of the war—that mankind can be crueler than I ever could have imagined; that men will, indeed, give up their lives for a friend, and share their last small piece of bread with a hungry brother. Most of all, I learned that I have a responsibility to be genuinely thankful to all the men and women who have given their lives to defend this great country. Visiting military cemeteries overseas, and seeing those miles of crosses on the graves, I realized that each body there interred had been a beloved son, father, brother, husband, uncle or friend of a grieving family back in the States.

As I look back at my life at the age of eighty-four, I can truly say it has been an adventure. I have never paid much attention to my age when learning or starting something new. My newest *accomplishment*—and I use the word lightly—is my use of the computer to type this book and e-mail chapters to my editor. I learned to snowboard in 1997 on a visit to the Colorado mountains, so I figure I should now be up to surfing the Internet. The manager of the store where I rented the snowboard looked strangely at the age on my application. "Is this supposed to be fifty-seven?" he asked, as I picked up my board. "No, it's seventy-five," I said, and headed for the checkout counter.

I have been blessed to start and own several businesses, including the first civilian outlet to sell the famed Corcoran Paratroop Jump Boot after the war; with my traditional airborne gung-ho operating system, I extended my Army Store business to five states and 113 employees. I've owned and flown a private plane, run for city council, replaced our county chairman, and was asked to run for the House of Representatives—an offer I quickly refused. I fathered five wonderful children—the accomplishment of which I am most proud—learned to ride a motorcycle at fifty, and carried the Olympic Torch on a leg of its journey through Navasota, Texas, in 1996. The brief thought that my seventy-four-year-old body might not be up to the task vanished ever so quickly when "USA! Go America!" and all things patriotic filled the air, as I ran through the streets lined with children who had been let out of school to witness the occasion. I do believe I could have run to Atlanta, I was so pumped up by the event.

All this experience sometimes makes me think about my old friend and gunner, Duck. My greatest disappointment of the war was our separation at Stalag IVB. After the war, we stayed in touch and laughed about the fact that we both had fathered so many children. The word in German prisons was that Hitler was feeding us something to make us sterile. Every time we had a new kid, we took it as a personal victory for the Allies, assuming the attitude, "Gotcha!"

Taking the Long Way
Back to Texas

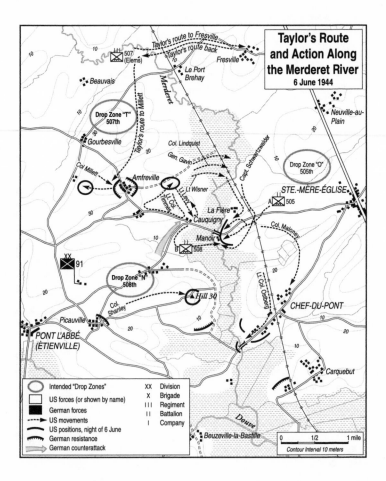

Taylor's Route and Action Along the Merderet River
6 June 1944